Dear Reader:

The book you are about to read is the latest bestseller from the St. Martin's True Crime Library, the imprint the *New York Times* calls "the leader in true crime!" Each month, we offer you a fascinating account of the latest, most sensational crime that has captured the national attention. St. Martin's is the publisher of bestselling true crime author and crime journalist Kieran Crowley, who explores the dark, deadly links between a prominent Manhattan surgeon and the disappearance of his wife fifteen years earlier in THE SURGEON'S WIFE. Suzy Spencer's BREAKING POINT guides readers through the tortuous twists and turns in the case of Andrea Yates, the Houston mother who drowned her five young children in the family's bathtub. In Edgar Award-nominated DARK DREAMS, legendary FBI profiler Roy Hazelwood and bestselling crime author Stephen G. Michaud shine light on the inner workings of America's most violent and depraved murderers. In the book you now hold, PERFECT BEAUTY, acclaimed authors Keith Elliot Greenberg and Detective Vincent Felber untangle the mystery behind a love triangle—and a murder.

St. Martin's True Crime Library gives you the stories behind the headlines. Our authors take you right to the scene of the crime and into the minds of the most notorious murderers to show you what really makes them tick. St. Martin's True Crime Library paperbacks are better than the most terrifying thriller, because it's all true! The next time you want a crackling good read, make sure it's got the St. Martin's True Crime Library logo on the spine—you'll be up all night!

Charles E. Spicer, Jr.
Executive Editor, St. Martin's True Crime Library

PERFECT BEAUTY

A True Story of Adultery,
Murder, and Manipulation
in Middle America

KEITH ELLIOT GREENBERG

DETECTIVE VINCENT FELBER

St. Martin's Paperbacks

PERFECT BEAUTY

Copyright © 2008 by Keith Elliot Greenberg and Vincent Felber.

Cover photo of Cynthia George and Jeff Zack © Jocelyn Williams / *Akron Beacon Journal*. Cover photo of tiara © Stockbyte / Getty Images. Cover photo of John Zaffino © Bob DeMay / *Akron Beacon Journal*.

ISBN: 0-312-94953-7
EAN: 978-0-312-94953-2

Printed in the United States of America

St. Martin's Paperbacks edition / April 2008

St. Martin's Paperbacks are published by St. Martin's Press, 175 Fifth Avenue, New York, NY 10010.

10 9 8 7 6 5 4 3 2 1

ACKNOWLEDGMENTS

This case was not solved by the work of one or two people. So it is with great humility that we acknowledge some of the many people who did not get mentioned.

First, we thank the entire Akron Police Department, with special gratitude going to Lieutenant Melissa Schnee, Sergeant Timothy McLeod and Detective Juanita Elton; Harrold Torrens and Aaron Reese of the Ohio Department of Public Safety, whom Detective Felber owes a great apology; Special Agents Peter Kacarab and Jennifer Higgins of the Department of the Treasury for lending their investigative and financial expertise to the case.

We would also like to thank all the brave men and women who suffered through the stress of testifying for the prosecution at both trials. Their only reward was knowing that they were doing the right thing. They should be proud of the fact that they performed their civic duty in such an admirable way.

Without the support of his family, Detective Felber would never have been able to write this book. His heartfelt gratitude goes out to Teri, David, Rachel and his parents. His co-author, Keith Elliot Greenberg, thanks his wife, Jennifer, and daughter, Summer. Dylan Greenberg's computer assistance was greatly appreciated.

Many thanks go to Mike Homler and Charles Spicer of St. Martin's Press, who bravely put their faith in a cop who had no writing experience and only a story to tell. We must also acknowledge Heather Florence for her legal assistance and advice.

And while David Whiddon is a major part of the story, Detective Felber was never able to express just how important he was to this case. Without his dedication, brilliance and friendship, this case would never have gotten off the ground. They worked side by side and nothing was done without his advice or presence. His belief in justice for all is heroic.

PERFECT
BEAUTY

ONE

"SIGNAL THIRTY-THREE."

Detective Vince Felber quickly maneuvered his unmarked car into the right lane of Interstate 77, and looked for the exit sign. He'd been heading home for lunch when the reports crackling over the police radio caught his attention. There'd been some kind of incident near BJ's, the massive wholesale outlet on the edge of the city, and cruisers had already been deployed. Now, it appeared, the occurrence was more serious than anyone had initially anticipated.

"Signal thirty-three," Felber heard his boss, Sergeant Ed Moriarity repeat. *"Detective Felber, we need you to go to Sixteen Seventy-seven Home Avenue."*

Felber was already on his way. "Forget about eating," he smirked.

WHEN "SHOTS FIRED" first flashed in yellow across the desktop computer screen at Akron police headquarters, Sergeant Moriarity had barely grunted. Shots were fired all the time in Ohio's former rubber capital, and the taciturn detective squad boss didn't make an issue of it unless someone was on the receiving end of a gunshot. Because the computer was connected to the dispatch system, the sergeant could read a summary of every call handled by the department's operators. He liked it when the lettering was green, signifying "non-emergency." Yellow was a little more serious, but no cause for alarm. So Moriarity briefly looked away from the screen, and went back to his paperwork. A paragraph or so later, the bulletin changed to "MAN SHOT," and the phones started ringing. Moriarity pushed his documents aside, picked up his radio, and keyed it to transmit to all available detectives. Then, he stood up to converge with them at the scene.

The moment Felber received the message, his focus shifted. Working to prevent his adrenaline surge from controlling his actions, he reminded himself that he was in an unmarked vehicle, and had to obey all local traffic laws. But this would not be an issue. Soon after Felber was dispatched, traffic slowed to a crawl.

Only rarely were Akron's gray skies penetrated by the sun, and today—June 16, 2001—was one of those days. The weather was warm, but not hot—a spectacular afternoon. Kids played baseball on sandlots all over the city. People Rollerbladed and rode bicycles. On this Saturday before Father's Day, stores were crowded with shoppers who seemed eager to get outside and take advantage of the fair temperatures.

The first report had come in while most of Akron's detectives were out on their lunch breaks. Even at its busiest, though, the weekend detective squad generally consisted of a skeleton staff, comprised of investigators from both the Crimes Against Persons Unit—devoted to physical crimes against individuals, including rapes, robberies, assaults and homicides—and the Property Unit—specializing in thefts, burglaries and B&Es (breaking and entering episodes). Despite its relatively diminutive size, Akron was not immune to the urban friction that sometimes permeated the industrial Midwest. Murders were no longer a rarity; the city of 212,000 averaged twenty homicides each year. When one took place, the Crimes Against Persons Unit occasionally borrowed a detective or two from the Crimes Against Property division.

Today, Felber was on loan.

At 39 years old, Felber was often mistaken for a doctor, lawyer or engineer—anything but a cop. And, indeed, his background reinforced this. After high school, he'd lived at home and commuted to Akron University, majoring in engineering. After taking a leave of absence from his studies, he registered at Kent State, and pursued journalism. Although he'd graduated with a degree in advertising, he felt too attached to the city of his birth to pursue the career in New York, Chicago or even Cleveland. As clichéd as it sounded, he wanted to make the world a better place. So in 1992, he joined the Akron P.D.

Because of his curly brown hair and vaguely Mediterranean features, Felber was often mistaken for Lebanese or Jewish; in fact, he was German and Italian. To some, he seemed introspective, to others, introverted—qualities he used to his advantage when interrogating a suspect. Despite his six-foot-three-inch stature, Felber could make himself virtually invisible, allowing a perp to blurt out the kinds of extravagant claims and contradictory information that prosecutors found invaluable.

In social situations, strangers were baffled by the detective's acidic wit, delivered dryly with a straight face. But his friends on the police department had no trouble deciphering what he truly meant. In fact, many shared the same sense of humor themselves.

"Why'd she do it?" a neighbor might ask a cop responding to a suicide call.

"Evidently," he'd reply without even a hint of a smile, "she wasn't happy."

Felber knew that these kinds of responses were simply a defense mechanism to shield the public from confidential information, and the officers themselves from the type of depression that arose after confronting misfortune and tragedy. Felber compared the mentality to the gallows humor soldiers relied on during wartime. Of course, despite the potential to suddenly find oneself in a life-and-death struggle on High Street or Mineola Avenue, war was a lot more severe than patrolling the streets of Akron. But in war, the enemy was generally a faceless menace from a foreign land. In Akron, police were seeing their own people at their worst. And if the job wasn't tough enough, there was the challenge of negotiating the political combat zone in the station house.

"It's not the people on the outside," went the slogan among Felber's peers, "it's the people on the inside who burn you out."

Still, the joking deepened the brotherhood between Felber and his fellow detectives. It was one of the things that he loved most about the job.

FROM I-77, FELBER switched to Route 8–North, exiting at Howe Avenue in Akron's Chapel Hill section, and passing under the Interstate. At first, there was nothing unusual about the sight on the other side of the windshield: a sunny parking lot crowded with traffic and people wheeling shopping carts. Then, he spotted the crime scene—a gas station situated in front of BJ's, the boxy store anchoring the nearby strip mall. Another 500 yards, Felber noted, and the Akron detective squad could have enjoyed a quiet weekend. That's how close the incident had been to Cuyahoga Falls, the suburb that abutted Akron just north of the city line.

For a moment, Felber felt a sense of detachment, observing the police cars and frantic officers from a distance, like a person watching some cinematic fiction in the darkness of a movie theater. Then, he was being waved through the barricades, steering around cruisers and exchanging nods with cops he knew from the station house. He couldn't help but flash back to his childhood, when he'd hear police sirens from his room and burst out the front door, running down the street to gape at the action. Always, the barrier was manned by some stern officer, holding back the curious and staring back, tight-lipped, when anyone tried prying loose a morsel of information. Now, all these years later, Felber was the object of curiosity, with the eyes of the public upon him.

Stepping out of his vehicle and past the yellow crime-scene tape, Felber felt a bit self-conscious and uncomfortable. On the day he graduated from the police academy, he'd crossed the line from onlooker to active participant. But this wasn't the time for contemplation. Sergeant Moriarity had beaten him to the scene, and taken it over, monitoring the activity in the parking lot closely while delivering instructions to investigators.

It was an odd place to kill someone. "If you think you're going to be murdered," the detectives often said, "go to the most public place possible. You'll scare the killer away."

Apparently, that strategy hadn't worked. The BJ's parking lot was one of the busiest places in the city—a familiar, seemingly safe location completely incongruous with murder.

The detective walked up to Moriarity, and received a synopsis of the morning's events.

Minutes earlier, an ambulance had removed the body of 44-year-old Jeff Zack, a prematurely white-haired businessman who'd seemed impervious to danger. As an Israeli paratrooper, he'd been trained to navigate minefields, and fight alone behind enemy lines against armor, attack helicopters and infantry. In the United States, he'd gained a reputation as a smooth-talking, strong-willed guy who used the knowledge of Arabic he'd acquired in the Middle East to enter into a number of business ventures with a network of Arab-Americans. On a good day, the six-foot-four-inch Zack seemed like a jovial man who didn't let the rigors—or responsibilities—of life bother him. But very suddenly, he could explode in anger, yelling, threatening and using his hulking size to intimidate.

Zack was a well-known character at BJ's—for all the wrong reasons. A serial adulterer, he was notorious for flirting with the female clerks. At first, his overtures seemed harmless. But after procuring the phone number for a pretty, 17-year-old clerk, he began badgering her with calls, even offering to pay her for sex. Eventually, her father contacted Zack, and informed him that the girl was underage.

"So what?" he replied.

Incredibly, Zack continued to phone the teen, prompting the other clerks to band together and report him to management. One month before the murder, Zack had been banned from BJ's.

Nonetheless, he was possessed with the uncanny ability to learn the intricacies of whatever business he was pursuing, whether it was scrap metal, insurance, credit cards or heating and air-conditioning. In fact, he'd procured his Ford Explorer at an employee discount, after a transaction with the automaker. He currently divided his time between, among other things, an Akron flooring company, a landscaping operation and a vending machine enterprise. It was that last that initially aroused interest in investigators. He'd shop at BJ's to purchase candy in bulk to fill his vending machines. And, rumor had it, the business was secretly bankrolled by Zack's former paramour, Cynthia George.

Around Akron, the stunning George was described as a "socialite." A coal miner's daughter, Cynthia had turned her back on her past, and reinvented herself as the wife of wealthy restaurateur Ed George. With her sparkling eyes and engaging smile, Cynthia was an ideal hostess at her husband's night spot, the Tangier, a local institution characterized by purple neon and an Arabian Nights motif. She'd also entered beauty contests, taken hula lessons and consumed self-help tomes. At the Georges' 8,100-square-foot palace outside of town, Cynthia seemed to live in splendor with her Christmas card–perfect brood of children, jewelry and furs, and a troupe of servants.

While Ed George supported his wife's lifestyle, Cynthia came and went as she pleased, attracting the attention of men of varied backgrounds and often forceful temperaments. With Ed away at the restaurant, Jeff Zack was a regular guest in the wing of the house Cynthia had all but claimed for herself. For eight years, they carried on an affair, and even had a baby together—a child Cynthia's unsuspecting husband deeply loved and raised as his own. Some were shocked by her lack of discretion, but Cynthia didn't care. She'd long ago liberated herself from the conventions of her childhood. In her mansion, ensconced in opulence, she was indifferent to the jealous condemnation of others, indulging instead in the freedom afforded those of her station.

But a month earlier, the romance between Cynthia and Jeff had come crashing to a halt. There had been tears and angry phone calls and—as was common when Zack found himself in a predicament that didn't suit him—threats. To the few who knew her well, Cynthia had confided that she feared Zack exposing their relationship and love child to her husband—resulting in divorce and, even more terrifying, the evaporation of the prosperity she'd labored so long to procure.

But Cynthia was far from the only person in Akron engaged in an adversarial relationship with Jeff Zack. The alliance between the former Israeli warrior and his Arab business partners was always tenuous at best. And because of his penchant for bouncing from one scheme to another—many bordering on the illegal—some described Jeff as a man who acquired new enemies with every personal and professional transaction.

Today, on possibly the prettiest day of the year, the wrong person had caught up with him. As Felber discussed the crime with Sergeant Moriarty, a call came in from Akron City Hospital. Shortly after his arrival there, Zack had died from the bullet to the head he'd received while pulling up to the gas pumps.

It would be Felber's first homicide, and he realized that there was a great task ahead of him. He'd always prided himself on being a thorough detective, but it was obvious that this case was going to receive a lot more scrutiny than a breaking and entering at a florist's shop. Every report would have to be written with greater contemplation and detail. Every observation would be dissected by supervisors, prosecutors, defense attorneys and, ultimately, judges. In the years to come, Felber would find himself battling reluctant witnesses, obstructionist attorneys and incompetence within his own department. But he didn't care. He was looking forward to it.

Nobody, he reasoned, should get away with murder.

TWO

DETECTIVE FELBER DIDN'T know it yet, but he was personally connected to one of the central figures in the case. Seventeen years earlier, before he'd ever considered a career in law enforcement, Felber had worked for Cynthia George's husband, Ed, as a bartender at the Tangier.

Edward Joseph George was considered one of the wealthiest men in Akron—one of eight children in a tight-knit, accomplished Lebanese-Catholic family. As a teenager, he attended St. Vincent–St. Mary High School, west of downtown—the place basketball star LeBron James first received national exposure before being recruited by the nearby Cleveland Cavaliers. Then, Ed moved on to John Carroll University and Michigan State, en route to taking over the family business.

His father, Ed, Sr., had opened the original Tangier in 1948. After it burned down, the family purchased a chunk of land adjoining a cemetery on West Market Street, and rebuilt the facility into a dining and entertainment emporium that featured acts like the Beach Boys, Frankie Valli, Charlie Daniels, Tina Turner and James Brown. In 1990, President George Herbert Walker Bush spoke at a Republican Party fundraiser at the Tangier. Eight years later, his son, Texas Governor George W. Bush, also delivered a speech there.

The facility was adorned with photos of these celebrities, often posing with Ed George, who claimed to operate "the best steakhouse in Ohio." Apparently, the Tangier was the largest restaurant of its type west of New York and east of Chicago. Why it was situated in Akron—the founding city of Alcoholics Anonymous and center of the All-American Soap Box Derby—and how it remained in business was a bit of a curiosity.

The lower-middle-class people with whom Felber grew up thought the Tangier was the classiest place in the state. And the management played to them, boasting of its "Vegas-like atmosphere." One of its eleven banquet rooms was called the Casbah. Another featured a Roman fountain in the center of the floor. Diners ate amongst opulent statues, faux painted walls, stained glass and domed ceilings decorated with imitation clouds.

To some in Akron, the Georges were admired and adored, particularly in the Arab-American community, where they reportedly contributed millions of dollars to charities in the Middle East. Ed's brother, Robert, owned a health food store in Cuyahoga Falls. Another brother, David, ran Bell Music—directly across the street from the Tangier—a company that supplied pool tables, juke boxes, video arcades and cigarette machines to bars and businesses all over the Akron area. In addition, Bell Music installed what could best be described as "gambling machines" in various facilities.

In other parts of Ohio, a related branch of the George family leased machines specializing in lottery-style tickets and video poker. But in 1991, authorities seized six such devices from fraternal clubs in greater Columbus. Philip George, Jr., of George Music, told the press that his company provided these machines to charitable groups for amusement, not gambling.

"We can't be responsible for someone taking the machine and using it in a wrongful way," he said.

Law enforcement was less than convinced, and Philip

was eventually convicted of gambling-related activities and sentenced to over 20 years in prison. Although an appeals court would later overturn the verdict, the legal fight—among rumors of other episodes—left a lingering impression that the George clan had underworld ties.

Felber first entered the Georges' universe in 1983, after answering an ad in a local newspaper for a Tangier bartender's position. Upon stepping through the doorway, the future detective noted that the decor and other accoutrements bordered on the outlandish. The color purple ran through the general design of the complex, and the booths were backed in camel hair. At 22 years old, Felber's previous experience behind the bar had largely involved pouring shots and beers at a college pub. But he was bright, and good-looking in a Mediterranean sort of way. And, like most of the people the Georges hired, he was willing to put in long hours.

Mark Barbuto, a handsome guy in his late twenties, ran the restaurant in the evenings with Ed George, and was Felber's immediate supervisor. They would later discover that they were distantly related through marriage. But it seemed to make little difference in the Tangier work environment. To Felber, Barbuto had the personality and finesse of an insurance salesman. Still, there were moments when the two found themselves communicating about weighty issues: Ed's management style and, then, years later, the death of Jeff Zack.

What Felber needed at this stage of his life was money, and the Tangier seemed to be a place filled with material possibility. Initially, he was promised that his earnings would increase with his seniority. The pledge was so enticing that he turned his back on his college studies, moved out of his parents' home, and settled into a house with three other Tangier bartenders.

The restaurant was one of the first to use computerized liquor dispensers. The concept was appealing enough—until Felber realized that it took the individuality out of bartending, along with the accompanying tips. The machines poured slightly more than one measured shot. If a good customer asked for a particularly strong drink, he was out of luck. He received the same measured drink as every other client. The mechanized system also prevented a bartender from doling out a free drink to a preferred patron. Without the ability to do the customer a favor, imbibers were disinclined to leave a little extra on the bar for their server.

Because of the computerized dispensers, patrons were oblivious to the type of liquor that they received—unless they requested a specific brand. If they asked for a Canadian Club and Coke, for instance, that's what was delivered. If they made the mistake of simply ordering a "whiskey and Coke," the bartenders went to what they called "the well," stocked with the cheapest products Ed could find. Yet, as the customers reclined on purple vinyl seats below glass chandeliers, many clung to the belief that they were getting the best. After all, they'd been told, that's what the Tangier served.

While the Tangier never watered down its drinks, the bartenders were forced to use crushed ice, which melted as the liquor was poured and—aesthetically, at least—suggested that the cocktails were more potent. Ice cubes were frequently added as well, to enhance this effect.

The carafes of wine so proudly touted by the restaurant staff were often left open on shelves. Although sold at a premium, the carafes were regularly filled with the type of cheap box wine found in grocery stores. About once a month, Felber claims, a carafe would be returned after a customer noticed a dead roach in his or her drink.

Cockroaches were a problem at the Tangier at the time. When Felber worked in the kitchen, pouring drinks for the waitresses, he recounts, the computer boards connected to the liquor dispensers regularly shorted out—the result of insects becoming electrocuted while crawling across the circuits.

Some of the Tangier waitresses made a decent living. Others earned about the same as servers in franchise restaurants. Nonetheless, working for Ed George was as challenging as waiting on the customers—some of whom were splurging for an anniversary or other special event and, thus, felt entitled to demand more than they would in their workday lives. After the Zack murder, police would track down a veteran waitress who'd recall Ed's combustible disposition: "His temper would get the best of him," she said, describing how he threw items around the kitchen. "He would make irrational, spur-of-the-moment decisions, based on his temper. Some of those decisions were bad for business, and ended up costing him money."

Yet, once he cooled down, he was able to continue working alongside the objects of his rage, with no grudges held.

On one occasion, Felber became so angry while witnessing an Ed George eruption that he thought about confronting his boss. A line of waitresses were waiting for drinks at the kitchen bar when one rushed into the room, slipping on the greasy tile floor. She was hurt, and an experienced waitress ran over to assist—setting down a tray of six dinners. In the frenzy of the moment, she forgot that she was violating one of Ed George's rules about placing trays on certain counters. A few moments later, Ed entered the kitchen himself and surveyed the scene. Looking away from the fallen waitress, George zoned in on the tray teetering on the forbidden counter. Reddening, Ed grabbed the tray and hurled it across the kitchen, shattering dishes and splattering the room with meat, vegetables and silverware.

Spewing obscenities, he laced into the helpful waitress, vowing that the cost of the dinners would come out of her wages.

As Ed stomped out of the kitchen, Felber turned to the waitress: "Are you all right?"

Shaken by the intensity of the verbal assault, she slowly nodded. That's when Felber offered to drag Ed back into the kitchen and force him to apologize.

With tears streaming down her face, the woman replied, "He isn't worth it."

"There's no way," Felber said, "that he can make you pay for those dinners."

The waitress looked at him with beaten eyes. "Yes, he can," she answered. "I need the job."

Felber never found out whether Ed eventually calmed down and withdrew his threat about forcing the woman to work for free for the next several weeks.

BY THIS POINT, whenever Felber heard a friend or neighbor boast about a night at the Tangier, he shook his head in befuddlement. Once in a while, a waitress would come into the kitchen, telling the staff that a customer had complained about a fellow patron eating slovenly, without any table manners. The workers would laugh when they realized that the offensive diner was actually Ed George.

On Monday nights, Ed often squandered hundreds of dollars in poker games at the restaurant, while obsessively cutting corners on the most trivial expenses. For instance, the bowls of whipped butter on each table were returned to the kitchen at the end of meals, and scraped into a tub for re-use.

Banquets were the Tangier's specialty. Ed George knew the secret to not only turning a party into a spectacle, but attracting customers with relatively inexpensive prices. To counter these reasonable fees, Felber heard, the hors d'oeuvres were rarely thrown out.

Bartenders at these events were paid up to ten percent of the bar bill—to a maximum of $50. It was hardly a living wage. In fact, Felber realized that he'd earned more money while working at the college pub. Aware that in the rest of the world, customers generally left a 17 percent tip, Felber suggested that this fee be automatically added to the bill. It was unlikely that the patrons would mind, and the bartenders stood to nearly double their pay. Night manager Mark Barbuto laughed at the proposal.

"What's so funny?" a confused Felber asked.

"Ed George already calculates a twenty percent tip into the bill."

"*Twenty* percent? What happens to the ten percent we're not getting?"

Barbuto shook his head and smiled. "What do you think happens to it? It goes into Ed George's pocket."

"Do the customers know this?"

"Don't make trouble, Vince. If you need extra money, steal it from the register. That's what Ed expects you all to do anyway."

Felber was speechless.

"He figures theft into your salaries," Barbuto continued.

Not long after this discussion, Felber quit the Tangier and returned to college. During his entire tenure at the restaurant, he couldn't remember having a single conversation with Ed George—but *had* noticed that, even though he tended to angrily demean loyal employees like Barbuto, Ed never directed his wrath at Felber. A fellow employee explained that Ed liked Felber because his register generally logged the most money.

Still, in Felber's estimation, Ed wasn't all bad. Unlike others in his field, George apparently restrained himself from flirting with the waitresses. And, about a year into Felber's employment, he noticed a stunning woman with short blonde hair, waltzing through the kitchen, without acknowledging anyone else's presence.

"Who's that?" Felber asked one of the waitresses.

"Oh, that's Cindy. Ed's fiancée."

Soon, Cindy would begin filling in as a hostess at the restaurant, as well as a greeter in the Tangier's small concert hall, known as The World-Famous Cabaret. Reportedly, she also played a role in hiring important employees, and overseeing the Tangier's renovations.

In time, her presence at the complex would loom as large as her husband's.

AFTER JEFF ZACK'S murder, investigators, reporters and even old friends would attempt to paint a psychological profile of Cynthia George. Yet, the woman at the axis of the scandalous crime maintained her mystique—able to compartmentalize sections of her life, as well as her past. To this day, many longtime associates claim that they never really knew her.

To one segment of her peers, Cynthia was well-mannered, kind-hearted and driven by faith. Friends from church and other venues were impressed by her ability to quote Scripture. Members of the Fairlawn Country Club remember her smiling countenance, as she drove onto the grounds with a car full of happy children. Others found her controlling, aggressive and almost sociopathic in the way she'd disregard the fortunes of everyone else to achieve her goals.

She began life as Cynthia Mae Rohr in North Canton, Ohio—site of the first Hoover vacuum cleaner factory—growing up in a home more than 200 square feet smaller than the garage adjoining the house that she'd share with Ed George. At one stage of his life, her father, Glen, labored in the coal mines, while neighbors worked for Republic Steel, the Belden Brick Company and Timken, a manufacturer of—among other specialties—ball bearings. The family struggled, but Glen and his wife, Helen, kept their one-story bungalow freshly painted and tidy, instilling in their four children a devout Catholicism that Cindy clung to deep into middle age.

At North Canton High School—then housed in a two-story brick building near her home—Cindy stood out as a pretty, popular and intelligent girl with the potential to achieve anything she tried. Although people would later view her as a bit of an enigma, as a teen, Cindy was the consummate joiner, who blended well with others and had a sense of charity, volunteering at a local hospital. On Thursday nights, she was a regular at the Pep Club, painting signs to spur on the school's sports teams to victory. As a junior, she was voted into the Homecoming Court. The next year, she became president of the Booster Club.

Unfortunately, the realities into which she'd been born prevented many of her dreams from being realized. She'd hoped to study art and design in college, but her family's financial condition precluded her from attending. She fantasized about modeling and entering the Miss America contest, but, at five-foot-four, she was too short. There were discussions about joining the Peace Corps, but these went nowhere.

After her 1972 graduation, she claimed, she hitchhiked west, ending up in Wyoming, Montana, even Alaska. Although the journey may have been motivated by Cynthia's disillusionment over her limited options, the very fact that she busted out of her somewhat parochial surroundings indicated that this was a woman with a sense of adventure, who would not be constrained by the Buckeye State and its accompanying mores.

Back home, Cindy still did fairly well for herself, eventually working in US Airways' VIP lounge in Pittsburgh. She had plenty of willpower, but limited cash. When she finally met Ed George—at the Tangier, six years after her high school graduation—Cynthia was apparently living on a farm in a small trailer, feeding the animals to cover her rent. She told friends that she was booking musical acts, and her initial exchange with Ed was supposed to be purely professional. Then, apparently, Ed complimented Cynthia on her "radiant smile." Soon, they were dating, and Ed—who lived at home into his forties—was paying her expenses, and purchasing her rapidly expanding wardrobe.

"We knew that it would be forever from the minute we met," she'd tell the television show *Dateline*.

Some would later assert that Cindy viewed the restaurateur as a father figure.

In 2002, when police questioned one of Cynthia's friends about the affair with Jeff Zack, the associate grew incredulous. "Cindy would never fool around," the woman insisted.

She claimed to know this because Cynthia had always stressed that she'd been a virgin on her wedding night.

The 1984 ceremony and reception were so notable that the *Akron Beacon Journal* featured it alongside news about Jesse Jackson and the Cleveland Browns. Twenty-nine-year-old Cindy returned to her hometown triumphantly, shimmering in her white wedding gown, as she walked the aisle at St. Joseph Catholic Church in Canton. Her family—who could never afford to send the ambitious young woman to college—now watched in wonder, as the 44-year-old groom picked up the tab for the kind of event neither they, nor members of their social circle, ever imagined attending.

Cindy's mother Helen performed two solos in the cathedral, in front of a chorus of sixty. The 500 guests then converged on the Tangier, where every table was adorned with an Italian wedding cake, and each invitee received a souvenir cake knife decorated with Jordan almonds.

The couple arrived at the ceremony in a white carriage pulled by a horse of the same color. Observed a former confidante of the bride, "She *had* to have a carriage."

Despite the extravagance, though, Ed kept an eye on the bottom line. The reception was deliberately held on Monday in order to ensure that the banquet room was available to anyone wishing to pay for it on a weekend. And he assured a reporter who covered the festivities that his wife was in complete agreement.

"I'm glad Cindy understands this," he said.

Cynthia seemed ecstatic throughout the evening, delighting guests at one stage with a Hawaiian dance she'd learned.

Not long after the gala, her photo went up in the Tangier, beside those of Jerry Lee Lewis and the Temptations. With the arrival of each of her seven children, the George family picture gallery would expand.

Cindy's defenders remember how she used the connections of the George family for charitable means, installing candy machines in various locations, and contributing proceeds to a children's hospital. "After a while, Cindy wasn't around to refill the inventory," remembers Mary Ann Brewer, one of several nannies who worked for the family, "and Ed would have to send someone from Tangier to do it instead."

Mary Ann, a skilled home health nurse, began her thirteen-year stretch working for the Georges in 1987, when doctors demanded that Cynthia remain in bed during her second pregnancy. "I had four pregnancies in five years," Cindy later told the Cleveland *Plain Dealer*. "With the pregnancies, I have a certain condition where I can't even stand up to take a shower. I have headaches the whole time. They had to nail blankets on the windows so the light wouldn't come in . . . It took a toll on me. But we were always happy. We always considered each baby a blessing."

At the time, the family was living modestly in a condominium in Granger Township, outside Akron. Among the neighbors in their complex was an even-tempered scientist named Lionel Dahmer, whose son, Jeffrey, is said to have committed his first murder in nearby Bath.

Then, in 1992, the Georges made a dramatic life change.

Built at the point where the suburbs and country melt together, Cynthia and Ed's new dream home stood apart from the modest farm houses found on the rolling fields of Medina County, about 20 miles from Akron. Before the foundation was even laid, the Georges were featured in a local newspaper, driving a spike into the ground on their eighteen-acre homestead, a small-town celebrity couple flaunting their rank on an uneven playing field, a neighborhood where no one else even cared to come close.

From the street, a driveway ran about fifty feet toward a four-bedroom, 1,500-foot farm house, originally constructed in 1870. But this was not the Georges' citadel. It was simply the servants' quarters. Another hundred yards, and the path turned in the direction of a five-bedroom, five-bathroom, French/English mini-mansion, with giant chimneys and a 1,429-square-foot, four-car garage. A decade later, the home would be appraised at $1.4 million—a pittance in Beverly Hills or South Beach, but an enviable sum below the Western Reserve in northeastern Ohio.

"Cindy helped design a lot of the house herself," notes Mary Ann Brewer. "It's a mammoth house. But there still wasn't enough room for seven children."

Still, Cynthia managed to enjoy her comforts behind the walls of her personal compound. Separated from the rest of the household, Cynthia's upstairs bedroom was an apartment unto itself—with its own microwave, refrigerator and towel warmer. Cynthia and Ed each had separate dressing rooms, and shared a black-and-white tile bathroom, with "his" and "her" sinks and a Jacuzzi.

By contrast, the children's bedrooms have been described as sparse. "When I left the Georges in October of 2000, the kids' rooms still had plasterboard on," Mary Ann contends. "They weren't wallpapered. They still had construction lights up. And the downstairs—it wasn't really furnished. I mean, they brought a lot of things from their condo over there. But, really, Cindy didn't buy that much for that part of the house."

Police would also observe tall weeds in the Georges' yard, and Christmas lights still hanging months after the holiday season.

According to Mary Ann, at one stage, Cynthia hired a Russian housekeeper, installing her in the farmhouse, in a small room with a black-and-white television, pull-out couch and microwave. Although she'd apparently been promised weekends off, the woman often found herself working Saturdays and Sundays from 8 AM to 7 PM. If

Mary Ann wasn't around, the duties occasionally included babysitting. The woman complained that she frequently didn't receive her salary unless she pestered the Georges for it, and a green card sponsorship pledge never materialized.

As the months wore on, the woman grew despondent, showering in the big house after the long work day, then bringing a plate of food from the kitchen back to her room. Without access to mass transportation in the country, she was overcome by a feeling of isolation. So one night, she arranged for a friend to pick her up, and shuttle her to a center assisting Jewish immigrants from the former Soviet Union. With the group's help, the housekeeper fled to Cleveland and, ultimately, New York.

The morning after her departure, Cynthia—noticing that her employee had failed to show up for work—personally walked down to the farm house, where she was dismayed to discover that her housekeeper, and all her possessions, were gone.

BEFORE HIS MARRIAGE, Ed George had purchased a condominium on Vanderbilt Beach in Naples, Florida. In the coming decades, during those rare occasions when he was able to free himself from the restaurant, he took the family south. But, even on vacation, Cynthia apparently found a way to exert her independence from the rest of the household.

"Ed would be golfing," Mary Ann says. "And it seemed like Cindy was always gone. In the evenings, the kids and I would be playing cards on the patio, and we'd hear the door opening and closing. And it would be Cindy, leaving."

At times, the nanny claims, the children would wake up and ask for their mother. On at least one occasion, Mary Ann says, she was personally awoken by Ed George.

"Where's Cindy?" he asked. "Where's Cindy?"

"I don't know."

"Isn't she here?"

"No, she's not here."

"It's one o'clock in the morning. Where is she?"

The whereabouts and mindset of Cynthia George would eventually become a preoccupation of police as well—as they tried sorting out the events surrounding the midday murder of Jeff Zack.

THREE

THE FIRST CALL was received by the Akron police dispatcher at 12:09 PM:

> Dispatcher: *What is your emergency?*
> Man: *I need immediate help. We have a gunshot wound at BJ's Wholesale Club, Sixteen Seventy-seven Home Avenue.*
> Dispatcher: *Where's the victim?*
> Man: *Pardon me?*
> Dispatcher: *Where is the victim?*
> Man: *He is in his car. A motorcycle drove up and shot him . . .*
> Dispatcher: *. . . Okay, the police and fire department are on the way, sir.*
> Man: *He has a gunshot wound to his face. He is bleeding profusely.*
> Dispatcher: *Is he conscious?*
> Man: *Barely.*
> Dispatcher: *Okay, he is breathing right now?*
> Man: *Well, we think so . . . I'm just watching right now . . .*

The caller then placed a female witness on the phone:

Dispatcher: *Did you see the motorcycle driver?*
Female: *What?*
Dispatcher: *Did you see the motorcycle driver?*
Female: *Uh, I could not tell you his face, hon.*
Dispatcher: *Okay. Was he black or white?*
Female: *That I cannot tell you . . . Get an ambulance fast.*
Dispatcher: *They're on the way. Which way did he go? Which way did the motorcycle go?*
Female: *Uh, it went out of the parking lot. It went past me . . .*
Dispatcher: *. . . Is anyone with the guy who was shot?*
Female: *No. Uh, no. No, there is nobody with the guy. He is still in the car by himself.*
Dispatcher: *Are any of your people with him that can tell us if he is still breathing?*
Female: *Uh, we do have a policeman here right now.*
Dispatcher: *Okay. Go talk to him. Thank you very much.*
Female: *You're welcome.*

WITH THE AFTERNOON sun reflecting off the police vehicles surrounding the gas station in front of the big chain store, Detective Vince Felber did his best to hide his anxiety. *He* knew that this was his first homicide case. He just didn't want anybody else to detect his nervousness. Sergeant Ed Moriarity was busy delegating commands, and looked like he didn't want to be bothered. At least not yet. So Felber made his way toward Jeff Zack's SUV, conscious of every move he was making. He wasn't about to disturb a shard of glass or step in a splatter of blood, and become responsible for polluting the crime scene.

The driver's-side door was still open, its window blown apart. Just below was the collection of reddened cloth that the medical team had used as they attempted to alleviate the victim's bleeding, while they waited for the ambulance to arrive. The spot Jeff had occupied in the final seconds of his life was replaced by a puddle of blood shimmering on the passenger's seat; for some reason, the driver's seat was fairly clean. A pair of loafers also rested on the passenger side of the vehicle. As Felber began walking toward the other end of the SUV, he heard a cell phone ring. He followed the noise, and noticed that the device had been left behind on the hood.

As a rule, Felber avoided answering other people's telephones. But the circumstances today were unique. Could this be the killer—or some accomplice—calling to see if the task had been completed? Felber grabbed the phone.

"Hello," he said.

"Is Jeff there?" a female asked.

Felber could hardly contain his curiosity: "No, can I take a message?"

Click.

Several minutes later, the phone rang again.

"Hello," Felber answered, imagining himself breaking down the voice on the other end into a confession.

Click.

A little different from TV, Felber thought, carefully depositing the phone into an evidence envelope.

The contents in Zack's pockets would also yield little. Doctors eventually turned over, among other items, a tiny bag of marijuana. To the untutored, this may have seemed like a vital clue. Was Zack's death drug-related? But detectives believed that they knew better. To them, finding a small bag of marijuana on a murder victim was as significant as unearthing a calculator on an accountant.

The answers would have to come from the people who knew Jeff Zack.

DETECTIVE DARRELL PARNELL did things his own way and at his own speed. At 55, he was among the oldest detectives in the department—and one of two African-Americans in his unit—after joining the Akron police in 1992 when his prior employer, General Tire, pulled out of the city. As four other detectives and four uniformed officers applied all their forensic skills at the crime scene—gridding off areas of the parking lot, utilizing metal detectors in the nearby grass, marching single file with their eyes trained on the ground—Parnell surveyed the Explorer, and mentally drew an image of the murder. Stepping a few paces back, he twisted his fingers into a gun, and followed the path where he imagined the bullet had traveled. Then, with his colleagues scrambling to detect a DNA-laden cigarette butt or some other clue around the SUV, Parnell unearthed the smashed-up projectile next to a concrete wall less than 100 yards away.

It was the slug that had exited Zack's head, and broken the passenger-side window—and the only piece of crime-scene evidence that prosecutors would deem useful.

AT THIS POINT, detectives had already fanned out around the shopping area, canvassing all the surrounding businesses. Robert Falkowski, the manager of BJ's, told Felber and Detective John Bell about finding Zack sitting upright in his truck, with the engine revving. Before calling 911, Falkowski had reached through the window and turned off the ignition.

When Felber and Bell asked the manager if he'd known the victim, Falkowski replied with a grimace. Yes, he knew Jeff Zack—the man who'd propositioned his underage clerk. There weren't going to be many people in BJ's who'd have positive things to say about Jeff Zack, Falkowski pointed out.

But he offered something that detectives hoped would help solve the case quickly: the surveillance tapes from the two cameras dangling from each end of the gas station's roof, pointing inward toward the pumps. Like so many store surveillance systems, the tapes were rarely changed. Instead, images were recorded over and over and over each other, diluting the quality with each rotation. Nonetheless, the detectives accepted the manager's overture.

The Akron Police Department had a station set up in its Crime Scene Unit to monitor surveillance video. Felber had spent two years in the Crime Scene Unit, and understood the system's inadequacies; the equipment was pitifully out of date, and frequently didn't function. The station was connected to a computer that supposedly could capture screen shots of criminals in the act. Unfortunately, the device hardly ever worked. So Felber—who spent much of his free time tinkering with computers—attempted to fix the problem. Instead, higher-ups blamed him for creating it.

It had been three years since he'd left the Crime Scene Unit, but virtually nothing had changed. In fact, Felber found the department's equipment so unusable that, at one point, he took the surveillance tapes home and tried playing them on his personal VCR. As the store manager had predicted, the quality was extremely poor. The recording alternated between shots from both cameras—five seconds from the camera at the north end of the station, then five seconds from the camera at the south, and so on. The view from the northern camera was relatively clear. The southern one was so distorted that it was impossible to discern that a vehicle had even been at the scene. As fate would have it, the southern camera was the one pointed directly at Jeff Zack's auto.

Felber and his colleagues placed their faces next to the monitor, hoping to uncover any piece of crucial data from the hazy video. An SUV-like object *could* be distinguished driving behind the pumps, with something that may have been a motorcycle following close behind. As soon as the Explorer stopped at the service island, though, the shot switched to the northern camera. By the time it switched back, most likely, the shooting had already occurred.

At least that was the conclusion that the detectives drew. But they weren't willing to surrender. Because dilemmas like this had occurred in the past, the Akron Police Department now worked with engineer Hugh Aylward at NASA's John

H. Glenn Research Center in Cleveland. His specialty: video enhancement. When Felber phoned him, he graciously offered to assist.

In a television drama, Aylward would have inserted the tape into a high-tech machine and—using some secret algorithm—brought crystal clarity to the vague shapes. Detectives would have been able to identify not only the killer, but the make and model of the gun, and the assassin's license plate number. In reality, Aylward did clear up the recording a touch, but in no meaningful way. His most significant contribution was digitizing the video and placing it on a computer disc, eliminating concern over the tape degrading with each subsequent viewing.

Detectives were disappointed, but still not defeated. Felber contacted a local studio said to have state-of-the-art video enhancement capabilities. The owner volunteered his services—an enormous help, since the department was far from willing to absorb the cost itself. But the company's well-intentioned efforts produced no better results than the NASA attempt. Felber also viewed the surveillance footage from the camera near BJ's front door to see if the victim had entered the store before the attack, and if the killer, for some reason, opted to follow him. All to no avail.

With no video evidence, it appeared that authorities would have to rely on the accounts of people who'd been shopping or working in the area, and happened to catch a few glimpses of the crime.

THIS MUCH WAS consistent: cars were flowing in and out of the crowded parking lot when the killer appeared on what was described as a black, white and lime green Ninja motorcycle. To some observers, the cyclist seemed to be going faster than the other drivers, and there was a certain frenzied energy with which he made turns. It was nothing extraordinary, a witness would later tell police, "just a little odd."

The motorcycle blazed into the gas station, and began circling the pumps.

Carolyn Hyson was working the gas station's cash booth, situated in the center of the pumps, and could see every vehicle being fueled. Just as she stepped outside to stretch her legs, she noticed a white-haired man parking a Ford Explorer at the pump twenty yards away. On a normal day, she'd never have remembered the vehicle—or the motorcycle that screeched up next to it, on the opposite side of the pump. But when she turned away, toward a Fazoli's franchise to the north, an ear-splitting *bang* forced her to double back and take notice.

Facing her was a man wearing a full-faced helmet and dark clothing, now positioned next to the driver's side of the Ford Explorer. Questioningly, she returned his stare. But she could see neither his eyes nor his face through the helmet's tinted shield. Apparently convinced of this, the man turned back toward his motorcycle, slipping something into the small of his back. Then, he calmly mounted the bike and took off through the parking lot.

Randall Addison was fueling his van when the shot rang out. But his vehicle blocked any view of the crime scene. With Hyson's screams now filling his ears, Addison ran around the van to see a motorcycle screeching out into heavy traffic on Home Avenue.

Some fifty yards away, Nate Zappolo was stopped at the traffic light when he felt the air trembling behind him. Peeking into the rear-view mirror, he spotted the motorcycle flying up on his vehicle, hugging the road's double yellow line to avoid a collision with oncoming traffic. Suddenly, the cyclist veered to avoid Zappolo's left side mirror, then recklessly cut in front of the other vehicles into a parking lot adjoining a Circuit City electronics store. From there, the cyclist jumped a curb and sped through a field of grass toward the access road leading to the expressway.

Once he'd disappeared, Carolyn, the gas station's cashier, turned her attention back to the SUV. The horn was blaring, filling the air with one continuous burst. The driver's-side window was shattered and, through the broken glass, she saw the white-haired man slumped against the steering wheel. Blood was dripping down his face. Knowing that the phone in her booth didn't work, she let out a panicked scream, hoping someone would call 911.

"WE HAVE A *medical emergency.*"

Dr. Sheila Steer was shopping when she heard an unusual announcement come over the public address system at BJ's. A shaken voice proclaimed that there'd been a crisis nearby, and a medical professional was urgently needed. Dr. Steer left her shopping cart behind, and hurried to the front of the store, where manager Robert Falkowski motioned her outside.

Jeff Zack couldn't have received better medical attention if he'd been shot inside a hospital. Steer, an emergency room physician, rushed into the parking lot to discover that three nurses had already removed an unresponsive Zack from his SUV, and gingerly placed him on the asphalt. The bullet had entered his face below his left eye, tumbled through his head, and exited just below the right ear. Shattered glass had peppered his face with red speckles. One of the nurses ran to her car to retrieve a CPR mask, and the four took turns, trying to stabilize Zack until an ambulance arrived. But, as Zack lay on the ground, Dr. Steer heard an all-too-familiar gurgling sound, and recognized that the man was drowning in his own blood.

Still, she jumped into an ambulance with the EMS unit, briefed the technicians on Zack's condition, and—as the vehicle blared toward East Market Street—valiantly continued her effort to save this complete stranger. Deep down, though, she realized that Zack's luck had run its course. When he died, shortly after his arrival at Akron City Hospital, Dr. Steer was not surprised.

NEARLY THREE HOURS later, a tow truck removed Jeff Zack's Explorer from the parking lot, hauling it to the Akron Police processing garage for further inspection. With the truck gone, the officers and detectives also began to fall off. By 4 PM, anyone pulling up in front of BJ's would have no inkling that, earlier in the day, a man had been murdered at the gas pumps.

Before he left the crime scene, though, Sergeant Moriarity faced the press. He knew the name of the victim, but couldn't reveal it before Zack's family was notified. Moriarity's instincts told him that this was nothing short of a hit. Yet, it seemed too early to show his hand; the longer the suspect believed that cops were clueless, the more likely he was to discard caution, and engage in some other incriminating stunt. A few reporters mentioned road rage, and Moriarity said nothing to discount that theory.

Within hours, he prepared a press release, requesting information from anyone who might have witnessed "an altercation involving this style motorcycle and a blue Ford Explorer." As a result, the Cleveland *Plain Dealer* reported that some type of exchange had occurred between Zack and his assailant, further fueling the road rage premise.

THE PROCESS OF canvassing Jeff Zack's neighbors was tedious and time-consuming, yet, with the dearth of hard evidence at the crime scene, it was an essential means of gaining a glimmer of understanding into the life, and possibly the death, of the victim. The Akron police needed every spare body to perform this chore, and Felber was among a team of six detectives—under the leadership of Lieutenant David Whiddon, a 250-pound, barrel-chested, former high school football star—charged with walking past the two-story colonial homes, well-trimmed lawns, red fireplugs and tall shady trees in the Akron suburb of Stow, and interviewing reticent acquaintances in their doorways and garages. The vast majority claimed that their interactions with Zack had consisted of exchanging quick waves, then going about their business.

But the shadowy entrepreneur had had a tendency to linger around homes inhabited by attractive women—he'd allegedly lost a job as a heating and air-conditioning repairman because he spent too much of his time flirting with female clients—and had become embroiled in a feud with a next-door neighbor over what the man characterized as harassment of his wife.

Allegedly, Zack had enjoyed spying on the woman when she was sunbathing or swimming in the family pool. On one occasion, she'd doused him with the hose when he entered her property sporting a three-piece suit. Another time, he'd apparently come into her yard and uttered a number of inappropriate comments, prompting her spouse to physically snatch Zack and grapple him off the property.

Reportedly, Zack had threatened to shoot the man with an AK-47.

A short time later, the husband was raking leaves in front of his home when Zack suddenly drove toward him, then swerved out of the way before making contact. Looking back, the woman admitted that she'd never believed Jeff intended to harm her husband. Zack had simply been using his vehicle to toy with a person he didn't like.

The more police probed, the more they saw a pattern. At his son's school, Jeff had asked teachers for dates. People in the neighborhood told detectives about a 1996 incident at a hardware store, in which Zack had grabbed and kissed an underage sales clerk, telling her that he'd be willing to go to jail for having sex with her. He'd been charged with sexual imposition, but pleaded guilty to disorderly conduct, and received a year's probation. Still—as with the father of the 17-year-old girl from BJ's—detectives would have to find the youngster's family, and ensure that the murder wasn't some form of revenge.

It was also apparent that several of Zack's neighbors knew a salacious detail about his distant past, a 1981 arrest related to his involvement with an Arizona escort service. Apparently, after having sex with two girls aged 15 and 16, Jeff had persuaded them to become prostitutes. Zack later told authorities that he'd worked as a bodyguard and driver for the escort service because he was broke. He avoided prison time—receiving 2 years' probation—by testifying against two others. Nonetheless, the news upset Zack's fellow suburbanites so much that one resident actually called a neighborhood meeting about it, and handed out documents related to the arrest.

ALTHOUGH ZACK HAD regularly regaled friends and acquaintances with tales about his days in the Israeli military, he was actually an American, the eldest of Alvin and Elayne Lieberman's three sons, born in Detroit in 1957. Jeff's parents divorced when he was nine, and the boy was so emotionally wounded by his father's departure that he cut the man off emotionally. For the rest of his life, Jeff would become extremely volatile when he suspected that someone was rejecting him.

He was also upset that his mother was one of the few women in the neighborhood who had to leave her children each day and go to work. Often, Jeff found himself alone with his brothers, babysitting. He resented this situation so much that, at age 16, he briefly moved to Florida on his own.

By this time, Elayne was remarried to David Zack, and Jeff and his youngest brother Marc had adopted their stepfather's surname. For some reason, the middle brother, Rick, remained a Lieberman.

Jeff always kept himself in shape, playing football

and lifting weights during his teens. But his rebellious spirit triggered eruptions in school and, for a period, there was concern that he wouldn't be able to graduate from Southfield-Lathrup High School. When he did, William Tyndale College, a now-defunct Christian school once known as the Detroit Bible Institute was among the few willing to accept him. Teachers characterized him as bright, but easily bored and restless. He eventually dropped out.

Although he later told his wife that he'd attended Michigan State University for one year, she doubted his story. According to one close associate, Jeff spent his late teens selling marijuana and Quaaludes.

At one point, Jeff became engaged to a girl he'd met in high school. When she broke off the relationship, he exploded, moving his former fiancée's belongings out of her apartment, and into the home where they'd planned to live together.

Friends attributed the episode to Jeff's abandonment by his father, and the pain of being rejected. "It was the reason why he behaved the way he did," his mother said after his death.

In 1975, Jeff inexplicably vanished. Three months later, he called his mother and informed her that he was living on a *kibbutz*—or collective farm—in Israel, and had enlisted in the Israeli Army, becoming a dual citizen of the United States and the Jewish homeland. There was no question that, unlike other American Jews unwilling to risk their lives to maintain their ideal of a Jewish nation, Jeff was ready to shed his blood for his principles. He planned to become a pilot in Israel's storied air force, but his eyesight hindered him. Instead, Zack told family members, he was a paratrooper, comparing his training to that of the Navy SEALs. He also claimed to have engaged in clandestine anti-terrorist campaigns, boarding airplanes dressed in civilian clothing, wielding a suitcase containing an Uzi submachine gun. Compared to many of Jeff's later business schemes, in Israel, he was driven by a sense of mission, and placed himself in harm's way, not out of defiance, but dedication to the Jewish state.

It was during this period that he displayed an incredible fortitude for learning languages; by the end of his life, he'd claim to speak English, Hebrew, Arabic, Russian and Spanish. But he also boasted that, while in Israel, he indulged in a bit of freelancing, transporting and unloading kilos of hashish. Zack later described this era as the happiest in his life.

His post-military pursuits involved a succession of jobs and careers. When he'd get settled into one enterprise, he'd grow dissatisfied, and start looking for something else. At one stage, he went into the recycling business with his step-father. But the two clashed when the older man fired Jeff after accusing him of swiping scrap metal after hours, and reselling it.

In 1986, Jeff was working as a headhunter in Phoenix when he first encountered Bonnie Boucher, who'd tired of her job with a cable company, and was searching for a change of pace. Within three months—against the advice of Bonnie's family—they were married in Boulder, Colorado. The two loved the state, with its mountains, old mining towns and bike and hiking trails, so much that Jeff transferred to an office in Denver. In time, he earned his stockbroker's license, and began working for a brokerage firm southeast of Boulder, in the small town of Louisville.

Yet Bonnie's family was always distrustful of Zack. Early on in the relationship, Jeff's father-in-law, Robert Boucher, had a friend at the Mesa, Arizona, police department run a background check on Zack—and discovered his arrest on the prostitution charge.

"I was only driving the girls around," Jeff said. "I didn't know what was going on."

On another occasion, Zack's mother-in-law accused him of walking into the bathroom, exposing himself and urinating in front of a female relative.

In 1988, while Bonnie was pregnant, the couple moved to

San Diego, where Jeff took a job with a new brokerage company. But, as with other aspects of his life, scandal was never far away. After his boss allegedly began scamming money from investors, Jeff contacted the Securities and Exchange Commission. At one point, a California neighbor claimed, the supervisor suddenly appeared at her home, irritably inquiring about the whereabouts of Jeff Zack. There were also apparent threats delivered to Zack and his family.

Before the Zacks left San Diego in 1991, Jeff sold off many of his personal possessions, the neighbor said, including his prized boat. Jeff claimed that his mother-in-law was ill, and they needed to return to Ohio to care for her. But it seemed like he was trying to cut his ties with California in a hurry.

The company's owners were eventually imprisoned for their role in the plot. Although Jeff was cleared of any wrongdoing, his involvement with the brokerage house provoked an IRS investigation. In the fallout, Zack was forced to file for bankruptcy.

In 1997, Jeff phoned his brother Marc, who was living in Utah with his wife. Jeff was in town on a skiing trip and needed a place to stay. The couple was about to embark on a vacation, and didn't feel comfortable leaving Jeff to his own devices in their condo. As the conversation became more heated, Jeff asked to speak to his sister-in-law, then began abusing her over the phone. Marc took back the receiver, and told Jeff never to call him again.

There were moments in Jeff's life when he appeared to be on the verge of achieving some type of stability. Yet his flirtation with risk continuously undermined him. He told a co-worker about a plan to divorce Bonnie, and replace her with a woman from the Middle East. Love had nothing to do with the motive. Once the bride received her green card, Zack would terminate the relationship—pocketing a $6,500 payoff. Although the plot never took shape, a scheme involving stocks yielded high dividends at first. As the months passed, though, Jeff's profits dwindled away until he lost his entire investment. He hadn't been able to maintain a steady job since.

THE TASK OF visiting the Zack home went to Bertina King, a confident, six-foot-tall detective who'd earned some deference among her fellow African-Americans for her "take no shit" attitude. Other detectives thought this *I am woman, hear me roar* manner helped make her a favorite with Captain Elizabeth Daugherty. Because of the perception that Bertina would ask the questions that no one else could, she was temporarily removed from a rape investigation and teamed up with a victims' assistance advocate, as well as representatives from the medical examiner's office and Stow Police Department. Their assignment was not an enviable one: informing Zack's wife, Bonnie, and 12-year-old son, Brian, of Jeff's death, then questioning them about his potential enemies, as well as his copious faults.

The Zack home sat above a landscaped yard, the bottom floor fronted by brick, the upper level with tan siding. The suburban setting may have contrasted with the ramshackle neighborhoods where Bertina first earned her reputation, but her techniques never wavered. When no one answered the front bell, Bertina went around to the back—wondering what the neighbors might think, surveying this statuesque black woman peeking through the Zacks' sliding glass doors. The entranceway was open, and Bertina was debating whether there was another victim inside when a black Cadillac pulled into the driveway.

Bonnie Zack was home.

"Who are you?" she demanded. "And what are you doing behind my house?"

It was a reasonable question, and it took Bertina several minutes to establish her credentials. She'd been through this process so many times before that Bonnie was soon making candid revelations.

Despite the self-confidence she projected as a real estate

agent, Bonnie was very much a long-suffering wife, whose good looks couldn't mask the fact that her husband's myriad indiscretions had aged her. Beneath his jolly veneer, Jeff could be an obnoxious womanizer who bolstered his immense ego by heaping verbal abuse on family members. Yet, although Bonnie freely conceded that her fifteen-year marriage to Jeff had been rocky, she was visibly shaken by news of his death. Sitting down at the kitchen table, she admitted that she couldn't bring it upon herself to phone Jeff's mother and other relatives, and Bertina offered to perform this delicate chore herself.

When the conversation resumed, it was obvious that no one in the family would buy into the road rage theory. Yes, Jeff was known to drive fast and cut people off. At times, he seemed to enjoy angering strangers, and never backed down from a confrontation. But he was practiced at these types of encounters, and probably wouldn't have continued to the gas station afterwards to fill up his tank. If someone had wanted to take him to task for his driving, Jeff would have pulled over to the side of the road and settled it there.

But this was not the side of Jeff that his son chose to remember, and Brian Zack was devastated by the murder. The boy had adored his father. Jeff had been Brian's mentor and friend. For all of Jeff's limitations, he was absolutely devoted to his son. Zack sincerely believed that Brian could be the best at anything he tried, and supported the boy wholeheartedly, attending every basketball game—and every practice.

Brian knew his father as a guy who'd volunteered with a pets-for-kids program at local hospitals, and recalled Jeff's pride in describing his time in the Israeli military. Zack had often shown his son photos from this era—he once also displayed an Israeli assault rifle to a co-worker—and Brian was happy to view the pictures again and again.

On the last day of his life, Jeff had invited Brian to help him power-wash a deck. But before they'd left the house, Jeff wanted to change a lightbulb.

"Bring that chair over here," he requested.

Brian took his time—he was in the middle of breakfast—and Jeff started to yell. As Bonnie rushed forward to calm her husband, the boy retreated to his bedroom. But through the door, Brian heard a familiar diatribe: "I'm out of here. I want a divorce. You'll see what it's like when I'm gone. You won't know what to do without me. You need me to the do the landscaping and everything else around here."

Naturally, Bonnie was worried about the way the murder would affect her son. And, because of the nature of their marriage, she realized that authorities had reason to suspect her. But Bonnie wasn't guilty and didn't act that way. Rather than hiding behind her legal counsel, she remained forthcoming, answering questions about everything—including her sometimes negative feelings toward Jeff.

Without pausing to conceptualize a chain of events, Bonnie rattled off her activities that morning. She'd spent the early hours at home, dropped off Brian at a miniature golf course, returned to clean the house, then went to Kaufmann's department store. She was there fifteen minutes when her son phoned, asking for a ride. She swung back to the golf facility, picked up Brian and a friend, and drove them to Maplewood Park, where they went swimming. Eventually, she headed into her office, and was stopping off at home to retrieve a client's phone number when she came across the police.

Although Bonnie certainly appeared innocent, she was quick to add that there were others she assumed wanted to hurt her husband. To prove the point, Bonnie walked Detective King over to the answering machine, and played a message she'd saved from three days before the shooting. What unnerved Bonnie was the fact that her normally brash husband had seemed to become worried as he listened to the words.

The call was less than thirty seconds long, and had been received at 2:55 PM on June 13, 2001:

*"All right, buddy. You got one way out, so you need to
start answering your cell phone—okay? I'll be talking to
you, or should I call your mom and dad's house in
Arizona? Whatever. Answer the phone, boy."*

Jeff hadn't identified the caller, but Bonnie thought that
it sounded a bit like Mike Scranton, a onetime business associate who'd fallen out with Zack over a dispute involving
a few thousand dollars. Bonnie didn't think the clash was a
big enough issue to culminate in murder, but she readily
acknowledged that Jeff had kept his business deals to himself, and she was often ignorant to "the whole story" regarding many aspects of his life.

Police initially believed that Scranton was such an important suspect that a detective was flown to Florida to interview him near his home. Yes, Scranton confirmed, he
and Zack had exchanged unfriendly words over a financial
dispute. But that was it. Scranton possessed neither the
criminal leanings nor the resources to hire a hit man.

Still, another name kept resurfacing in conversations
detectives had with Bonnie Zack and, it seemed, virtually
everyone else: Cynthia George. Her affair with Zack was
an open secret; even Bonnie Zack's relatives knew about
the relationship. In fact, Bonnie had been with her husband
on the night he met Cynthia, during a lavish gathering at
the Tangier. Bonnie and Jeff were having drinks when
she'd caught him staring at the dazzling woman with the
body of a fashion model and the deportment of an heiress,
on the opposite side of the bar.

Well accustomed to her husband's wandering eye, Bonnie made the best of what could have been a turbulent situation. "Don't even think about it," she chided Jeff. "She's
well beyond you."

"You think so?" Jeff smirked back. "Well, go watch.
Watch me."

With his wife looking on, Jeff sauntered up to Cynthia
and made some jocular remark. This was Zack at his best—

the amiable salesman capable of soothing strangers into a comfort zone where they quickly let down their guard. Soon, Jeff had his arm around Cynthia, and—just to prove that his intentions were purely innocent—drew Bonnie into the conversation, and the good humor.

When Ed came by, Zack complimented him on his beautiful spouse.

"If you can afford her," Ed jokingly replied, "you can have her."

Jeff whispered into Cindy's ear, "You deserve more than this."

Before long, Jeff was a member of Cynthia and Ed George's social network—while his own family came to regard the arresting blonde as Zack's "special friend."

FOUR

CYNTHIA GEORGE'S NANNY, Mary Ann Brewer, had a theory about why her employer, self-indulgent in so many other ways, was willing to endure miscarriages and bed rest to produce a family of seven children. "Cindy wanted one more child than Ed's mother," Mary Ann says. "But Cindy only had seven kids. Her mother-in-law had eight."

Perhaps this explains why, even when Cindy was pregnant with one child, she agreed to adopt a little girl from Lebanon as Christians, Muslims and outside armies warred in her husband's ancestral nation.

One Monday evening, Cindy and the kids swung by the Tangier before Ed repaired to a friend's house for his weekly poker game. As the family ate dinner, Cynthia happened to mention, "The baby was born today."

She was referring to the bi-racial boy she'd arranged to adopt.

Ed was less than pleased. He was worried about the way society would react to an African-American boy in a family of Lebanese women. "We're not getting another baby," he insisted.

"Yes, we are."

"No, we're not." He turned to the nanny: "Mary Ann, tell her you're quitting if she brings home another baby."

It was a pointless argument. The plan was already in motion. As Mary Ann recalls, "She was the boss. She was the boss of everything."

Within days, the boy was living in the George home. Ed fell in love with the child instantly, and doted over him.

Five of the George daughters attended Our Lady of the Elms, a Catholic school that placed a high premium on parental involvement in their children's education. Ed was a regular attendee at the school's basketball games. Cindy played an active role during the six-month period when one of her children was preparing to spend her summer in Nicaragua with Amigos de las Américas, a social service organization.

Despite his workaholic reputation, Ed was ever-present in the children's lives. Every Saturday morning, no matter how late he'd been at the Tangier the night before, he cooked the kids breakfast. On weekday mornings, he'd ferry them to school, running a brush through the little girls' hair as they walked out the door. While he seemed genuinely enthusiastic about bonding with the youngsters, he may have wondered why his wife wasn't doing more. Staffers occasionally had to babysit the George kids at the restaurant because Cynthia seemed too busy doing something else. A Tangier employee eventually told police about hearing Ed grumble that Cindy didn't make herself available enough to pick up the children from school and other outings.

To Mary Ann, it also appeared that Cynthia didn't have much interest in participating in family meals. "I'd cook dinner and we'd all be sitting at the table," the nanny recalls. "She'd come in, go upstairs, shower, change and go back out again."

Although Cynthia seemed to enjoy her freedom, she allegedly complained that Ed didn't give her the kind of money she needed to support her lifestyle—and told associates that she'd contemplated leaving him.

Whether this was bluster or not, it was apparent that

Cynthia had an eye for other men. Her lawyer, Michael Bowler, noted that Ed's compulsive work habits "probably left a hole in their relationship, and a hole in their marriage." At the Tangier, while Ed lorded over the kitchen, Cynthia regularly flirted—often with the best-looking man in the place.

Even so, the relationship with Jeff Zack was unusual in its conspicuousness. To some observers, it appeared that Jeff and Cindy were always together—even in front of Ed. George had purchased a $40,000 baler from Jeff to compact cardboard, and the restaurant phoned Zack whenever a spare part was needed. The staffers at the Tangier immediately recognized Jeff's voice when he called—sometimes unremittingly. When Jeff stopped by the club, he was known to head directly into Ed's office, where the two would hang out like childhood friends. More than one employee observed that they were similar types of guys: overbearing, rude and uncouth. Behind Ed's back, Jeff would gossip as if he had the inside story on the Tangier—claiming that the restaurant was losing money, and Ed's brother's company, Bell Music, was keeping the business afloat.

Brian Zack would later tell police about meeting the Georges when he was about 7 years old, and visiting their home to play with their children. One of the girls even spent the night at the Zacks' house a few times. And while visiting Ohio from her home in Arizona, Jeff's mother, Elayne, had attended parties at the Georges' residence.

To acquaintances, Cynthia occasionally introduced Jeff as "Dr. Zack." Jeff smiled, and played the part of a confident medical professional, never letting on that, in some ways, his paramour regarded him as more of a handyman.

"Cindy had him doing all kinds of repairs around the house," Mary Ann maintains, "building shelves, putting up Christmas trees, hanging decorations and lights all over the place."

When Ed wasn't home, Jeff would occasionally enter

the George house, greet the kids and the help, then stroll into Cynthia's bedroom. Sometimes, the two disappeared into the attic together, locking the door behind them. There were days when several of the children would be running around the house searching for their mother, while she was blissfully concealed in some quiet corner of her faux chateau with her boyfriend.

One afternoon, Mary Ann noticed one of the children giggling.

"What are you laughing about?" the nanny asked.

"I just saw Mommy kissing Jeff upstairs. I was playing underneath the crib. I saw them kissing."

Even more disquieting was Mary Ann's contention that Jeff appeared to focus an inordinate amount of attention on the Georges' oldest daughter. There were moments, the nanny said, when that became uncomfortable, watching Cynthia's lover grab and hug the teenager.

"You should really talk to your father about this," Mary Ann told the child.

She wasn't sure if the girl ever followed the advice.

IN EARLY 2000, an Akron vending machine company received a call from Cynthia about making a purchase. The same day, she arrived at owner Azeem Syed's office with two of her daughters, as well as Zack. Apparently, she was interested in putting her boyfriend into business.

Zack's Mid West Vending company installed machines providing soft drinks, coffee and snacks. Jeff often brought his son Brian with him to fill up the machines, and purchased candy in bulk at BJ's. Syed said that Jeff liked to haggle to get the best deal. But the Arab entrepreneur actually admired his Israeli customer for this. No one catches a break in this world, Syed reasoned, unless he asks for one.

Zack bragged that his wife was leading her real estate office in sales, and rarely engaged in transactions worth less than several million dollars. Yet, when Zack was delinquent in his payments, Syed phoned not Bonnie Zack, but Cynthia George—who always made sure that the debts were quickly settled.

Early on in the relationship, Bonnie's relatives noted that Jeff seemed to spend a great deal of time bicycling with his attractive companion. From the day he met Cynthia, Bonnie later confided to police, "I was nothing." Zack even gave his son an electronic planner with three emergency numbers programmed into it—including one marked "Cin" for Cindy George. Although Jeff initially described Cynthia as a good friend, he later revealed their romantic relationship to his son, pointing out that he'd stayed in the George home overnight when Ed was elsewhere. When police later asked the boy why he thought his father had disclosed something like this, Brian replied that he and Jeff were close, and didn't keep secrets from one another.

"Jeff was happy to have this relationship with Cindy," observed Zack's mother, Elayne. "I liked her a lot. She was a fun-loving, beautiful girl, very charming. She seemed to be very sweet. And, apparently, her husband didn't pay very much attention to her.

"As far as I knew, the relationship between Cindy and Jeffrey was intimate. But nothing was ever described to me. I just assumed. Because when he came out to visit me in Arizona, the phone rang all the time, and it was always Cindy. They would talk for hours on his cell phone. And she was always there when I came to visit Jeffrey in Ohio."

Yet, Elayne was certain that Jeff and Cindy would never leave their respective spouses and legitimize their affair: "I don't think she would have married him. She was living this life of wonderful wealth. She had this mansion, and anything she wanted."

On the few occasions that someone dared to question Ed about his unusual marriage arrangement, he replied that women were now "liberated," and didn't assume traditional roles or behaviors. Friends also theorized that, Cynthia's misconduct notwithstanding, Ed's pious and strong-willed

mother would never have allowed any of her children to vio-
late Catholic doctrine by terminating a marriage in divorce.

DURING CYNTHIA'S FINAL pregnancy, Mary Ann began to
suspect that her employer had become anorexic. "I had to
make her eat," Mary Ann says, "because even though she
was pregnant, she did not want to gain a lot of weight. After the pregnancy, Cindy also seemed obsessed with keeping her weight down—in ways I didn't really feel were
healthy.

"She didn't eat. All she did was drink water—and eat
this popcorn, hot air popcorn that she'd make in her bedroom, upstairs, while the rest of the family was at the table,
eating real food."

Later, Cynthia would describe the conception of her
seventh child in frightening terms, claiming that Zack had
shown up at her home on a night when Ed was away, demanding admittance. "He was saying, 'Let me in,'" Cindy
told the Cleveland *Plain Dealer*. "I locked that door, and
then I saw him go to the next door." Cynthia sobbed as she
recounted the story to a reporter. "That was a bad night."

Before leaving, she told the newspaper, Jeff taunted her,
"Your life is not your life anymore . . . Call the police. Call
your mother. Who's going to believe you? Didn't you in-
vite me over when your husband wasn't home?"

She claims that she initially believed that her youngest
daughter was the offspring of her husband. Similarly, Ed
perceived the birth of the seventh child in the family as
"God's will," tending to the baby late at night when she'd
awake, coughing from a respiratory ailment. "It was *his*
child," Mary Ann contends. "He loved that child. Honestly,
even if he knew the truth, I think he was too caring of a father to act any other way."

In Arizona, Jeff's mother was unaware of the addition
to *her* family: "I never knew that she was Jeffrey's daughter. He never told me."

By the time Jeff died, though, Bonnie was astute enough to ban Cynthia from the Zack home. The beauty "always dressed flashy and flirty," Bonnie would testify in court, with more than a trace of disdain in her voice. Brian Zack told police about an argument his parents had had about six months prior to the murder. Jeff had asked Cindy to stop by the house. "I don't want to see her," Bonnie shot back, "and she's not welcome here."

According to police, Bonnie had begun to suspect that her husband was having an affair with Cynthia in 1998, while listening to one of Jeff's phone conversations from a bathroom next to the Zacks' bedroom.

"I can't get enough of being inside you," Jeff had reportedly said.

When he hung up, his wife confronted him. "You're hearing things," he insisted. Not only had he not made the comment, he maintained, but he wasn't even talking to Cindy.

Bonnie was apprehensive, and continued to listen for other hints. One day, she heard Jeff arranging to meet Cynthia at the Cuyahoga Falls Sheraton. Bonnie quickly found a babysitter for Brian, then staked out the hotel. When she spotted the couple, she stepped out in front of them, and demanded an explanation. They responded with silence. Spinning on her heels, Bonnie stormed out of the building—and was deeply hurt that Jeff never made an effort to follow her.

Jeff "really liked his wife," his mother Elayne told Jim Johnson, a reporter who covered the waste disposal industry for a publication called *Waste News*. But he "was just unhappy a lot and always seeking attention." As a result, he "went after other women."

In 1999, Bonnie overheard Jeff and Cynthia on the phone again. This time, they were arguing. Afterward, the normally emotionless Jeff appeared visibly shaken. He confirmed that he and Cindy had been having an affair for years, and even shared parentage of a child. But now, he emphasized, the relationship was over, and he never intended to see Cynthia again.

Almost as soon as the words had left his mouth, Jeff was denying that he'd fathered any of Cynthia's children. And when he resumed his association with Cindy, he assured his wife that the relationship was purely platonic. Bonnie tried to convince herself that her husband was telling the truth.

Although these anecdotes may have reinforced the theory that Bonnie was the culprit in her husband's killing, Brian had his own theory. The day before the murder, Brian told police, he'd been watching the ABC news magazine show *20/20* with his father. When a story about a professional hit man aired, Jeff turned to his son. "If anything ever happens to me," Zack stated, "look at Ed George. He has money and can hire someone to do me in."

THE SCENARIO MADE perfect sense: a man finds out his wife is cheating, and forces her boyfriend to pay with his life. Detective Felber attempted to pursue this angle by phoning Cynthia's mother, Helen Rohr. "We're interested in talking to you about Jeff Zack, as well as your daughter," he said.

"I hardly know Jeff Zack," she replied. "I really can't tell you anything."

"I understand. But I'd still like to talk to you, as well as your other daughter, Jane."

Helen promised to telephone Jane, and possibly arrange a time for Felber to interview the pair at the same time. "I'll call you back in a half hour," she said. But forty minutes later, Felber was still waiting for the call, and decided to phone Helen again.

"I wasn't able to get ahold of Jane," she insisted.

"Well, I'd like to figure out a time when we can meet. How's Sunday for you?"

"Sunday's not any good. I have a birthday party on Sunday. How about I call you on Monday to set something up?"

"Can I have Jane's number in the meantime?"

"I really can't give it to you. It's unlisted."

Felber contained his frustration—and received the phone number after patiently explaining that he was a detective investigating a homicide.

When he phoned again the following Monday, though, Helen informed him that she had a heart condition, and was concerned that it could be aggravated by a discussion about Ed George's possible involvement in a murder. As a result, her attorney, Robert Meeker, had advised her not to speak to the police. Jane was also retaining Meeker, and received the same recommendation.

The detective started phoning the couple's friends. Initially, several agreed to speak. But within twenty-four hours, they'd call back and claim that a newly hired attorney had suggested that they decline the police department's invitation. On more than one occasion, Felber noted that the friends appeared to be represented by lawyers affiliated with Ed George.

Having a suspect evade an interrogation was a normal part of the investigative process. But it seemed extreme to have so many associated with the couple making the same excuse.

BEFORE ZACK'S MURDER, Felber's biggest case had involved the apprehension of Richard Curley—a.k.a. "The Curley Monster." Curley was a master burglar, who'd studied human behavior and realized that most people placed their wallets and keys on counters close to windows. Working between the hours of 2 and 6 AM, Curley would quietly cut the screens of first-floor windows, reach in, and empty billfolds and snatch jewelry. From time to time, he found an open door, helped himself to items in the home, then sat down in the kitchen, brazenly snacking on cereal, cake and leftovers. Numerous houses were hit on more than one occasion.

Police suspected Curley of several burglaries, but never

grasped the level of his proficiency. Because burglaries were occurring three to four times a week in various parts of the city, some hypothesized that a gang of thieves was responsible. But when Felber and Lieutenant Ken Ball finally questioned Curley, they broke him down to the point that he confessed to more than 600 thefts over a five-year period. The detectives even convinced him to participate in a ride-along, where he pointed out more than 150 homes that he'd burglarized, describing the technique used at each individual house. It turned out that several owners had never even filed police reports; they hadn't known about the crimes until the detectives told them.

Around the time of the Zack investigation, a thief named Labron Yeager was stopped for a minor traffic violation. Both Felber and Detective Darrell Parnell believed that Yeager was a member of a gang of burglars who regularly crashed stolen vehicles through convenience store doors, hauling off cigarettes and disappearing into the night. The enterprise was so widespread that convenience stores in Akron now block their doors with two solid pillars. After the traffic infringement, the detectives talked Yeager into meeting them in a neutral location—a spot behind a hamburger joint—to discuss the gang's activities. When he arrived, he claimed to be nothing more than a lookout, and thus assumed that he was immune from prosecution. Felber and Parnell said nothing to dissuade this notion, as Yeager began to grumble over the fact that his juvenile step-son had been recruited into the group. Despite pressure to arrest Yeager at the scene, the detectives took a risk, and agreed to let him leave and reconvene with them in the near future. This act of good faith—along with Parnell's black man–to–black man talk to Yeager about setting things straight—prompted the thief to lead police to nine other gang members over a two-week period. Of course, he was soon arrested, as well.

In less than a decade on the Akron police force, Felber had logged more than 1,000 arrests. In fact, while sitting in a car, pressing an organized crime associate into inquiring about the Zack murder, Felber spotted a wanted thief jiggling door handles of nearby vehicles. Excusing himself, Felber told the aging mobster to go home, then chased the thief over a bridge, and cornered him at the edge of the river, until backup arrived.

FELBER DESPERATELY WANTED to speak to Ed George. Although it was his first homicide, the detective believed that his onetime employment at the Tangier, along with his track record, could make a difference. But the Georges had already been visited by Major Paul Callahan, Captain Elizabeth Daugherty, Sergeant Moriarity and Detective Bertina King—and the decision to send this quartet to the George mansion had been anything but arbitrary. Callahan and Ed George already knew each other. Callahan was the lead singer of an Irish band that performed at the Tangier every St. Patrick's Day. In fact, Ed had contacted Callahan in early 2001, claiming that someone was harassing Cindy. Callahan suggested starting a paper trail by filing a police report. Ed seemed hesitant.

"Do you know the guy?" Callahan asked.

"Yeah."

"Who is he?"

"I don't want to say."

"Well, if you know who he is, tell him to leave your wife alone."

Two weeks before the murder, George had called the major again, leaving a message about the matter on Callahan's voice mail. With all his other responsibilities at the police department, Callahan never had a chance to return the call. But he wouldn't have been able to provide a great deal of assistance, anyway. Since the Georges lived outside the Akron city limits, there was nothing that Callahan could actually do, save for recommending that the restaurateur call authorities in Medina County.

Nonetheless, on the day after Jeff Zack's murder, Callahan and his subordinates pulled up onto the Georges' property. With their civil servant salaries, they couldn't help but be impressed by Cindy's hulking dream house. But there was a shabbiness that reminded them of the neglected dwellings they'd encountered in the lower income districts of the city. Three-foot weeds wafted in the wind in the front yard. Christmas decorations from more than half a year earlier had never been removed.

The group knocked, and a nanny admitted them into the house. Not only was much of the home cluttered and messy, but the Christmas tree was still standing. The detectives asked to speak to Ed, and were told that he was golfing. Only Cindy was available. This promised to be an ideal situation. With Ed unable to influence and scare his wife, maybe Cynthia—distraught over her lover's death—would reveal the truth.

Although polite, Cynthia's movements and demeanor were just a little bit off-kilter; from years of interviewing drug-impaired suspects, the detectives wondered whether she was heavily medicated. At a certain point, Moriarity and Callahan left the room, hoping that Cynthia would feel more comfortable with the two females. When they asked about her husband's whereabouts on the day Zack was murdered, Cindy had a ready answer: "At the restaurant with some city of Akron health inspectors. There was some kind of sewer backup."

She even remembered the timeline. Ed had apparently left home at about 8:30 AM, and she didn't see him again until approximately 1:30 PM. City health inspectors would later verify this assertion. Cindy could also account for her own schedule. She'd spent the entire morning with her seven children, getting ready for a 2 PM wedding at St. Vincent. But she wasn't interested in discussing much else with the two women, and asked to speak to Major Callahan. The female detectives excused themselves, and Callahan entered to meet with Cindy alone.

Callahan would later tell his investigators she was less than obliging. To many of the questions, she responded, "Don't you think I should wait for Ed to come home before I answer that?"

"How did you hear about Jeff's murder?" Callahan said he probed.

"It must have been Sunday morning. Ed came in with the newspaper." George was apparently the one who'd notified his shocked wife about the crime, then read part of the article aloud, as she shook her head in disbelief.

Callahan tried delving deeper. But Cindy claimed to be confused by the process, and unsure of what to do next.

"Remember when Ed spoke to me about that person who was bothering you?" Callahan ventured. "Was that Jeff Zack?"

"Yes."

"How did you know Jeff?"

"We were friends."

"Were you more than friends?"

Cindy looked down and paused. "No," she finally answered.

"Well, why do you think he was bothering you?"

Cynthia shrugged, and mumbled something inaudible.

Callahan opted not to pursue the conversation, and the four detectives left a short time later.

The next morning, Callahan reached Ed George by phone.

"Can you believe this?" Ed mused.

Once again, Callahan inquired if Jeff Zack had been the man who'd been harassing his wife.

"Yes," Ed answered.

"Could you come down to the station with Cindy so we can talk about this more?"

"Let me talk to Cindy, and we'll be there right away."

Less than an hour later, Robert Meeker—the same attorney affiliated with Cynthia's mother and sister—arrived instead. Meeker radiated dignity and importance. A former starter on the Notre Dame football team, Meeker sat on the board of trustees of both Edwin Shaw hospital, and St. Vincent–St. Mary High School, Ed George's alma mater. A Catholic Youth Organization (CYO) basketball and football coach, Meeker was a past president of the Notre Dame Club of Akron, as well as the Dapper Dan Club, an organization that donated thousands of dollars to youth sports in the city. Although his specialty was personal injury, few police viewed him as, or treated him like, an ambulance chaser. When Meeker entered a room, everyone else was generally deferential.

On this day, Meeker had a short but predictable message to deliver: Ed George would not be doing any interviews with the Akron Police Department. With those few words, the lawyer effectively barred any law enforcement agency from speaking to the man most detectives viewed as the number-one suspect.

FIVE

AS THE WEEKS progressed, detectives remained fairly certain of Ed's guilt; few could remember a case in which an innocent person had hired a lawyer, then refused to talk to authorities. When police called one of the Georges' nannies, she replied that her employers had told her to bring their lawyer, Robert Meeker, to the interview.

"Why?" Detective Felber asked.

"For my protection."

"For *your* protection?"

"Well, maybe for their protection."

Still, some of Ed's behavior was completely uncharacteristic of a killer. For example, why would a man as savvy as Ed George call Major Callahan to complain about Jeff's phone calls, then have him murdered two weeks later? Ed wasn't that stupid. Perhaps he was simply cocky enough to believe that he was above the law. And why wouldn't Cindy cooperate? There were so many questions only she could answer. Wouldn't this devoutly religious woman want to see justice served?

Legally, she was under no obligation to discuss the case any further with police. In fact, if investigators continued to pursue her, they ran the risk of being charged with harassment. One lazy afternoon, a group of detectives found themselves studying photos of the George family and pondering these questions. Aware that two of the children were adopted, they quickly spotted the bi-racial boy, then tried detecting the girl born in Lebanon. In the process, Bertina King noticed that another one of the girls lacked Ed's dark complexion.

"Well, Cynthia gave birth to her," Felber argued. "The kid looks like Cindy."

"Maybe it's Zack's kid," Bertina countered, remembering Bonnie Zack's recollection of the conversation in which Jeff had admitted to siring a child with Cynthia, before quickly recanting the story.

The banter continued. But soon, the detectives concluded that Bertina appeared to be correct. The Georges' youngest daughter looked an awful lot like Jeff Zack. Now, a different scenario came into play. Could Zack have been murdered so Ed could protect his family?

The theory made as much sense as any, and police realized that they now had the right to request a DNA test. But there were ethical questions plaguing the individual detectives. Lieutenant Whiddon had a 6-year-old daughter of his own, and felt less than enthusiastic about submitting an 8-year-old child to an exam that could prove that her biological father was not the man who raised her, but a guy who'd been murdered at a gas station. Although Felber had the same reservation, he insisted that a paternity test could establish a clear motive in the case. After several days of debate, Whiddon relented.

The Summit County Prosecutor's Office concurred. There was enough evidence to obtain a search warrant forcing the Georges to take a paternity test. The problem with the search warrant, though, was that its contents would be accessible to the media. No one wanted the child's possible illegitimacy publicized in the press.

As a professional courtesy, Mary Ann Kovach, the chief counsel for the prosecutor's office, offered the Georges the opportunity to take the test voluntarily. But over the next four weeks, their attorney, Robert Meeker, failed to provide law enforcement with an answer from his clients. The more he stalled, the less sympathy detectives felt for the family. Despite their feelings about Ed, police were going out of their way to protect a child's privacy. Yet, the Georges appeared uncooperative—and ungrateful. When a deadline set by the prosecutor's office was also ignored, a warrant was signed and executed. On August 24, 2001, the Georges and their daughter showed up at St. Thomas Hospital in Akron, where they were met by police and a nurse.

The procedure was relatively simple. In a small office, the nurse would place an oversized Q-tip in the child's mouth, and rub it against her inner cheek. Ed appeared fairly relaxed, pleasantly greeting police, and calming the girl in a fatherly fashion. But after he stepped into the hallway to leave Cynthia and the child alone with the nurse, the mood changed. As the nurse delivered instructions, Cindy told the child that she did not have to obey. Feeling her mother's discomfort, the girl continuously turned her head away from the Q-tip.

After fifteen minutes, Ed reentered the room, wondering why the process was taking so long. Sensing his daughter's apprehension, he gently placed her on his lap. After a few minutes, the girl agreed to open her mouth for the nurse. It took less than twenty seconds for the swabbing to be completed.

With Cynthia nervously leading the family out of the room, Ed remarked, "Honestly, I don't care what the tests show. You're my daughter, and I love you."

Three weeks later, the state crime lab at the Bureau of Criminal Identification and Investigation released its results. Now, police knew that the youngest George daughter was indeed Jeff's love child.

In the George home, Cynthia was forced to break the news to her older children. Her daughters would later say that the reality was difficult to grasp, but they grew to forgive their mother—and accept her explanation that Ed would always be the "dad of [the child's] heart."

Meanwhile, detectives were busy running down other leads.

"JEFF ZACK WAS a hated man."

The information was relayed in the most unlikely of settings, over the supermarket checkout counter. At first, the customer thought little of the cashier's comment. But as the weeks passed, the patron concluded that she had no choice but to report the remark to the police.

The conversation had begun at the Tops grocery store some 200 yards from the site where Zack was killed, after the clerk surveyed a customer's identification, and noted that the woman lived close to the Zack family. "There was something going on with this guy, and the wife of the guy who owns Tangier, Ed George," the cashier mentioned. "Jeff Zack was a hated man."

When police learned of the exchange, they visited Tops, and tracked down the clerk, known to acquaintances as Diane C—for Cantanese—a chatty woman who seemed to enjoy the novelty of talking to a detective. After rattling off a number of facts she'd gleaned from newspaper and television stories, Diane started to question Detective Felber herself.

"Did Ed George hire someone to kill Jeff Zack?"

"Don't know."

"Was the Mafia involved?"

"Doubt it."

"Are you worried that someone might kill *you* for getting too close?"

"No."

Within a half hour, Felber thanked the woman and moved on, concluding that she was a little too caught up in the rumors and media buzz concerning the murder. Only later would he realize that she was closer to uncovering the real story than she'd ever imagined.

AT THAT MOMENT, at least, the staff at the Tangier seemed likely to provide more reliable information. It had been at least fifteen years since Felber had spoken to some of these employees, but they filled him in on developments at the restaurant, as well as the personal lives of Ed and Cynthia George.

Although Ed seemed to know about and condone the affair, some staffers theorized that he'd grown tired of the public humiliation, and commissioned an underworld associate to wipe out his rival. The budget-conscious restaurateur could now spare himself the cost of a lengthy break-up, and subsequent alimony payments, as well as adhere to his mother's—and his Church's—prohibition against divorce.

In the years since Felber had left the Tangier, he learned, the workers had monitored Cynthia's behavior closely. She'd entered the Mrs. Ohio America contest in 2000 at age 46, impressing judges and fellow competitors with her poise and beauty. Despite the complications of her life—seven children, a husband and a long-term extramarital affair— she'd shined on the stage, placing an impressive third.

The same year, the *Akron Beacon Journal* featured Cindy in a section on local celebrities and their reading habits. Her favorites: *Original Goodness*, an uplifting book inspired by the Beatitudes of the Sermon on the Mount, encouraging readers to release the love and hopefulness within themselves, and *Eat Right 4 Your Type: The Individualized Diet Solution to Staying Healthy, Living Longer & Achieving Your Ideal Weight*.

To some, Cynthia seemed like a woman exuding positive energy. To others, she was a troubled person desperately trying to find happiness. And now, not only was her relationship with Zack a source of anxiety, but business at the Tangier had started to decline. Although hailed as a bona fide Akron landmark, the restaurant no longer had a lock on the market. Newer, more contemporary restaurants were luring in younger consumers, as were eateries situated in the suburbs, where many of the Tangier faithful had migrated.

"I grew up in a different era," Ed conceded, fully aware that the Tangier's survival depended largely on a costly renovation.

DETECTIVES LEARNED THAT a woman named Patricia Lauck had happened to be in Fazoli's restaurant, close to the crime scene, when Zack was killed. This was an interesting coincidence, given her credentials: former Tangier bartender, purported friend of Cindy George and longtime girlfriend of Mark Barbuto—the man who'd hired Felber at the restaurant some fifteen years earlier. Could she have been positioned in the strip mall to ensure that the hit came off successfully?

Patricia told police she'd been purchasing sandwiches when she heard the gunfire, then rushed to the site of the shooting. As a nurse, she was ready to offer assistance. But when she saw other medical professionals working on Jeff, she continued to BJ's, where she'd arranged to pick up her mother.

Felber set up a meeting with Barbuto at an Akron diner to discuss this and other issues. They hadn't seen each other since Felber quit his job at the restaurant, but the detective assumed that there'd still be a bond. Throughout the meal, Felber recounted old stories, hoping to relax his interview subject. But Barbuto was guarded, answering questions with retorts like "I'm not sure," and "I don't remember." Whenever Felber tried looking his subject in the eye, Barbuto glanced away, fidgeting and gazing around the restaurant, clearly wanting the reunion to end.

Although he'd left the Tangier several years earlier, Barbuto still considered Ed George a friend. Sure, they'd exchanged some angry words around a hot oven or in the bar area. But the restaurant business was a high-stress industry, and didn't always bring out the best in people. Despite everything, Barbuto was loyal to Ed. If a crisis ever arose, Barbuto was certain that his old boss would quickly come to his aid.

"How well did you know Jeff Zack?" Felber asked.

"I knew that he and Ed were friends. I'd see the two of them talking together in Ed's office."

"What about Jeff and Cindy?"

"They were friends, too."

"That's all?"

"As far as I know."

Barbuto insisted that he'd never heard Ed utter a negative comment about Jeff, and there was no way the restaurateur could possibly be responsible for Zack's murder. Ed had too much to lose by becoming embroiled in something like that.

"When's the last time you saw Ed?" Felber asked.

"We just spoke a couple of days ago."

"Any mention about what happened to Zack?"

"It's never come up."

Furthermore, the rumors about Ed's ties to organized crime were false, Barbuto added, maintaining that he'd never seen any criminal types in the Tangier.

At this point, Felber concluded that Barbuto was being less than candid. The detective reminded Barbuto of the questionable characters they'd both known at the restaurant. But this was not a chat between friends, and Barbuto refused to concede a thing. As the conversation progressed, Felber made a mental note to subpoena the phone records for Barbuto and his girlfriend, Patricia Lauck. If Patricia had been stationed as a lookout on the day Zack was murdered, the documents would indicate that she called either her boyfriend or a member of the George family to confirm the hit.

THE ROLL CALL room on the fourth floor resembled a large classroom, with long tables replacing school desks. Generally, a supervisor addressed detectives from a podium near a big-screen TV, muted and tuned to ESPN. Typically, reports were interrupted by groans, as those assembled turned their attention to a clip of a Cleveland sports team suffering yet another loss. Other times, the supervisor's remarks were punctuated by commentary from the detectives.

"The victims were walking home from a friend's house on Bellows Avenue," Felber remembered one report beginning, "when the suspect approached and pulled out a revolver. He told the victims to give him everything they had. They gave him four dollars in cash and a wallet. He handed it back to them, said, 'Don't say nothing,' and walked off."

"Ain't it a bitch," one of the detectives hollered, "to be so poor, you ain't even worth robbing?"

On another occasion, the investigators were told about a young woman who'd been pressured by her parents to go to the hospital for a rape examination. "Victim is a white female, twenty-four," the supervisor said. "The only description of the suspect is 'black male.'"

"That wasn't no rape," came a remark from deep within the call room. "Some white girl's parents caught her having sex with a brother."

As politically incorrect as some of these comments seemed, the repartee added to the solidarity the detectives felt, as they helped one another face humanity's failings head-on.

Felber was engrossed in the investigation in the late summer of 2001, when he passed Captain Elizabeth Daugherty on the police department stairway. "Did you hear about that plane crashing into the World Trade Center in New York?" she began. He hadn't. But as she described the incident, he envisioned a small, private airplane going off-course, and clipping a radio tower attached to one of the buildings. It wasn't until he reached the roll call room that he sensed that the country had experienced an unprecedented horror.

As he entered the room on September 11, 2001, the mood was strikingly different. Today, the dark quips were replaced by a sound Felber had never heard at roll call—stunned silence. He took a seat and, for the next four hours, stared, dazed and shaken, at the screen with forty of the seemingly most insensitive members of society. Except for an occasional gasp or burst of anger, the detectives remained awestruck. Not much police work was accomplished that day.

Because of the nature of their job, most police officers convince themselves that they're indestructible, and can get out of virtually any situation alive. But the images of New York's Finest—arguably the toughest police officers in the United States—caught under mountains of steel and stone and smoke forced every brother in blue to question the bravado they'd all mustered through the years, and lingered for a long time to come.

WITH MUCH OF the canvassing complete, the detectives now took on the grueling challenge of wading through the paper trails woven by each major player in the case. As predicted, Bonnie Zack was cleared relatively quickly. With her lawyer's blessing, she turned over copies of the family's financial records. Excepting a number of charges from hotels Bonnie claimed never to have visited, investigators found nothing to link her to the murder.

But if Ed George had hired someone to kill his romantic rival, perhaps his own financial documents would tell the story. Detectives contacted the banks favored by the George family, and discovered seven separate accounts listed for Ed or Cynthia. Banks tended to be cooperative when police subpoenaed these types of records, but in this case, the officials appeared to slow the process by demanding that detectives submit every shred of paperwork. After several weeks—and a number of additional subpoenas—the institutions released documents for a six-month period beginning in January 2001.

For investigators, the overriding question was "What qualifies as suspicious?" There were lots of withdrawals and deposits, but it was difficult to discern how the withdrawals had been spent, or the sources of the deposits. Detectives were forced to obtain a court order to gain possession of the documents that would match the check numbers with actual names. Still, they joked, they were unlikely to find the one check made out to "Hit Man," above the notation, "For the Murder of Jeff Zack." This was a fishing expedition, they understood, and they had to throw a lot of lines into the water.

Felber tried placing himself in the suspect's position, imagining each step the killer had taken. As a result, the detective hypothesized that the person who contracted the murder would want to speak to the hit man, as soon as the job was completed. Therefore, police planned to order the entire set of phone records for the Zacks and the Georges. Very quickly, investigators discovered that, as with their bank accounts, the Georges had many phone numbers—cell phones, work phones, home phones—and changed them frequently. Once authorities knew these numbers, they faced the challenge of tracking down the individual phone companies—Ameritech, Cingular, Alltel, along with their competitors and subsidiaries—and sending subpoenas to each for the desired time period. Despite the urgency to solve the case, detectives realized that these services were not provided for free. In fact, because of the substantial fees, police were forced to scale down their requests, eventually to only seven months of partial records.

Once the estimate for this undertaking arrived at police headquarters, though, the detectives had to minimize their efforts even more. Simply put, the Akron Police Department was not going to exhaust another $10,000 on an exercise that could likely go nowhere. Because of this, $1,500 was devoted to rounding up a fractional portion of calls made within a three-month span.

When the records finally arrived, the detectives were immediately overwhelmed. The records were not made for public consumption.

Columns were identified with notations like "OR," "PER," "FEA," "CL," "M," "T" and "AK." With the help of Dan Kovein, a phone expert in the prosecutor's office, detectives attempted to interpret the codes. But the task was nearly impossible. Telephone companies were constantly buying one another out, and changing the notations on their bills. New employees were completely unaware of the coding systems previously used. As a result, a lot of questions concerning the phone records went unanswered.

Throughout this period, Lieutenant David Whiddon regularly received calls from Jeff's wife, mother and other family members, inquiring about progress in the investigation. Whiddon had recently been promoted to his position and—unlike other high-ranking police brass who attained their status secreted behind desks, and taking exams—he had the respect of the rank and file for being a tough street cop. Yet, while Sergeant Moriarity was known to use intimidation to make headway in a case, Whiddon tended to rely on his intellect and verbal skills. As the inquiries came into his office, Whiddon would have been within his rights to assign a subordinate to respond to the family's concerns. But the lieutenant felt obliged to answer each question personally. A realist, he'd tactfully advise callers to lower their expectations—at least, in the short term. But, in his heart, he'd already made a vow to solve this—and every other—homicide.

The trustful rapport with Zack's relatives would prove

beneficial, as the family helped close some of the holes in the Jeff and Cindy saga. At its best, the relationship was an explosive one. With the demands of their respective marriages and families, the lovers were not always able to put in the time needed to make their affair work. This added to the natural friction caused by two strong, and sometimes difficult, personalities. At a Christmas party at the Tangier in 1999, for instance, the couple had had a loud argument as the other guests uncomfortably looked on. During those times when Cynthia attempted to end the romance, Zack had never been the type to tend to his emotional wounds in silence, devoting himself instead to reclaiming his lover's affections.

He had an unusual way of achieving this, however. Bonnie Zack would later tell police about listening to her husband lambaste Cindy on the phone, calling her incredibly foul names. "Wow," Bonnie thought, "he's as abusive to her as he is to me."

In 2006, Cynthia told the Cleveland *Plain Dealer* about a day in 1997 when she'd threatened to tell Bonnie Zack about the affair. "Come on over," she quoted Jeff as saying.

When she arrived at the house, she claimed, Bonnie wasn't home. Instead, she said, Zack had sucker-punched her in the garage, shouting, "You toy with me? You toy with me?"

He then allegedly dragged Cynthia upstairs by the hair, where he stuffed her into a garbage can and shoved an AK-47 in her mouth. She maintains that Zack had threatened to skin her alive, and hang her on the flagpole in front of the Georges' home—a gruesome image for her children to behold when they awoke the next morning.

Then, according to Cindy, Zack had handed her a two-page handwritten letter demanding that she page him every four hours, and only leave her home in the company of her children or husband. If she disobeyed these orders, Cynthia told the newspaper, Jeff had vowed to terrorize her family members and torture her to death.

"I'd wake up in the middle of the night, and he would be standing over me," Cynthia told reporter Christopher Evans, "talking about how to make a nail bomb, and wouldn't it be a shame if one of your kids opened the package when it came to the door, and how it would feel to be buried alive and live long enough to hear your kids crying."

Cynthia also claimed that Jeff spoke about pouring acid down her throat and setting her on fire—shoving gas rags in her face to amplify the warning.

Mary Ann Brewer remembers how obsessive Zack could become when he thought that Cindy was withholding emotions. He'd call the house constantly, hanging up if Ed or one of the children answered. Sometimes, in an effort to lure Cynthia to the phone, he'd disguise his voice. But Mary Ann knew his intonations well, and, during these exchanges, would simply ask, "What do you want, Jeff?"

"Where is she? She won't answer her cell phone. Do you know where she is?"

"No, Jeff, I don't."

"She won't answer her pager. Where could she be?"

"Jeff, I really can't help you."

"I think you know more than you're telling me."

In time, Jeff generally managed to track down his partner—through a mixture of persistence and harassment.

"Zack had the computer dial our number every ten minutes all night long," Cynthia told the *Plain Dealer*. "My kids were in severe depression. Edward, I don't think he knew what to do. He saw his wife lose thirty pounds, the phones ringing and ringing, and there were bruises."

"When all the ranting and raving was going on," Mary Ann says, "all the screaming and crying and carrying on, I told Cindy, 'You don't have to put up with this. Why are you taking this from him?'"

Cynthia answered the nanny in a trembling voice: "You don't understand."

"What don't I understand?"

"Jeff and I have a child together. He will take my

daughter and move her to Israel. And I'll never see her again."

The nanny knew how profoundly Ed loved the child, and wondered whether the loss of his daughter would be the one issue that would propel him to leave Cindy. Mary Ann theorized that Cynthia was less concerned about losing Ed than sacrificing the lifestyle they shared in their big house. "She was afraid of becoming penniless," Mary Ann said. "She couldn't stand the thought of being penniless."

Whatever the circumstances, by 2001, Cynthia's doctor had prescribed the anti-depressant Remeron. That same year, after many break-ups and reconciliations, the couple severed ties for the final time. Brian Zack told police that about a month before the murder, he'd heard his father on the phone to Cindy: "Change your phone number, okay? That way, I won't be able to call you anymore."

Not long afterward, Brian accompanied his father to a job at a construction site. The boy noticed Cynthia driving by—in tears.

ZACK'S CO-WORKER, BEN Fluellen, recounted a similar experience. Sometime in May, Ben and Zack were doing a landscaping job when an SUV pulled up in a driveway across the street. A woman was at the steering wheel, with a child behind her in a car seat. Zack crossed the street to talk to them. The conversation lasted for close to two hours.

When Zack returned, Ben recounted, he was crying. "I miss my daughter," he said.

"I thought you only had a son," Ben replied.

"I also have a daughter—from outside my family. That's who I was talking to, my daughter and her mother. I don't know if I'm ever going to see that little girl again."

IN THE EARLY days of the investigation, detectives became hopeful with each snippet they learned about the major players in the case. But the mood changed after months of inconclusive probing. Bonnie Zack and her relatives were cleared. The survey of Jeff's estranged business associate Mike Scranton had gone nowhere. The Georges weren't talking, and apparently neither were their friends. As authorities clung to the hope that the phone records would yield new possibilities, the homicide squad shifted their attention back to some of the other unsolved murders in Akron.

Then, one morning at roll call, Felber glanced at a list of stolen vehicles, and noticed a white, black and lime green motorcycle on the registry. The detective imagined a number of possibilities. The motorcycle might have been legitimately stolen, then used to kill Zack. Or it was possible that, after murdering Jeff, the perpetrator had filed the report as a way to distance himself from the crime.

As it turned out, the bike had been stolen nine days after the homicide. The owner had never been in trouble with the law, and made no attempt to hide the fact that he'd been riding the vehicle during the period when the shooting took place. And—as he took great pains to emphasize—*his* motorcycle had "cow fur," a covering resembling cowhide.

Felber closed the lead—only to hear about the same motorcycle much later in the investigation.

EVENTUALLY, THE PHONE records arrived—and Felber and Lieutenant Whiddon swiftly concluded that, for all their experience, they'd never examined these types of documents. Unlike a telephone bill, the records were not formatted for customers, but for technicians. Each telephone company had its own set of abbreviations. And some of the notations were so cryptic that virtually no one in the department could figure out what they meant.

Felber and Whiddon initially concentrated on Jeff Zack's records, and realized that the lists of calls he'd dialed and received contained only the phone numbers—no names. The documents were literally piled two feet high, and thousands of pages had been subpoenaed. How were the detectives going to accomplish their task? It seemed impossible—until they decided to isolate three days of Zack's records. More than 300 calls were listed. Fortunately, many of the numbers were identical. Within days, Persons Unit secretary Carrie Stoll helped the detectives identify fifty recurring numbers. Still, this left hundreds more—including the threatening phone call made to Zack on June 13, 2001, and the mysterious one Felber had received when he picked up the victim's phone at the crime scene. There was only one way to solve these riddles: compile the bewildering numbers, and write a subpoena for each. Once the judge signed the subpoenas, they were sent to the individual phone companies. It was months before the conglomerates got around to responding to these requests.

But on those occasions when numbers were matched to names, detectives were amazed, and even amused, by the turns in the lives of the central figures. For example, they learned that in May 2001, Jeff had flown out West to visit his family. On the flight to Arizona, he'd met a married woman, and commenced a whirlwind affair, independent of his relationships with Cynthia and Bonnie. After Zack returned to Ohio, he told his wife that he was going on a bike trip, and instead jetted out to Vegas to meet his mistress. The woman became infatuated with Jeff, and was the voice Felber heard when he answered Zack's cell phone in front of BJ's.

At 12:30 PM on June 16, 2001—twenty-five minutes after the homicide—detectives discovered that Cynthia George had placed a call to her husband. However, she'd already told police that Ed had been busy that morning, and the couple was planning to attend a wedding later in the day. Therefore, Cynthia was acting like a wife checking in with her husband, as opposed to a participant in a murder plot.

There had certainly been a great deal of communication between Cynthia and Zack, though. Between March 1 and May 10, 2001, Jeff had phoned his mistress's cell phone 351 times, and her home on 131 separate occasions. Were some of these the harassing calls that Ed had discussed with Major Callahan? It seemed likely. But many of the exchanges went on for five minutes or longer. If Cindy felt plagued by her persistent lover, wouldn't she have hung up immediately? Detectives also noted that Cynthia had called Zack twice herself during the first ten days of May. Then, on May 11, a little more than a month before the murder, it appeared that Jeff's phone calls stopped for good.

The records raised a lot of questions. But there were only two people who could answer them. One was dead. The other was hiding behind her attorney, Bob Meeker.

ON HIS OWN, Felber created a database to manage the voluminous amount of phone calls, using Microsoft Access software. There was no precedent for this at the Akron Police Department; the detective was charting new technological territory. Within three months, 400 identifiable numbers were included in the system, along with information about how many times that number had been called, and the inventory of records where it could be found. By the end of the investigation, the phone numbers in the database totaled more than 1,000.

Along the way, police also had the opportunity to view the cell phone records for Mark Barbuto's girlfriend, Patricia Lauck. Yes, she'd called Barbuto after learning of the crime, but that wasn't strange: anyone who came upon a shooting in the course of a shopping day would probably feel compelled to tell a close friend about it. And there were no calls to Ed or Cynthia George. When police asked Patricia to come to the station to discuss the other numbers on her bill, she hesitated, not wishing to be dragged further into the homicide investigation. When she did show up, she brought along Tom Adgate, a quick-witted attorney who, coincidentally, had once represented Felber. When a client is guilty, it's common for a lawyer to interfere during this process. By contrast, Adgate appeared relaxed during the questioning, only stepping in to clarify a point, or object if a query seemed inappropriate. In the end, Lauck's story changed little from her first meeting with detectives more than two months earlier, making the incident seem nothing more than a coincidence.

ON MAY 13, 2002, as a new spring was running into summer, Felber and Whiddon slid into a police vehicle, and steered it onto I-77. The two were starting to get used to each other. Because he usually arrived at work earlier and found a spot in the department's small, basement parking garage, Whiddon generally drove when they traveled together. Whiddon had an uncanny sense of direction. As a high school football fan, he frequently used his knowledge of nearby stadiums to find his bearings. Felber had enormous respect for Whiddon—a perfectionist on the job, whose wife was a nurse in a ward for terminally ill children—and tolerated his occasional concentration lapses while driving. His habit of changing radio stations, and preference for country music were more difficult to accept.

"I don't know why you keep switching stations," Felber protested, as they passed Killian Road, near Akron Fulton International Airport. "All the songs are the same—the twang, the guy losing his girl, crying over a beer, the pickup, the trusty beagle . . ."

"What trusty beagle?"

". . . It's redneck hip hop."

"How can you make that kind of comparison? I don't hear anything about cop killing in country music. Or drug use . . ."

"Isn't alcohol a drug? You know what I think? I think

you secretly like classic rock. But you won't play·it because you know I hate country!"

The argument continued for close to a half hour, until the pair rolled into North Canton, Ohio, and stopped in front of a small, neatly kept home. The detectives ran the plates for the two cars in the driveway, and confirmed that one was registered to Cynthia George's sister, Jane Harper.

Knocking at the front door, they were met by a small, somewhat fragile woman who identified herself as Cindy's mother, Helen Rohr. Very delicately, Felber explained that he wanted to talk about Jeff Zack.

Helen seemed non-plussed: "I don't really know him." She described Zack as a friend of her daughter's, who'd been a guest at one of the Georges' baptism parties.

"Was that the baptism for his youngest daughter?" Felber followed up.

"No, it wasn't."

Suddenly, Jane marched to the door. Studying her face, the detectives were able to detect a resemblance to Cynthia. Both were very attractive women, although Jane was heavier. To Felber, she bore the coal-miner's-daughter qualities Cindy never wanted to evince in adulthood—with an attitude that seemed completely antagonistic. "Why are you asking these questions?" she demanded. "We don't know anything about Jeff Zack. And you're upsetting my mother."

"We're not trying to upset anybody," Felber replied. "Is there someplace where we can talk about this?"

"We can talk right here," Helen suggested, motioning at the open porch where the detectives now stood.

"It's raining," her daughter pointed out. Jane grudgingly invited her visitors to meet them on the screened-in porch on the side of the house. But this would not be the private conversation that police wanted. Helen stood in the doorway of her kitchen, monitoring the conversation, while Jane did most of the talking.

She claimed that she and her sister were close and spoke

regularly, that Cynthia and Ed had a wonderful marriage, and that Jeff Zack's name never came up in family conversations.

"Do you know about his affair with Cindy?" Felber interjected.

Neither Jane nor her mother reacted strongly. Like others close to the Georges, the women feigned ignorance. Worried about unnerving Helen, Felber asked if Jane would prefer speaking to detectives alone. When she and Helen declined, Felber continued his line of questioning: "And did you know that Jeff is the father of one of Cindy's children?"

Before Jane could respond, Helen exclaimed, "She looks like her grandfather."

Felber turned to the older woman. "How do you know which child I'm talking about, if you never thought Cindy and Jeff had an affair?"

When neither woman provided a logical answer, Whiddon took over the discussion. "Jane, did Cindy ever talk to you about Jeff Zack's homicide?"

"No."

Helen looked concerned. "Is she a suspect?"

Felber shook his head. "She isn't. But I can't understand why she won't talk to us."

"Her attorney won't let her," Helen said.

"It's not really her attorney's decision to help the police with a murder investigation," Whiddon responded. "It's Cindy's. If one of my friends was killed, I'd do everything I could to help find the killer."

Helen couldn't help but nod in agreement. On the verge of tears, Jane threatened, "I'm calling my lawyer. We don't have anything more to say. I think you better leave."

The detectives complied, driving back to Akron hoping that they'd at least "shaken the tree." The next day, their aspirations were confirmed when the chief counsel for the prosecutor's office, Mary Ann Kovach received an angry phone call from Bob Meeker. Why had she allowed the police to speak to Cynthia's family without consulting him first? Kovach hadn't known about the visit in advance, but now she calmly promised the attorney that she'd call the detectives' superiors. Within hours, Whiddon was sitting in Captain Elizabeth Daugherty's office. No one had done anything inappropriate, she stated. But Meeker complained that Felber had been overly aggressive.

"That isn't true," Whiddon answered, and the matter ended there. But there was still a sense of unease among the detectives. Powerful people were watching, dissecting and reporting their behavior. Neither could recall another case where they'd been asked to explain why they'd dared to approach a suspect's relatives.

"**ANYBODY WANT TO** follow up another bad lead on the Zack case?" Narcotics Detective Shawn Brown asked from the other end of the phone.

It had been two days since police visited Cynthia's family, and Detective Richard Morrison already had a smirk on his face. When Vince Felber entered headquarters dressed in a brown shirt and matching pants, Morrison set the mood of the day by cracking, "I didn't know you worked for UPS on your time off."

"You've never been a clever detective," Felber replied with a half-grin. "And you're not a clever comedian. Ever think about law school?"

Now, Morrison was holding the phone, summoning Felber to the receiver. Detective Brown had a confidential informant who earned a good deal of his income dealing drugs. Recently, the man had mentioned a customer who'd attempted to relieve a debt with a black, green and purple Ninja motorcycle. Felber took down the informant's information, and called him.

"It's not a good time to talk," the man said. "Give me your number, and I'll call you back."

Four days later, Felber managed to get the man on the

phone again. The informant attempted to end the conversation, until the detective mentioned that he was interested in talking about the motorcycle.

"Shit, I thought you wanted to arrest me. If I'd known you were calling about the motorcycle . . . Well, that's an entirely different situation."

Around the time of Zack's murder, the informant recounted, he was given a motorcycle that he was sure had been stolen. There was no plate on the bike. And when the informant heard about the homicide, he'd broken the motorcycle into parts, and had them crushed inside some dilapidated autos. Still, he'd held on to the motorcycle's engine block, and was willing to provide it to police.

Now, detectives tried tracking down his drug customer. The client was an addict, and didn't have a permanent phone. But by searching through the man's arrest records, police discovered his mother's address. The woman lived on a well-manicured city lot in a decent neighborhood. But when Felber and Whiddon visited the house, they found not the addict, but his brother, a hostile man with a jailhouse demeanor.

"We'd like to speak to your brother," Whiddon began.

"The answer is *no*."

Both detectives realized that the addict was hiding in the house, coaching his brother from behind the door. But at that point, they had neither a warrant nor a legal justification to obtain one. Instead, they returned the next day, and tried their luck with the mother.

The woman was nothing like her sons. But that wasn't a surprise. Often, the worst offenders were raised by polite, hard-working women. She'd banned the addict from her house, she said, after he stole her television. His brother had probably snuck him into the home while she was away at work.

Once again, it was a story the detectives knew all too well.

Yet Felber wasn't ready to veer off this road. He called Detective Brown's informant again—to thank him for his help. The detective took no joy in expressing gratitude to a drug dealer, but maybe the man could be of assistance in the future. As it turned out, he claimed to have another lead.

Felber listened with a cynical ear. Occasionally, sources fed off the excitement concerning a big case. Before they became lost in the drug world, after all, they'd been raised with a sense of right and wrong. Assisting the police brought them back to a place where they were helping the good guys. It also built up credit for the next time they got into trouble—and made them feel important.

Although, ultimately, this bike had no connection to the crime, the informant opened a new window for detectives. Convinced that he possessed a crucial piece of evidence in the Zack murder, the man had mentioned the engine block to his boss, Tim Cantanese. Tim owned some lawnmowers, a few pickup trucks, and some basic landscaping equipment. By sheer happenstance, he was also the son of Diane C, the Tops supermarket clerk who'd met with Felber and ended up grilling him about gossip related to the case. As it turned out, Cantanese was also dating a woman who apparently knew quite a bit about the Zack homicide.

WITH HER STREAKED blonde hair, almond eyes and outspoken manner, Christine Todaro often attracted attention—both wanted and otherwise—in the bars on State Road, the Cuyahoga Falls strip where she spent a good deal of her leisure time. She lived a block or so away from the thoroughfare—handy, as the old car she drove ran infrequently—on the ground floor of a two-family house, in an apartment equipped with the bare essentials: an inexpensive dining-room table, couch, television and Sony PlayStation. The walls were bereft of photos or decorations. Christine had trouble making her rent, and was about to be evicted.

She'd also been married to John Zaffino, a name detectives had yet to encounter in the Zack investigation.

On the surface, Zaffino had quite a bit in common with

Jeff Zack. While Zack might have been more of a natural charmer, Zaffino exuded a kind of rough charisma, and had the ability to step into a new profession and pick it up quickly. Both enjoyed bragging of their macho exploits: Zack wove tales about his days as an Israeli paratrooper; Zaffino made it a point to mention that his biceps measured eighteen inches.

They also each shared a fascination with Cynthia George.

Zaffino had spent his youth in Warren, Pennsylvania, a onetime logging and oil town described by its boosters as the gateway to Allegheny National Forest. Steeped in Revolutionary War history, and peppered with historical homes, Warren nonetheless lost much of its younger population in the late 20th century, as local factories shuttered and jobs moved elsewhere.

Despite its outward beauty, Warren could be a tough place, and few considered themselves tougher than Zaffino, who tore up roadways with motorcycles and trucks, and, despite a squat appearance, bench-pressed as much as 300 pounds. Zaffino's wing of the family was known for their short fuses, and John rarely lost a fight—often describing the damage he'd inflict before unleashing a volley of blows.

John and Christine were married from 1999 to 2001. Each was divorced with a son, and, in some ways, their scorching personalities seemed to mesh. But Christine describes their two tempestuous years together as insufferable. She admits that she hit him on more than one occasion, and claims that he broke her arm in another altercation. Another time, she contends, he punched her 13-year-old son in the face, knocking him out.

"I don't know if John Zaffino had a good side," says one detective. "If he did, not too many people brought it up to us. He was extremely hot-tempered, to the point of being dangerous. He did seem to be very intelligent—he might have a high IQ, actually. But there's a sick, sadistic side to him, too."

Nonetheless, Christine and Zaffino continued to communicate after their divorce, which is how Tim Cantanese first heard about John's connection to the case. During those times when Zaffino phoned his ex-wife, Cantanese listened to the conversations, and heard John boast about killing two people. The first victim allegedly lived in Pennsylvania. The second, Zaffino insinuated, was Jeff Zack.

Zaffino first spotted Cynthia George sometime in 2000 at Jillian's, an establishment featuring a "sports video café," jazz bar, hibachi grill, cigar bar and a tiki bar/dance club called the Groove Shack. Cindy has claimed that Ed was supposed to have met her that night and, when he failed to show, she started to leave. That's when Zaffino stopped her and introduced himself.

"You can't walk out by yourself," he said flirtatiously. "There's dangerous people out there."

"I'm married," Cynthia replied, "and I have seven kids."

"Does that make you Catholic or Amish?"

Cindy smiled.

Zaffino handed the middle-aged beauty his phone number. "Will you call me when you get home, just so I know you got there?"

Soon, Cynthia was sneaking away from her husband for liaisons with this new man in her life, as well as Zack. As the romance with Jeff deteriorated, Cynthia's relationship with Zaffino escalated. "I tried to say goodbye," she told Cleveland *Plain Dealer* reporter Christopher Evans, "but I stayed.

"He was very patient and very kind. He would make sure that I ate, and we would go for walks."

In order to communicate easily, Cynthia purchased John a cell phone, reserved exclusively for their conversations. At some point, he began referring to her by the nickname "Sparky."

"Zaffino was the lower-class type," opines Mary Ann Brewer, "somebody that she wouldn't pick up normally. He was a bully. And he had no money—he had nothing. I couldn't understand why she took up the affair with him. Now, I believe she got him, she worked him and she used him."

As was often the case, Zaffino was broke, and relegated to living with a friend. Yet, shortly after becoming involved with Cindy George, associates noticed that he had his own apartment, and didn't seem concerned about paying his bills. At one point, he was hired as a salesman for a chemical company. He knew nothing about the field, but because of his raw intelligence, educated himself about the industry in an astonishingly short amount of time. According to Zaffino's former co-worker, Cynthia seemed uncomfortable with this scenario, and made him quit. It appeared that she preferred him being dependent on her generosity— and available to meet her demands.

Police would later hear rumors that the couple had made extravagant plans for the future. Cynthia had apparently promised that, when the workaholic Ed George died, John would run the restaurant. The dream of overseeing some hundred staffers at one of the most storied establishments in the Midwest no doubt captivated the small-town Pennsylvanian. But it wasn't going to be realized it seemed, without a price.

SIX

ACCORDING TO TIM Cantanese, Zaffino told Christine that he'd used his computer to research information about Zack, then began following the unsuspecting man by motorcycle. When the opportunity had presented itself, Zaffino fired the fatal shot into Jeff. Then, he'd apparently thrown out his evidence-laden computer hard drive.

Felber listened as Cantanese described how Christine heard that Zaffino had been initially hired by a guy named "Ed" to rough up the victim. When Zack refused to make himself scarce, Zaffino told Christine, "Ed" ordered a fatal hit.

The detective was excited, but couldn't betray his emotions. In a monotone voice, he continued asking Cantanese to clarify his remarks. Felber always tried to ask enough questions to maintain consistency in a story—but never so many that the witness began to feel like his honesty was being challenged. It was a delicate balance. Because of a rule about hearsay evidence, Cantanese could never be put on the stand; he hadn't heard Zaffino's confession directly. Sitting alongside Lieutenant Whiddon and Detective Brown in the department conference room, Felber said, "It would really help if Christine spoke to us herself."

Cantanese shook his head from side to side. Christine

was deathly afraid of Zaffino, and would never repeat her story to the cops—let alone in court.

"You know how important this case is," Felber started.

"And you know how indebted the department would be if you made things happen," Brown cut in.

The detectives were appealing to Cantanese's ego, and their efforts seemed pretty transparent—at least to them. But suddenly, Cantanese blurted out, "What can I do to help?"

Felber was cautious about asking Cantanese to secretly record Christine. It was common practice to wire a snitch to obtain information from a criminal—but recording a deeply personal story from a civilian? The thought disturbed the detective, particularly because Cantanese and Christine had an intimate relationship, and she would never expect this man to betray her disclosures. Once Christine was on tape, police would have her in a corner. If she refused to cooperate, they could arrest her for obstructing justice. Sometimes detectives concluded that the only way to catch people was to lower their own morals.

Cantanese was willing to play. When the detectives gingerly suggested wearing a wire, Cantanese seemed unruffled. "Sure, no problem," he answered, adding that he didn't even like Christine that much. He was simply dating her, he claimed, because she was "a good time."

Late that afternoon, Tim Cantanese was walking out of the station—with a cheap digital recorder the department had purchased at RadioShack.

TWO DAYS PASSED without a call from Cantanese. None of the detectives were surprised—and there was no legal way to force him to cooperate. Still, Felber felt that it was imperative to stay on top of Tim, and move the case along.

"Did you talk to her?" the detective asked when he finally got Cantanese on the phone.

"I was supposed to see her last night, but I had to work late."

"When are you supposed to get together again?"

"Tonight. I'll call you in the morning, and tell you how everything went."

"Thanks, Tim. We really appreciate your help."

When Cantanese failed to phone the detectives the next morning, Lieutenant Whiddon notified Captain Elizabeth Daugherty. "Have Felber call him again," she suggested.

It was only about noon, and Felber was hesitant. He knew that Cantanese liked to party, and was likely still sleeping it off. Felber also worried that if he pushed Cantanese too hard, this valuable resource might back away. Still, Felber followed orders and made the call.

It was three hours before Cantanese finally got around to answering the phone. "How'd it go with Chris?" the detective asked.

Cantanese sounded testy: "I was out drinking with some friends, man. I'm just getting up now. I didn't see Chris last night. And, to tell you the truth, I don't know when I'm seeing her again." He paused. "I'm beginning to think this might not be such a good idea."

It was time to talk Cantanese back from the edge of the cliff, and Felber reiterated his gratitude, emphasizing Tim's role in possibly solving this high-profile homicide. Before hanging up, Cantanese promised to reach out to detectives in the very near future.

Felber didn't push him for a date.

When three more days passed with the same disappointing results, the detectives strategized their next move. Captain Daugherty suggested picking up Tim, and intimidating him into assisting. Felber strongly disagreed. Intimidation may have worked on television, but—at least in Felber's experience—it was an ineffective tool in the real world. "We just have to give the guy time," Felber argued.

A few days later, Cantanese called the department on his own.

"I saw Chris last night," he began. "I couldn't get her to talk about Zaffino."

Felber was less than overjoyed; Tim's tone was troublesome. "He didn't come up in conversation at all?"

"Hey, it's a sensitive subject. Honestly, I don't know if I'm *ever* gonna get her talking about Zaffino. And forget about recording it."

Felber wondered if Cantanese was looking for a way to cut off his relationship with the Akron Police Department. But the detective was not about to let his source evaporate. "If you were another kind of guy," Felber stated, "I'd kind of understand. But you're a pretty smooth talker. I think we all know that. You could probably get a woman to do anything . . ."

Cantanese chuckled.

"I'm right—aren't I?"

Nonetheless, Felber was less than confident when the discussion ended, and he walked over to the Persons Unit to find Whiddon.

"Here comes your stalker," secretary Carrie Stoll jokingly remarked to the lieutenant.

Felber half-smiled.

"Either you get a restraining order against this guy, or I'm going to do it."

Felber gestured for Whiddon to speak to him around a corner, in private. "I have an idea," Felber said. "Why don't we send someone over to Christine's place ourselves, and ask her a few questions?"

"Won't that blow things with Cantanese?"

"No, the way I'm looking at it is, even if she clams up, she'll want to call Cantanese and talk about our visit."

"And Cantanese might be able to help us then—really loosen her up, 'cause she's so freaked out, seeing two detectives at her door."

"Exactly."

Once Daugherty signed off on the tactic, Felber phoned Cantanese to inform him about the plan. Tim's enthusiasm seemed to return: "That's a great idea. I'll set up a date with her after you guys leave, and see what she says."

Lieutenant Whiddon suggested that, as the most knowledgeable detective on the case, Felber should visit Christine. Captain Daugherty wanted Bertina King to go along as well, given her experience, gender and ability to relate to just about anyone. While the detectives were contemplating their next move, FBI Agent Robert Charnesky strolled into the station. Charnesky had been working with the Akron Police Department on cultivating an underworld character who'd implied that he had ties to Ed George. But Felber now asked the agent to attend the meeting, as well. Although Charnesky initially declined the offer, he soon changed his mind. Every quality law enforcement officer loves a good mystery—and the Zack murder was among the most enticing.

On June 12, 2002, Charnesky, Felber and King knocked on the door of Christine Todaro's split-level home, and expressed an urgent need to speak with her. Felber made a big production out of introducing Charnesky as an FBI agent.

"What took you so long?" Christine asked in the ballsy, disarming style that law enforcement would come to admire. She politely made way for her guests to enter the apartment, shooing her 16-year-old son away from his PlayStation console, and into another room.

While she was nervous about discussing Zaffino, she conveyed information adequate for police to conclude that this was a violent man—one with enough of a problem to be prescribed Effexor for anger management. She'd left Zaffino, she explained, after he'd knocked out her son. When she returned to the home to retrieve her belongings, Zaffino held her hostage for two hours. During that time, he twisted her arm behind her back and told her that he intended to break it. A moment later, he made good on his threat.

"Does John own any guns?" Felber asked.

"He has two long-barreled ones."

"What about a motorcycle?"

"As far as I know, he hasn't had one since he was a kid."

"Do you have any idea why we're asking you about him?"

Christine shook her head from side to side.

"You don't know about any illegal activities he may have been engaged in?"

"I don't."

Felber dropped the bomb: "We think he may be involved in a homicide."

"A *homicide*?" Christine appeared alarmed. Plus, now *she*'d been dragged into the case.

"He never talked to you about anything like that?"

"*No*," Christine said a little too forcefully.

The investigators knew that she was lying and, under different circumstances, would have worked on dismantling her story. But now, they actually eased their questioning, hoping that Christine would come to view them as friends later on, when they really needed her cooperation. Obviously, the seed had been planted. Christine was so rattled that she unburdened herself to Tim Cantanese the moment he stepped through the door that night.

He recorded everything.

"Two fuckin' homicide detectives and an FBI agent came to my house this morning, looking for John," she complained. "Looking for John. I don't know what to do."

"For John . . . ?"

"My ex. The jackass of a husband . . . I am not going to jail for that guy."

"Oh, I wouldn't either."

"I am not going to jail."

"Why go to jail for someone that's acted ignorant, and broke your arm? . . . Didn't you tell me something about . . . how he shot the guy [Zack] in the face or some shit?"

"Yeah, he goes, 'Oh, I guarantee you he's going to have a hard time parting his hair now,' is what he told me."

"He said what?"

"He said, 'I guarantee you he'll have a hard time parting his hair now.' "

". . . Fucking tell them. Tell them what he told you. That's what I'd do."

". . . If he found out I said anything about that, he would kill me."

"This guy sounds like a real lunatic."

"He is."

"Didn't he say something about he killed someone in Pennsylvania, too?"

"Uh-hum."

". . . What is he, a hit man?"

Christine laughed nervously. "Yeah, for Ed George."

"Who?"

"Ed George."

"He's a hit man?"

"That's who he whacked that guy for, Ed George."

"Why would Ed George, why would a guy be so pissed off at a guy to have another guy whacked?"

At this point, Christine seemed to confuse her facts, claiming that the eruption centered around the restaurateur's daughter.

"The guy that John killed," Cantanese questioned, "was sleeping with . . ."

"Ed George's daughter."

Cantanese was quick to mention that he thought there was a $25,000 reward for the capture of Zack's assailant. He was wrong.

"You give me twenty-five grand," Christine declared, "and I'll spill my guts." Seconds later, though, she was once again expressing her fear of Zaffino.

"There's a witness protection program," Cantanese told her. "I'm sure they would make sure that you're a safe person . . . I'll tell you what. With that guy's background, they ain't going to have a hard time believing that he done something like that . . . they're getting closer and closer to busting him."

Still, Christine was worried about the police coming to her home, and questioning her again—particularly if her son was around. So Cantanese came up with an alternate proposal: he'd personally bring her to the station, where she could reveal everything she knew in a protected setting.

ON JUNE 13, 2002, Tim Cantanese phoned Felber at 10:30 in the morning. Chris and Tim had been up all night, discussing the visit from Akron's Finest—and everything was captured on tape.

"She's ready to come in and talk to you guys," Cantanese said. "But I need to ask you one favor. I have to get some sleep."

"Don't worry about it. What time do you think you'll be in?"

"I don't know. Maybe five o'clock or something."

"I'll be here, waiting for you."

No one expected Cantanese to arrive with Christine at 5 PM—witnesses rarely showed up on time—and they didn't. But fifteen minutes later, Felber received a call from Tim, explaining that the couple hadn't eaten all day, and wanted to stop for a meal on the way into police headquarters. Felber knew that there was always the risk that Christine would change her mind about speaking to authorities midway through her dinner, but his instincts told him to maintain good will. Ultimately, the police would get more from Christine if she believed that she was assisting by choice, rather than coercion.

"What time do you expect to be here?" Felber asked.

"About seven-thirty."

At 7:35 PM, Captain Daugherty noted that Felber, Whiddon and Sergeant Terry Hudnall had been on overtime for nearly four hours, waiting for the couple, and she was growing impatient. The captain held a private meeting in her office with Whiddon.

"How well can Felber handle witnesses?" she asked.

"He's good."

"Well, maybe he should call these two and get them in here."

Felber did not want to obey the order. But he wasn't about to defy his captain, either. He phoned Cantanese, and later admitted to feeling relieved when no one answered.

Daugherty's impatience seemed to be building by the second, and her underlings were now more focused on calming their captain than on interviewing Christine. When there was still no answer at 8 PM, Daugherty ordered the detectives to physically bring the couple to the station. This was a problematic task. Police knew nothing about the pair's whereabouts, and even if they did, there was no legal foundation to round them up.

"What does she want us to do?" Felber grumbled to Whiddon. "*Kidnap* these guys?"

A few minutes later, Cantanese called with some troubling news. Christine had spoken to a retired detective who claimed that Ed George had mob connections, and that she might die if she cooperated with police. "Zaffino's called her twice today," Cantanese said. "The guy's watching her. If he finds out what's going on, it's not gonna be good."

This wasn't the first time Felber had encountered this type of rationale. "A lot of these mob stories are nothing but hype," he told Cantanese. "The mob's not really a threat in Akron anymore. These days, the only places they have any clout are on cable TV, and in Martin Scorsese movies."

"What are you talking about?" Cantanese fired back. "I'm Italian. I know a couple of made guys, and so does Chris."

"So you know what these guys are like," Felber countered. "And I bet you're not too scared of them."

The effort to stroke Cantanese's machismo seemingly worked. "Not really," he answered, and agreed to show up in a half hour.

But Daugherty wasn't pleased about the change of

schedule, and ordered Felber to find out where Cantanese was situated at the moment.

When the captain was out of range, Felber turned to Hudnall: "You know what would happen if I did that? He'd tell me, 'Why do you want to know?' He'd feel like I was treating him like a perp. She really wants to blow this case, doesn't she?"

Felber picked up the phone and dialed. He'd later say that he received a busy signal, "or maybe dialed the wrong number." Regardless, he never reached Cantanese. So at 8:45, Daugherty ordered detectives to look for him.

Felber and Hudnall exited the department, ready to drive aimlessly around Akron, on the off-chance that they might catch Cantanese and Todaro exiting a diner or waiting for a light to change. As the detectives stepped into the parking lot, they were jolted by a shout:

"*Felber, over here!*"

Tim Cantanese and Christine Todaro were standing in front of the station house door. Felber walked up to the pair, and shook Cantanese's hand warmly. "Christine," the detective said, "I really appreciate you coming in."

She smiled in response.

"Hey," Cantanese asked, "where were you guys going?"

"I left something in my car," Felber replied, ushering the two up to the sixth floor.

FBI Agent Robert Charnesky was waiting there, once again eager to lend his support. Captain Daugherty began doling out assignments. "I know Christine Todaro," she stated. "She used to work at this place where'd I'd go for pizza." Indeed, Christine and her first husband had run a popular pizzeria. Apparently, the captain believed that this connection enabled her to assist in the interview. She designated Charnesky and Whiddon to accompany her, while Felber and Hudnall were asked to go into a separate room with Cantanese.

Felber was stunned. He was convinced that he knew more about the case than any other member of the department, and wasn't about to be left out of the most important interview of the investigation. As he watched Charnesky and Daugherty enter a conference room, Felber motioned for Whiddon to speak to him in the hallway.

"Look, I've been *living* this case night and day. I'm the one who . . ."

Whiddon stopped Felber mid-sentence. "You don't have to convince me," the lieutenant said. "Let's switch places."

Daugherty shot Felber a glare as he rambled into the conference room and took a seat opposite Christine. Resting in the center of the table was one of the twenty-dollar tape recorders issued to the detective bureau.

Todaro began speaking. She claimed that an older, Italian-American man had been following her around—at John Zaffino's behest, she assumed. The police paid polite lip service to Christine's allegation—witnesses were often paranoid, and investigators all but took it for granted that the elderly man was a figment of her imagination.

They asked about her relationship with her ex-husband. She reminisced about meeting Zaffino in 1995, while both were working for the same trucking company, and the interview began in earnest. "Can you tell us about your marriage to John?" Daugherty asked.

"Horrible, absolutely horrible."

"What happened?"

"He's very abusive . . . You know, he almost strangled me to death once in front of my kid."

". . . Did you make a police report on that, do you remember?"

"Actually, he called the cops and said I started it."

On another occasion, she continued, Zaffino had become so angry at her that he kicked her out of his car, leaving her stranded on the side of the road, miles from home. Always, there was the threat of violence. Because of this, Christine contended that she was careful never to drink around Zaffino. "I needed every ounce of energy I had to fight him," she explained.

She was also fairly positive that, shortly before the murder, John had described a fistfight he'd had with Zack: "He said that he had beat the shit out of this Jeff Zack, didn't use the name, but I knew who he meant."

"How did you know who he meant?" Daugherty asked.

"Because he talked about this white-haired Lebanese guy," Christine countered, apparently confusing Israel with its neighbor to the north. "When I saw it [Zack's photo] in the paper, I figured it out . . . He said this Zack guy started it. John beat the shit out of him in front of his posse. That's what he called it."

At this point, Daugherty began to take on a disbelieving tone, sometimes responding to questions with a curt "Okay." Felber wondered if the captain was trying to play "good cop/bad cop," or had become incredulous because of Christine's confusion about certain elements of the story. For instance, when Christine had failed to remember a phone number, Daugherty took on the demeanor of an interrogator confronting an impostor. When Christine mentioned that she'd seen Zaffino with a handgun, Daugherty asked her to specify the caliber.

"I think it's a thirty-eight," Christine answered.

"Tell me what you think a thirty-eight looks like."

"It kind of looks to me like a big nine-millimeter. I don't know. My dad's got a lot of guns and, you know, to me, it looked like a big nine-millimeter."

". . . You're sure about that?"

"Positive."

Felber and Daugherty exchanged dirty looks. Did the captain remember that the ballistics on the projectile found at the crime scene revealed that Zack had been killed with a .38? It appeared to Felber that Daugherty was focusing on the flaws in Christine's story, rather than the valuable information she was offering.

After Christine hypothesized that Zack had not been dating Ed George's wife, but his daughter, the captain stated, "Tie this all together for me, because I'm very unclear as to how or why it is that you think that Ed George is behind this."

Christine replied that Zaffino had told her that a man "got whacked because he was dating or messing around with Ed George's daughter."

It was obvious that Christine knew very little about Ed George or his motivations. But she continually provided her interviewers with observations that had the potential to bring the case into clearer focus. For example, Christine maintained, the woman at the center of the murder had allegedly promised to buy Zaffino a motorcycle.

Felber was not about to let this nugget pass by: "So the daughter of Ed George's, or whoever, was going to buy him a motorcycle?"

"I'm just speculating."

Throughout the interview, Felber did his best to concentrate on the content of what Christine was trying to communicate. By contrast, he felt that the captain was attempting to goad the witness into what police thought she *should* say: Ed George had hired John Zaffino to kill Jeff Zack because of the affair with Cynthia. Felber had seen rookie detectives treat a witness with disdain for delivering anything but the desired story.

"You asked him [Zaffino] directly, 'Did you do this?' " Daugherty queried.

"Oh yeah. I asked him point blank, and he would not tell me yes or no . . . He goes, 'Well, let's just say the guy has a hard time parting his hair now.' Which to me is a yes. To me, that's a yes."

"What else did he say about that?" Daugherty asked.

"He tried not to say very much, and I tried not to hear it. I didn't want to hear it. I didn't want to know it . . . because that makes me an accessory."

". . . Do you think he's capable of something like that, or do you think he's blowing smoke?"

"Oh, I don't think he's blowing smoke."

"You think he's capable? Do you think he's ever done

anything like that in the past? Has he ever got into a fight with anybody in the past like that?"

"Oh yeah. He's been in a million fistfights."

"Has he ever used a weapon that you're aware of?"

"I heard a rumor when I was in Pennsylvania that he killed somebody. But I don't know who, where, when, why."

When the tape ran out after a particularly heated session, and Daugherty left the room, Christine pointedly asked Felber, "What's *her* problem?"

"She's just doing her job. She just gets a little aggressive sometimes."

He stomped out of the room, toward Hudnall and Whiddon in the hallway: "We finally have a real suspect, and a witness who knows something—and the captain's gonna piss her off."

"Daugherty thinks she knows more than what she's telling us," Hudnall replied.

"I know," Felber answered sarcastically. "So does Christine. And you know what? If the captain keeps attacking her, she's gonna stop talking."

Hudnall and Whiddon were silent.

"Let her give us as much information as possible," Felber continued. "If she's lying, we'll charge her with obstruction. But she isn't lying—and if you ask me, any real detective would know that!"

He spun around and re-entered the room. When Daugherty returned, she waited before she inserted a new tape into the recorder. The captain asked Christine if she'd even been instructed to ditch the murder weapon, or cover up the crime.

"No," the witness shot back defensively.

Why did Zaffino kill Jeff? What was their connection? To Felber, it seemed like a scene from a black-and-white detective movie, minus the spotlight on the witness' face. When information came up a second time, Daugherty seemed to become agitated if the wording changed. Felber, on the other hand, cared little about the phrasing. When words don't vary, it indicates that the witness is lying—the responses are practiced. In his mind, the substance of Christine's remarks was consistent.

Then, the captain asked Christine to take a polygraph test.

"Why?" an offended Christine shot back.

Daugherty explained that it was the only way that detectives could gauge whether Christine was telling the truth. Felber cringed. Some studies claimed that polygraphs were reliable 90 percent of the time. Others listed the number at 60 percent. No researcher had ever reached the conclusion that a polygraph was 100 percent dependable. Because of this, a jury could never be informed that a witness had passed a polygraph test. But if the person failed, detectives were expected to dismiss nearly all of the witness' data as lies.

Christine stared at the captain, and demanded to know why her honesty had come into question. Was her word not good enough?

Daugherty raised her voice. She insisted that a polygraph would prove that Christine was telling the truth. "Are you on any type of medication?" the captain asked.

It was a common question for a polygraph candidate; certain types of drugs were known to elicit false results. But the timing was all wrong.

Christine glared at the captain.

Very quickly, Felber tried taking the conversation in another direction, asking about names of Zaffino's associates. In the midst of this, though, Daugherty cut in, asking Christine if she was willing to wear a wire, and record her conversations with Zaffino.

The novelty of assisting in a homicide investigation appeared to have run its course. Christine slowly explained that she no longer wished to play a role in John's arrest. She feared him—and feared Ed George.

Charnesky tried breaking the tension by switching

to non-offensive questions—like verifying addresses and phone numbers mentioned earlier in the interview. Then, the captain started zooming in on Christine again:

"Is there anything you've forgotten to tell us?"

By itself, this was a useful question. But it had to be uttered with the appropriate inflection, at the appropriate time. Given the stress in the room, the delivery once again indicated an uncertainty about the veracity of the witness' answers.

Christine ground her teeth. "No," she responded.

Daugherty started the recorder as Charnesky continued trying to soothe the witness, emphasizing how grateful he was to have Christine's cooperation. Felber also pointed out that if an arrest was ever made, police would rely on a variety of sources. Zaffino was not likely to trace his troubles directly back to his former wife.

The FBI agent eventually took over the questioning, revisiting much of the same material, but in a way that gave Christine the impression that he believed her. Slowly, she softened her stance, and again appeared eager to help.

"So you've talked about this with him more than once?" Felber asked, referring to her conversations with Zaffino about the murder.

"Yeah."

"A number of times."

"Right, many times."

"And he made comments that led you to believe without any doubt that he did it?"

". . . That's the impression that I'm getting from him, but he never comes out and says it."

". . . On the other hand," Charnesky said, "it's quite strange a person who's innocent, who knew nothing about it, I mean . . ."

"Wouldn't keep talking about it," Christine inserted.

". . . And . . . when you told him about our visit, even if he actually didn't admit it, he also didn't say . . . 'They're asking about me? About what?' "

"Right."

"No surprise reaction?"

Christine shook her head from side to side. "Nuh-uh."

She affirmed that this was why she was relatively certain that Zaffino had committed the homicide.

"What would it take to get him to say that?" Felber asked.

"I don't think he will. He hasn't yet."

When the interview finally ended, Felber escorted Christine into the hall where they met Hudnall. A confused and agitated Christine asked if she was now a suspect. The detectives assured her she was not.

With his good ol' boy charm and youthful grin, Hudnall had a way of inspiring the public's confidence. Besides being a SWAT team leader and a very tough cop, Hudnall loved hunting, football and beer. He referred to his wife as "Old Mean Sharon," and exhibited a certain pride in being henpecked. At one point, two of his sons were serving in Iraq, and the situation weighed on him heavily. Perhaps no one else in the department could succeed in making the types of inappropriate, off-color statements that came out of Hudnall's mouth without being disciplined. But the sergeant was given a pass—not because of his position, but the fact that there was never a modicum of malice behind his remarks.

Now, he actually managed to make Christine smile, particularly after he expounded on Felber's gibes about their captain. Both detectives insisted that Christine was the hero in the case. There was no way that she was going to be arrested. As she relaxed, Felber saw the opportunity to once again ask the witness to tape-record Zaffino.

Both Hudnall and Felber believed that Christine was a good person, and she could sense their trust. Someone had been murdered, they stated, and getting the killer off the streets was "the right thing to do." This moral argument often didn't work. But it apparently resonated with Christine.

"You only have to deal with us," Felber added, perhaps

a little too hopefully. "The captain won't even be in the picture. And you know what else? This is your way of making her look like a fool for accusing you. Because when this is over, that's how she's going to be looked at by everybody—like a fool."

Christine perked up, then grew solemn. "I'm just scared of the guy," she said, referring to her ex-husband.

"If we can lock up John Zaffino," Felber replied, "you'll never have to worry about him hurting you again."

The logic made sense to Christine. But what was going to transpire in the meantime? Could the detectives guarantee her that they'd protect her from John before an arrest was made?

"Yes, we can," Felber stated.

It was a vow that would cost him many nights of restless sleep, and countless waking hours of anxiety.

But it was a promise that he swore he was going to keep.

SEVEN

AT LEAST ONCE a day, detectives would notice Lieutenant Whiddon sitting at his desk, his head hunched down with a telephone receiver resting on his broad shoulders, as he listened to an agonizing, but familiar, refrain: "This thing has really destroyed my life." Always, it was a family member of a homicide victim at the other end of the line, begging the Akron police to make an arrest. Whiddon never delegated this chore to others, even though the exchanges sometimes lasted more than an hour, and callers yelled, pointed out that the system favored the wealthy, accused the lieutenant of insensitivity and—in those cases when the victim was black—occasionally blamed racism for the department's ineffectiveness.

Now, after a year of chasing around bad leads in the Jeff Zack case, there was the euphoric feeling that the police might finally have a real suspect. Whiddon could tell Jeff's family that the investigation was moving forward without lying.

During his few spare moments, Felber sifted through hundreds of pages of the Georges' phone records, hoping to find a number linked to John Zaffino. Several detectives told Felber that he was wasting his time. Regardless of their culpability, the suspects seemed too savvy to have called each other—creating a paper trail—around the time of the murder. Felber strongly disagreed. If Cynthia or Ed had commissioned the hit, he maintained, human nature would dictate that one of them would want to hear from the shooter immediately after the homicide.

His fellow detectives shrugged off the argument. For the time being, at least, Felber's search was going nowhere.

Investigators needed hard evidence, and finding the gun would have been a very good start. Captain Daugherty suggested sending a search team to skim the ponds near Zaffino's apartment. It was a good idea, but both Felber and Whiddon wanted to ensure that they were looking in the right place. Felber recommended having Christine inform Zaffino about the plan, and listening to his reaction on tape.

"I heard something on the radio," she told her ex-husband, "about the cops sending divers into those ponds by your place—looking for the murder weapon or something."

Zaffino laughed.

For two days, divers combed the tranquil waters. Nothing was found.

AS NEWS ABOUT the case spread around the Akron Police Department, a Persons Unit detective warned Felber to watch out.

"Watch out for what?"

In 1997, the detective responded, he'd been part of the team investigating the death of Dr. Margo Shamberger Prade, a popular physician found shot in her van outside her west Akron office. After months of tireless labor, detectives accumulated enough evidence to charge the woman's husband, Douglas Prade, with the crime. Douglas was a high-ranking captain with the Akron Police Department, and the case made national headlines. But when the awards were doled out, the supervisors received a good deal of the accolades, while the guys who did most of the work remained anonymous.

"I'm not worried about that happening here," Felber said. "I think I know a lot more about the case than certain people above me, and have a pretty good rapport with the witnesses."

"You've been warned."

LESS THAN HALF an hour later, Felber spotted the Persons Unit detectives entering a conference room, where Captain Daugherty and Major Callahan were already situated. He intercepted Lieutenant Whiddon in the hallway.

"What's going on?"

"Didn't anybody tell you? Daugherty and the Major called a meeting to go over the Zack case."

"No."

"Well, follow me."

Felber trailed his lieutenant and took a seat at the middle of the conference table. He'd spent much of the past twenty-four hours contemplating the department's best course of action, and concluded that—without a gun, fingerprints or witnesses who could positively identify the shooter—it was important for Christine Todaro to re-establish contact with John Zaffino, and entangle him in some type of dialogue about the homicide. Yes, Zaffino was being extremely cautious about what he disclosed. But he could not contain his curiosity about the way police were conducting the probe. Therefore, he needed to stay in communication with Christine. At first, Felber reasoned, detectives would instruct her to feed her former spouse data suggesting that police were on the wrong track. Emboldened by his belief that he was outsmarting the authorities, Zaffino might begin running his mouth. If this approach failed, Christine could suggest that, indeed, police were cultivating legitimate leads—worrying Zaffino into making compromising statements. Ultimately, of course, the goal was needling the suspect until he broke.

The meeting started with the captain delegating assignments. Detectives John Bell and Richard Morrison were to question an ex-boyfriend of Christine's—and an acquaintance of John Zaffino's—who might know something about the homicide. Sergeant Terry Hudnall was told to visit Zaffino's neighbors, and ask what they knew.

Felber attempted to interject. If detectives swarmed on all his associates, Zaffino was sure to become paranoid—and might even leave town. Wasn't it wiser to see what Chris could glean before the entire unit began busting down doors?

The captain ignored the suggestions. And Felber noticed the Major shooting him glares, as well. It appeared that Callahan was relying on Daugherty's advice, and now shared her distaste for Felber.

"There's something else we need to think about," Felber added. "I have concerns about jeopardizing Chris' life unnecessarily."

The remark hung in the air, disregarded.

When the meeting ended, Felber confronted Hudnall: "Is it a good idea to send all these people out there? Some of them don't know anything but the basics of the case. Isn't there a chance that someone could inadvertently say the wrong thing—particularly about Chris—and it could get back to Zaffino?"

"Maybe," Hudnall answered uncomfortably. "But she's the captain."

Felber turned to Whiddon. "Am I even still on the case?" He'd noticed that no one had given him a task that morning.

Whiddon smiled. "Don't overreact." He told Felber to set up a meeting with Christine and a narcotics detective who could show her how to use a recording device.

THE GROUP PICKED a vacant parking lot behind a school in Christine's neighborhood as a meeting point. The detectives arrived first, and watched as their witness pulled up in a red sports car that barely ran. Although Zaffino lived some twenty-five miles away, everyone was careful to be discreet. Nobody could risk the possibility of a Zaffino associate driving by, and reporting her collaboration to him.

Interestingly, Felber had never done undercover work, and was curious about the type of recording device the narcotics detective would bring. When he produced it, Felber seemed visibly surprised. The cassette recorder he'd had as a kid was actually smaller.

"Hey, this is Akron," the detective explained. "What did you expect?" He instructed Christine on the way to hold the apparatus up to the phone whenever she spoke with John. The microphone was sensitive enough to pick up the conversation.

"If I need to get ahold of you," she asked Felber, "do you have another number, besides the one at work?"

He shook his head.

"You don't have a cell phone?"

"The department never gave me one. I'm not important enough. Besides, I don't need one. Nobody ever calls me. I don't have any friends."

"It's true," the narcotics detective added.

They all had a laugh at Felber's expense.

WHILE CHRISTINE WAS willing to cooperate with authorities, she worried that John would become guarded if she brought up the murder. So detectives conceived a unique strategy: offering Whiddon to the *Akron Beacon Journal* for a story the newspaper planned on the first anniversary of the homicide. Felber warned Whiddon that the department might end up looking incompetent; readers were likely to grumble about the fact that a year had passed without an arrest.

"I don't care how it looks," the lieutenant replied. "I just want to solve this thing."

Felber asked reporter Stephanie Warsmith and her editor to let him know when the piece was going to run. That way, they could have Christine call Zaffino the same day to discuss the story:

WHODUNIT PERPLEXES DETECTIVES

. . . A year ago Sunday—June 16—Zack was parked at a Home Avenue gas station when a motorcyclist pulled up behind him, got off the bike and shot him in the head. The black-clad figure hopped back on the motorcycle and sped away.

To this day, the identity of the shadowy figure remains a mystery.

Police have not yet made an arrest, though they now believe a hit man was responsible. The case is sensational for the Akron area because of the method of the murder and the mystery. It's the type of tale that normally hails from a much larger, crime-ridden city.

"We haven't had anything like this ever," said Lt. Dave Whiddon, who heads the investigation.

CHRISTINE TODARO POSITIONED the newspaper near the telephone, and engaged in her first clandestine project for the Akron Police Department. "Did you see the paper today?" she asked her ex-husband, with the tape recorder rolling.

"No."

"You need to read the paper."

"What did it say?"

"It's in there about that guy, the guy you took out."

Zaffino tensed. "Chris, how dare you say that? . . . I'd appreciate if you didn't talk on the phone about stuff, please. Okay?"

"Yeah."

"'Cause, you know, they listen."

Having failed to gain an electronic confirmation of Zaffino's role in the Zack murder, Christine switched to another tactic, complaining about harassment from cops visiting her home and fishing for clues.

"Well, why don't you tell them you don't want to talk to them?" Zaffino said. "Then, they won't come around."

". . . How did I get involved in all this bullshit?"

". . . Listen to me. When you start panicking, then you start saying stuff that you don't even know what you're saying, and get it all screwed up . . . All you got to do is say, 'Hey, fuck you. Get the fuck out of here.' "

"I'm not gonna say that."

"That's all you got to say. Why not? . . . You would say it to me . . . You didn't do anything wrong."

"I know."

"And neither did I. I mean, none of us did anything wrong. They're investigating something and, uh, too fuckin' bad. . . . You need to work with me."

"I am working with you."

". . . No one's done anything wrong, Chris. And if you think otherwise, it's a misunderstanding on your part."

But Zaffino sounded less than confident, and eager to talk about the matter later that night, in person, where he assumed no one would be able to eavesdrop on the conversation.

Before they met, though, Felber, Hudnall and several narcotics detectives convened with Christine to wire her up for the encounter. Hudnall, a jocular guy who usually had plenty to say, seemed absolutely bewildered when Christine exited the car dressed like a teenager, in a tube top and skin-tight jeans. Wire in hand, he reached for different parts of her body, then pulled away. He was stumped; there was no place to insert a microphone that wouldn't betray a bulge.

"Oh shit," Hudnall said. "This ain't going to work."

Felber produced a mini–recording device loaned to him by the FBI, and suggested hiding it in a box of tissues in Christine's car. The narcotics detectives shook their heads. The tissues might muffle the sound. If John intended to get violent, they'd have no way of knowing. After some consideration, the detectives provided their witness with a pager, equipped with a built-in microphone.

Now, they delivered a series of instructions: make John get into your car, and do not go into his under any circumstances.

"How am I going to do that?" she questioned. Her vehicle was minuscule, and Zaffino drove a large pickup. But, the detectives explained, if she was sitting in John's passenger seat and he decided to take off, it would be impossible to stop him without alerting him to the sting.

Christine was also told to turn off her air-conditioner during the conversation; detectives wanted the audio transmission to be crisp. However, it was 85 degrees outside. How, Christine wondered, was she expected to explain her decision to forgo air-conditioning?

"Tell him it's broke," someone blurted.

"And if he tries to turn it on himself, and finds out it works, then what do I say?"

"Thank him for fixing it."

The plan was for detectives to follow Christine to her rendezvous point, in a lot near a CompUSA, and park their unmarked vehicles someplace where they could monitor the couple. If Christine was in trouble, she was instructed to wave her hands. One of the plainclothes narcotics detectives would then play the role of a Good Samaritan shopper, breaking up the confrontation.

Suddenly, Christine's cell phone rang. "Relax," she snapped at Zaffino on the other end. "I'll be there in a minute."

CHRISTINE THEN CONTINUED to her meeting with Zaffino. The four unmarked police cars scrambled for position in the busy parking lot. Because of interference from the stores and nearby traffic, detectives also had to park close enough for their receivers to pick up the proper signals.

Much to everyone's relief, Zaffino had been riding around with his son, and entered Christine's vehicle. Suspicious about being recorded, Zaffino checked above the visor, and visually inspected the car. Even if his ex-wife wasn't wearing a wire, though, he was clearly frightened that she might say the wrong things to authorities, and tried planting one consistent thought in her mind: "I honestly had nothing to do with this situation here . . . It has nothing to do with me . . . I don't know him [Zack]."

"If you didn't do anything, then you shouldn't be worried about talking to them," Christine challenged, referring to the police, "'cause that will get them out of my face."

She also seemed jealous of the mystery woman linking him to the case, a lady whose relationship with Zaffino may have overlapped with hers. "If you tell her the same stupid shit that you've told me," Christine said, "then what's keeping her from saying anything? What about that? You ever think about that?"

"Nah . . . last I knew, she moved."

". . . Who was it?"

"That fuckin' bimbo," Zaffino answered.

"What was her last name?"

"I don't know. I made her up . . . As far as any other bullshit goes, I mean, if you start pointing them [the police] my way, I don't have the money for an attorney."

"I'm not going to point them your way."

"There will be a kid over here who's fatherless."

"I know that. Don't you think you should have thought about that shit before you . . . ?"

"I didn't do anything. See, you believe I did something."

"That's because you told me."

"No, I didn't."

To the detectives dissecting the conversation, Christine Todaro was becoming one of the bravest people they knew. She was legitimately afraid of John Zaffino, and had every right to be. Yet, she never once backed down. Every time she raised her voice, the detectives—sometimes seated as close as 100 yards away—felt like running up to the car to save their witness before Zaffino exploded on her. But she managed to control the situation. Later on, when someone suggested tempering her tone, she explained, "I have to talk to him like that. If I wasn't fighting with him, then he'd *really* get suspicious."

Now, Zaffino implored her, "Just stay strong for me."

"I will."

"They'll leave you alone eventually . . . The less you tell them, the less they're gonna fuck with you."

Then, Zaffino returned to his pickup. As planned, Christine immediately met up with detectives in a residential area. Despite her composure with her ex-husband, she was actually so nervous that her knees were literally shaking when she exited her car. She returned her mini-pager, then mentioned that she was almost out of gas, and had very little money.

Felber reached into his wallet, and handed her 20 dollars of his own cash.

ON JUNE 27, Whiddon and Felber played Christine the threatening phone message that Jeff had received shortly before his death:

> *"All right, buddy. You got one way out, so you need to start answering your cell phone—okay? I'll be talking to you, or should I call your mom and dad's house in Arizona? Whatever. Answer the phone, boy."*

"That's John," Christine confirmed.

Covering their tracks, the detectives played her the tape two more times.

"Yeah, that's him," she verified.

Given her personality, Christine seemed genuinely excited by the thrill and danger of ensnaring a murder suspect—particularly a guy who'd broken her arm, and brutalized her son. Once she crossed the line, though, of setting up Zaffino, there was no turning back. The stress of misleading a dangerous man—whom she'd once loved—caused her to become physically ill. She felt like her life was in upheaval, and her usual challenges—finding a job, keeping her car running, maintaining custody of her son—seemed to magnify. She was having trouble controlling her anger, and handling day-to-day problems—depression symptoms all too familiar to police.

Chris' father was worried about the possibility of Zaffino finding out about his ex-wife's cooperation, and taking out his vengeance on her family. Her handlers felt guilty about this. After all, unlike those who play similar roles in other probes, Christine was not a reformed criminal. She'd simply ended up in her position due to an unfortunate combination of circumstances. Because of this, detectives were especially motivated. If someone was going to put themselves through so much personal anguish and peril, there had to be a payoff at the end. The police were determined to lock up Zaffino before he discovered the truth and murdered this selfless woman.

Nonetheless, the Cuyahoga Falls Police Department soon became aware of Christine for an entirely different reason. As she raced around the area to her various appointments, she had a tendency to ignore traffic regulations. Within a month, she'd received so many moving violations that her license was suspended. If Chris couldn't drive, she couldn't continue to meet with Zaffino. While discussing this with her handlers, Christine seemed relatively unfazed. "Just call Cuyahoga Falls," she suggested, "and fix the traffic tickets."

Neither Felber nor Lieutenant Whiddon had ever attempted anything like this before. When Whiddon broached the subject with the head of Akron's traffic bureau, the response was a basic one: "I don't think it can be done."

The lieutenant next contacted a traffic court judge married to an Akron police sergeant. "Once a ticket goes to the

Bureau of Motor Vehicles," the woman explained, "it's out of our hands."

Whiddon and Felber met to discuss their options. Captain Daugherty still had connections in state government. Since Daugherty might still suspect Christine of playing a role in the homicide, the captain would be in no rush to do her any favors. But Daugherty obviously wanted the investigation to move forward, so she agreed to contact her friend.

The official advised the Akron police to visit the Cuyahoga Falls Municipal Court and track down the judge overseeing Christine's case. If he could be convinced to dismiss the most recent traffic ticket, the official could contact the BMV about having Chris' license reinstated.

There was a catch, though. As soon as John Zaffino was arrested, the witness' license would again be revoked.

Felber never bothered telling Christine this detail. He'd spent enough time in government to safely assume that officials would eventually forget the stipulation.

Eventually, the judge asked the detectives to call the officer who issued the summons. Since the Cuyahoga Falls Police Department wouldn't phone him while he was off-duty, the Akron police found him at home. At first, he was cautious about the proposition. But when he realized that his one gesture might help solve a homicide, he called the judge and instructed him to negate the ticket.

With paperwork in hand, Whiddon and Felber now had to drive Christine to the BMV office in Canton, not far from the home where Cynthia George had grown up. As the detectives positioned themselves at the back of a line, Chris inquired, "You're the police. Why don't you guys just cut to the front?"

Felber nudged Whiddon. "She's right," he smirked. "Go pull some strings. I'm sure the nice people at the BMV won't mind."

With visible discomfort, Whiddon stepped around the roped area to address the BMW clerk. She immediately waved Christine and Felber forward, and pointed them toward a back room, where an office manager pleasantly arranged for Chris' license to be reinstated—and the recorded exchanges with Zaffino to continue.

THE MEETINGS THAT followed were interesting ones. Daugherty's husband, an FBI agent, accompanied the Akron police to one session, listening in as Zaffino spoke to his ex-wife on a device provided by the Bureau. John claimed that the police were so unscrupulous that they'd threatened to charge an 82-year-old woman in the homicide. While the allegation was false, the fact was that police *had* aggressively pursued an elderly woman: Helen Rohr, Cynthia's mother.

As time passed, Christine became cognizant of the fact that Cynthia George was not Ed George's daughter, but his wife. And, police confirmed, she had also been John's lover—while he and Chris were still married. Since Zaffino had been the one accusing *Christine* of cheating, this parcel of news enraged the witness. On July 15, she called her ex-husband, and began laying into him.

Nervous that Christine was going to blurt out the wrong thing on the phone, Zaffino told his ex-wife to meet him "now!" With the Narcotics Unit detectives already engaged, this presented a problem for the Akron Police Department. As Chris stalled for time, a number of detectives, along with a beat-up gray van containing five machine gun–toting SWAT team members were marshaled.

The van was stripped of most of its seating, so the officers awkwardly stood, as the vehicle maneuvered its way to the meeting point. In order not to draw attention, the team turned off the air-conditioning after the van was parked. Outside, the weather hovered above 80 degrees. Inside, the helmeted officers perspired in bullet-proof vests, as the temperature exceeded 100 degrees.

Highly emotional, Christine disobeyed police orders to

remain in her car, and stepped into Zaffino's Explorer. Radios lit up, as detectives tried coming up with a possible rescue scenario. It would be a complicated operation. Because they'd rushed to the scene so quickly, some of the law enforcement representatives were unaware of where the others were parked.

In Zaffino's vehicle, Christine, wearing a wire, angrily referred to Cindy as "that fuckin' whore you were with . . . that chick's cheated on her husband . . . she's been with so many different guys, it's unreal."

"I don't know anything about it."

"Yeah, you do. You're lying to me. Quit lying."

Zaffino countered that he and Christine were no longer married.

"We *were* married," she emphasized.

". . . I don't care about her."

"Fuck you."

For his part, Zaffino was becoming more paranoid. He boasted that his car contained a "bug detector" that could identify hidden electronic devices. Christine scrutinized the apparatus, chucked it into the back seat, and kept hammering the suspect.

"Look, if they pin this on me," Zaffino barked, "I'm gone for life."

"I understand that."

"And maybe the electric chair. But the only thing between me and there is you."

"No, *her*."

"No, you."

"No, *her*."

"No . . ."

"Bullshit. Don't fuckin' pin that on me, it's bull . . ."

"The only thing that would ever put me in prison and death is you."

"Fuck you," Christine screamed, reaching for the door handle. "I'm getting out. I don't buy that. No. You better check her out, and find out what her lips are saying. Okay?"

Felber sometimes contemplated the possibility of Zaffino zoning in on Christine's pager, and testing the mechanism to see if it worked. For that reason, Felber had planned to call the device while Christine was meeting with John. But narcotics detectives revealed that there was no telephone number. The department wasn't willing to spend the money to activate a pager that was only there as camouflage.

Now, as Zaffino and Christine spoke, Felber heard the suspect ask her if she wanted to get something to eat. As the detective shook his head from side to side, she agreed.

Zaffino pulled out of his parking spot. Lieutenant Whiddon quickly issued an order: follow them, but don't stop the pickup. In the confusion, some of the detectives ended up *in front* of Zaffino, rather than behind him.

The pair entered the drive-through ramp at a nearby McDonald's, and an unmarked police car fell in behind them. When it was the detectives' turn to order, they were afraid to decline and blow their cover. At the same time, they didn't want to lose John and Christine while waiting at the drive-in window.

Fortunately, the pickup became snarled in traffic soon after Zaffino paid for his food, and the police quickly caught up with him, following the suspect back to his previous parking spot.

ONE NIGHT AT 2 AM, Felber received a frantic phone call from Christine, speaking so quickly that the detective had a difficult time deciphering her words. Next, a Cuyahoga Falls police officer was on the line, explaining that someone in his department had noticed a car parked in a handicapped spot, and Christine exiting a nearby convenience store with her boyfriend, Tim Cantanese. When the officer began writing a summons, Christine launched into an angry, name-calling diatribe. He called for backup, and Chris became even more unhinged. Eventually, she was arrested for disorderly conduct and, when police checked the vehicle, some marijuana was located on the driver's side.

"Who's the driver?" the officer asked.

"I am," Christine replied, and was hit with a drug charge, as well.

Christine insisted that the drugs were not hers. Tim had lost his license, she said, and that's why she was driving his car. It was a lie, and the Cuyahoga Falls police knew it. Tim was one of several local characters on their radar, and when they saw him driving, they frequently pulled him over to add time to his suspended license. He'd been spotted behind the wheel earlier that night and now, as Chris had tried protecting him, the police were ready to punish her for her misguided valor.

Meanwhile, Cantanese watched the episode without once speaking up for his girlfriend. He was equally helpful when the case eventually went to court.

Felber tried telling the Cuyahoga Falls police that Christine was a vital part of a homicide investigation. But as they spoke, Felber could hear Christine in the background, continuing to shout and curse. If the officer wished to extend a courtesy to the Akron Police Department, Chris was not giving him many options.

"Let me speak to her again, please," Felber requested.

The officer handed Christine the phone.

"Chris," Felber began, "if you calm down and apologize to these guys, maybe they can cut you some slack."

"I'm not fuckin' apologizing to these assholes!"

There was nothing more that Felber could do.

The Cuyahoga Falls police later claimed that, as Christine was being booked, she kneed a cop in the balls. After Christine was bailed out the next day, she explained that this was a reaction to the cop's groping. Although the Akron detectives expressed sympathy, they didn't believe her; it was an excuse they'd heard dozens of times before. When the matter was adjudicated, they urged Christine to plead guilty to a misdemeanor. She followed their advice, and received probation. A short time later, the media reported a couple of town officers disciplined for, among other things, sexual misconduct.

Felber's attorney, Tom Adgate, agreed to represent Christine for one dollar. He also allowed her to use his name when Zaffino asked her to find an attorney to protect her from police harassment. At one point, Zaffino's lawyer, Larry Whitney, called to confirm this, and Adgate claimed that, yes, he was Christine's legal representative.

MEANWHILE, FELBER HAD been assigned to accompany Hudnall to Zaffino's old apartment complex, just off of Interstate 77, to gather information from neighbors. When the pair turned onto Nine Iron Drive, they immediately noticed the difference between Zaffino's lifestyle and that of his ex-wife. Nestled alongside a golf course, the buildings were new and well-maintained. The suites were comfortable, and designed for upper-middle-class sensibilities. Zaffino's neighbors were lawyers, financial brokers and other professionals who'd probably never seen the honky-tonks where the suspect imbibed and brawled.

The duo parked by the apartment manager's office and entered. Inside, they were greeted by the assistant manager of the complex, an attractive woman in her upper twenties, who admitted that Zaffino had once resided there. But when detectives asked to see related paperwork, she resisted.

"That's private information. We have a policy of not divulging private information."

Felber flushed with frustration. He was used to people in the inner city stonewalling police; many times, they feared retaliation from the perpetrators or their associates. But, here, the assistant manager was citing "policy" to hamper the investigation.

"I know you want to safeguard the tenants' privacy," he

began, "and I commend you for that. Your tenants have a right not to be harassed by salespeople or identity thieves. But we're trying to solve a homicide. Someone is dead, and I'm sure you don't want to keep us from finding the killer."

"I'm sorry," the woman replied icily, "but that's our policy."

"Fine, that's the company's policy," Felber shot back. "Let me tell you mine. My policy is to throw people in jail who refuse to cooperate in homicide investigations. You decide which policy you want to follow."

The woman paused. "Let me call my boss," she responded, repairing into a side office to use the phone. Five minutes later, she emerged with Zaffino's file, apologizing for obstructing the process.

"And I'm sorry I was a little impatient," Felber said.

The barriers melted. The woman described Zaffino as aggressive and annoying. Soon, she and the detectives were joking around, as Felber removed Zaffino's rental agreement from the file. John had signed the document in August 2000, and left the complex a year later, two months after the murder. Even more interesting was a name listed under "Emergency Contacts": Cindy Rohr.

Rohr, detectives instantly recalled, was Cynthia George's maiden name.

Jill Henry had lived next door to Zaffino, and described him as strange. She recounted a story he'd told her about a pet bird. According to John, he'd use a vacuum cleaner to freshen up the bird's cage—until one day, when he sucked his pet into the device. Zaffino thought that this was a hilarious story. Jill didn't.

She also remembered Zaffino having a motorcycle—it was "light green," she said, "and dark purple or black"—and a blonde girlfriend about 40. The woman often showed up at the complex in a dark gray Suburban, with a bike rack attached to the rear, and a Starbucks coffee holder affixed next to the steering wheel. She was "sickly thin," Jill remarked, so skinny that she looked like she could have worn kids' clothes.

AN HOUR AFTER returning to the station, Felber was called to the front desk, where he was met by a crazed Chris. She was near tears, and so mad that she could barely speak.

The detective had warned Christine never to come to the station. It wasn't safe. Ed George not only had friends, but relatives on the police department. Some cops—in an effort to seem important—had a tendency to speak loudly about issues that were supposed to be classified. And Zaffino's attorney, Larry Whitney, frequently visited the building himself. The last thing anyone needed was for Zaffino to know that she'd entered the lair of his enemies.

Chris' yelling drew Captain Daugherty and Sergeant Hudnall to the front desk. Eventually, Christine finally calmed down enough to make sense, and told the people in whom she was trusting her life that she had received a call from a friend who'd been visited by a couple of detectives. These detectives had asked a lot of questions—most of which dealt with her character and her possible involvement in a homicide. Her friend thought that she was the suspect.

But what angered her more was the fact that detectives had been questioning someone who knew both John and her. She felt that they were endangering her safety for no reason. She was afraid that the detectives would say something that would get back to John and let him know that she was working with the police.

Daugherty told Chris that they had to talk to friends of hers to verify that they could trust her. As far as they knew, Chris was involved in covering up the homicide. "How dare you accuse me of anything!" Christine shouted at the captain. "Why the hell would I volunteer to come down here if I had something to do with it? What the hell's wrong with you?! None of you people even knew who John Zaffino was before I told you!"

Daugherty maintained her position: "Chris, I'm going to meet with the police legal advisors to see if we can file charges against you for obstructing justice."

"What?!" Christine yelled. "You're going to arrest me?! For what?! Trying to help you?! You want to know something?! You're crazy!"

It had taken a year to find a witness who could lead police to Jeff Zack's assassin, and weeks of practiced persuasion to induce Tim Cantanese into bringing Christine to the station. Now that Christine had finally done the right thing, she was being threatened with incarceration. Worse yet, as far as Felber was concerned, was having detectives who knew nothing about the case or the people they were questioning recklessly placing Chris' life in jeopardy. It was too easy for a detective to unwittingly say something that would reveal that Chris was cooperating with the police.

"Chris!" Felber loudly interjected, forcing both the witness and the captain to turn to him. "You are not going to be arrested. Trust me. I won't let it happen."

The detective was banking on the likelihood that—despite the highly charged political atmosphere within the police department—Whiddon and Hudnall would back him on this issue. If they didn't, it was back to patrol duty.

"It's not up to you, *Felber*," Daugherty said, with an emphasis on "Felber." Then, she quickly stood and marched toward the Person's Unit.

Chris' faith in the department in general, and Felber in particular, was shattered. And now, she was in greater fear for her life. Felber did not blame her; he shared her anger. He whisked her out of the building, promising to call as soon as he discovered what had happened. Then, he wheeled around and stomped into the Person's Unit.

Felber found the detective in question—seated in a meeting with Captain Daugherty, Lieutenant Whiddon,

Sergeant Hudnall and others—and asked him why he was asking questions about Chris. Looking at Daugherty, he replied that this was what he was told to do.

"What?!" Felber screamed, his face turning crimson. "Was I lying when I told her we'd protect her? I knew this would happen!" Glaring at the captain, he shouted, "You're going to get her killed!"

Daugherty immediately ordered the detective into Major Callahan's office. Whiddon and Hudnall flanked him on each side. "Keep your fuckin' mouth shut," Hudnall whispered to Felber, "or they're going to kick you off the case. Then there really *won't* be anyone around to save Chris' life."

The suggestion pacified Felber—to the point that he didn't explode when the captain lit into him. Not only was he guilty of insubordination, she declared, but incompetence. In fact, she said, the reason that he'd initially been placed in the Pawn Unit was that he lacked the skills for real detective work. She also implied that he was misogynistic—and having an affair with Christine.

Felber almost burst out laughing. He'd never even hugged Christine. In fact, he wasn't even sure if they'd shaken hands. While Christine was certainly attractive, the detective realized that they were no match. Felber's idea of a good time was making a home-cooked meal and relaxing in front of the television; his early years as a bartender had turned him off alcohol and partying. Chris, on the other hand, was outgoing and social. He was far too sedate for a woman like Christine Todaro.

Now, he calmly made his point, using language that any legal bureaucrat could understand. If harm were to befall Christine because of police negligence, he stated, both the city and the department could be hit with a massive lawsuit.

He placed emphasis on the term "negligence"; it was often used in civil actions against police departments. There was no immediate response from either the major or the captain, but both appeared worried—and locked in deep thought.

Felber now stood, thanked the major for leaving him on the case, and exited the room. He spent the next twenty minutes on the phone with Christine, once again reminding her of the value of her efforts. As before, she agreed to continue working with authorities.

Whiddon and Hudnall allowed Felber to cool off for another hour before they approached him. The lieutenant emitted a rare smile, recounting his session in the captain's office, urging her not to fire the detective.

"I don't think I've ever seen you go crazy like that," Hudnall laughed. "I was afraid I was going to have to shoot you, like a mad dog."

Felber managed to smile back.

ON THE MORNING of July 16—less than twenty-four hours after a tense meeting with Zaffino—Christine called Felber with some alarming news: "John's on his way over here now."

"What?"

"He wants to take me to get a post office box, so the cops won't find my address."

"Do you believe him?"

"Yeah."

Felber was still worried. "Chris," he began, "I wouldn't go with him. Who knows what his real intentions are?"

"I don't have a choice," she countered. "What's he gonna think if I'm suddenly not here?"

The detective gave Christine some simple advice: when Zaffino arrived, Christine was to walk out to his car, pretending to be speaking to a friend on the cell phone. With John listening, Christine would mention that he'd just pulled up to her home, and was taking her to the post office. If Christine disappeared, Zaffino would know that police had a solid foundation to grill him about the situation. With all his other problems, he didn't need that. Christine followed the recommendation, and was back home in slightly more than an hour.

LATER THE SAME day, Chris told police that Zaffino's attorney planned to call them. Whiddon and Felber discussed the best way to handle this development. Certainly, they were interested in speaking to Zaffino—but not until they had enough evidence to nail him. Also, they deduced, the attorney would likely say that his client had no interest in talking.

Zaffino had already told Chris that, legally, no one was obligated to speak to authorities. "That's your memorandum of rights," he said, mangling the term for "Miranda warning."

If Zaffino's attorney did consent to a meeting, detectives knew that the lawyer would want to participate, cutting off police whenever John seemed vulnerable. It was better to wait, detectives concluded, and pick up Zaffino when he didn't expect it.

Two hours after Felber's conversation with Chris, Zaffino's lawyer, Larry Whitney, phoned. Lieutenant Whiddon replied that, no, police did not wish to speak to John Zaffino.

At this stage, it was better to keep him waiting for the ax to fall.

DETECTIVES SENSED THAT Christine sometimes assumed that she was under their constant protection. But this was a fallacy. "Protective custody," as defined in Akron, meant sending a cruiser by a person's house several times a day. What complicated her case was that she didn't live within the city limits. Fortunately, the Cuyahoga Falls police agreed to keep an eye on her.

Nonetheless, Christine's handlers were becoming more apprehensive by the day. At one point, an *Akron Beacon Journal* reporter called Lieutenant Whiddon, and mentioned a rumor that the hit man's ex-wife was cooperating with authorities. Clearly, there was a leak within law enforcement ranks. Was it possible that some of this inside information might also reach Zaffino? Then, one morning, when Christine walked to her car, she discovered that it had been vandalized the night before—with the word "SLUTE" carved into the paint with keys. No one became particularly alarmed until detectives remembered a note they'd found in the file at Zaffino's old apartment complex:

> *I am movine in August 2001 . . . I loved it here! Your greate girls.*
>
> > *Your friende, John.*

Was he terrorizing Christine because he knew something?

Akron detectives briefly discussed the possibility of asking the Cuyahoga Falls police to arrest Zaffino for criminal damage. But the evidence was weak and, even if he was found guilty, it was doubtful that he'd serve a day of jail time for such a minor infraction. More likely, he'd blame Christine for getting him into the situation—and possibly become more dangerous.

No one involved with the murder investigation wanted Christine to suddenly cut herself off from Zaffino—at least until he admitted to the murder. So detectives attempted to find an uncomfortable medium, warning her to maintain a physical distance from her ex-husband. "It's all right if you talk to him," she was told. "Just don't meet with him in person."

On the night of August 17, Christine received a 2 AM phone call. "I'm coming over," Zaffino announced with mildly slurred speech. This time, his intention wasn't a chat. He wanted a sexual interlude.

"Where's your girlfriend?"

"I ain't got a girlfriend. Go get some beer. I'm coming over."

"Get your own beer," Christine answered, hanging up.

A few minutes later, Zaffino phoned again. "I'll bring the beer," he insisted. "Where can I get some at this time of the night?"

Christine told John about an all-night convenience store, then hung up again. When he called a short time later, she didn't answer. Now, Zaffino was mad, and left her this message:

"Now, you're pissing me off. You're not answering your phone. You know what? [chuckles] *I don't have to tell you nothing. You know what happens to me when you don't answer your phone, so you better deal with it real fuckin' quick here, real quick."*

Frightened, Christine left her home, and went to Tim Cantanese's apartment. There, Zaffino finally reached her on her cell phone. But Christine just wanted to be left alone, and placed Tim on the line. This sent Zaffino into a rage. He told her in a subsequent message:

"You have a good night, sweetheart. Tell fucknuts [he] *better know what I look like. When I find him, he's done."*

The harrassment continued, with Zaffino calling back frequently, promising to stalk Christine in the bars along State Road. During one exchange with Cantanese, Zaffino dared the man to meet him behind the Tangier, implying that Tim was about to get whacked.

The next day, though, Zaffino conveyed a different tone when he called Christine. "Hey, you know about last night?" he began. "Forget about it. I said a lot of stupid shit I didn't mean. I'm sorry."

Christine shook her head from side to side. It wasn't like Zaffino to apologize—unless he had a motive. In this case, she sensed that he believed that he was in big trouble, and hoped to keep his ex-wife in his camp.

WHAT HE DIDN'T know was that another ex-wife had also turned against him.

The morning after Christine's visit to police headquarters, Captain Daugherty asked detectives to track down all vehicles registered in Zaffino's name. By noon, they'd located a 1995 Honda motorcycle, purchased from Midwest Motors in Uniontown, Ohio, on May 21, 2001—roughly a month before the homicide—along with two helmets, and a leather "tank" bag.

The captain personally called the dealership, and spoke to manager Chris Hause. "Could you describe the particular model Zaffino purchased?" Daugherty asked.

"I remember it was a black, Ninja-style bike, with a green or yellow stripe."

Saleswoman Kristine Peteya also remembered the customer fairly well. "He was pushy, and seemed to be in a hurry," she said. "It was like he needed the bike *today*." He only wanted it for a short period of time, he emphasized, and had to have the fastest one in stock. She recalled that Zaffino had paid in cash, and was accompanied by a woman Peteya could only describe as "thin and white."

Initially, Zaffino was hesitant to tell the saleswoman his real name, identifying himself as "John Smith."

Realizing how close detectives were to definitively breaking open the case, the captain arranged to visit Peteya at her apartment. There, the woman was shown an array of photos, but could not make a positive identification. Daugherty now asked the saleswoman if she could produce a picture of the motorcycle. Peteya sat down at her computer, logged on to Tradercycle.com—an Internet site specializing in motorcycle transactions—and typed in "1995, CBR-1000 Honda."

Only one bike was listed, and Peteya printed out the

page. The captain surveyed it, and realized that the listee had a Pennsylvania address not far from where Zaffino had lived with his first wife.

In the kitchen, Daugherty asked the saleswoman to call the phone number included on the website. If the seller was aligned with the suspect, Daugherty feared, a call from an Akron police captain would arouse suspicion.

A man by the name of Russell Forrest answered the phone, and mentioned that he'd received the bike from his fiancée's ex-husband, as payment for back child support. Forrest still had the motorcycle, he stated, and it was in pristine condition, save for a tire that had been replaced.

Peteya remembered that Zaffino had asked to have a tire replaced, prior to the final sale.

Back at headquarters, Daugherty contacted the FBI office in Cleveland. Agents there confirmed that the VIN number on Forrest's bike matched the one purchased by Zaffino. The captain then typed Forrest's address into a law enforcement search engine called ChoicePoint, and discovered that it was the same as that of Zaffino's first wife, Nancy Bonodio.

As the captain reviewed Peteya's sales file, she noticed something else. There had been 10,120 miles on the bike when Zaffino purchased it. A year later, there were only 11,008. For whatever reason, the suspect had used the motorcycle for a very brief period before discarding it.

Daugherty proposed sending Detectives Russ McFarland and Mike Schaeffer to Pennsylvania, to speak with Forrest and retrieve the bike. Felber objected. Forrest's fiancée, Nancy, shared a son with Zaffino. What if she warned him about the developments during some type of visitation transfer? As before, Felber was overruled.

But, this time, he had nothing to worry about.

RUSSELL FORREST'S BUSINESS, Forrest Motors, was located in a converted ranch house, built into a hill, in Washington,

Pennsylvania. Some twenty used vehicles sat on what had previously been the front lawn.

The Akron detectives entered with two Pennsylvania State Troopers, dressed in suits, and identified themselves to Forrest. "We're investigating a homicide," McFarland began, displaying an Akron Police Department vehicle impound waiver form, "and we have good reason to believe that a motorcycle you have could have been involved."

Forrest nodded.

"We'd like to seize the motorcycle for impoundment, and possibly confirm this."

Forrest didn't flinch. "You can have the bike. Where do I sign?"

McFarland pointed at the signature line, then tried diverting Forrest from the fact that police were interested in John Zaffino: "Sometimes, a person who uses a vehicle in a crime gets rid of it, and it passes from hand to hand."

Forrest wasn't fooled. "I know who you're looking for," he replied, pointing at Nancy. "That's my fiancée, and she used to be married to John Zaffino."

Nancy wasn't shy about describing her ex-husband's outbursts—although in her case, she claimed, Zaffino never crossed over from verbal to physical abuse. After their divorce, Zaffino had been a troublesome presence in her life, battling with her over custody issues. But after a domestic violence hearing involving Christine Todaro, Zaffino had been prescribed the medication Effexor, and it had apparently changed his moods.

"From the time John started taking Effexor," Forrest told detectives, "he was a different guy . . . the last couple of years have been pretty good."

"How was he before that?" Schaeffer inquired.

"Stressful."

Forrest described a phone message he'd received shortly after he began dating Nancy: "He had gone to some court hearing in Warren [Pennsylvania] for child support, and he called my house, and pretty much said, 'You tell that

Photo: Akron Police Department

June 16, 2001. Former Israeli paratrooper Jeff Zack is murdered at the gas pump in a busy shopping center just within the Akron city limits. Detectives wondered why the killer chose such a public location to execute his victim.

Photo: Vince Felber

The George family first opened Tangier, billed as "the best steakhouse in Ohio," in 1948. Over the years, the dining and restaurant emporium played host to dozens of prominent figures, including two American presidents. Patrons called the effervescent Cynthia a welcome presence at her husband's etablishment.

John Zaffino, street fighter and alleged wife beater. Although prescribed medication to manage his anger, detectives believed he was eager to kill to please Cynthia George.

Photo: Ohio Department of Rehabilitation and Correction

Always the beauty queen, Cynthia George managed a slight smile—even when booked for her connection to the murder of lover Jeff Zack.

Photo: Summit County Jail

Photo: Deborah Lovelace

Detective Vince Felber once worked for Cynthia George's husband, and devoted himself to the murder investigation. Even when urged to back off, Felber angered brass by persistently pursuing the case.

Photo: Vince Felber

Mike Carroll, the distinguished prosecutor detectives regarded as a storybook hero in the Jimmy Stewart mold.

Assistant Prosecutor Brad Gessner was perceived as young, aggressive—and quick on the attack.

Photo: Vince Felber

In an Akron Police Department interrogation room, an arrogant John Zaffino briefly waived his right to remain silent. Detective Vince Felber would comment, "A cocky suspect is a talking suspect."

Photo: Vince Felber

Lieutenant David Whiddon (seen with Persons Unit secretary Carrie Stoll) patiently fielded phone calls from victim Jeff Zack's family, anticipating the moment when he could reveal a break in the case.

Photo: Vince Felber

Photo: Paul Tople / *Akron Beacon Journal*

November 16, 2005. George is accused of conspiring with her lover, John Zaffino, in the slaying of Jeff Zack, with whom she had an eight-year affair that ended about a month before he was killed in June 2001.

Cynthia George gives her husband, Edward, a kiss and hug in court. Despite her indiscretions, Ed remained by her side throughout the investigaion.

Photo: Paul Tople / *Akron Beacon Journal*

Photo: Jocelyn Williams / *Akron Beacon Journal*

Cynthia George and Jeff Zack appear to be enjoying one another's company. This photo was used as evidence by prosecutors to establish their relationship during John Zaffino's murder trial.

fuckin' whore, cunt, bitch woman' . . . It just rolled and rolled . . . The wording was so intimidating, it scared the shit out of me."

And lately, Forrest pointed out, Zaffino had begun acting skittish again. For some reason, he was asking Nancy to return the helmets that had come with the motorcycle. Zaffino claimed he had a buyer but, when detectives heard the story, they wondered whether the suspect was worried that a crime-scene witness might recognize the headgear. Regardless, Forrest had no intention of returning the items.

"I told Nancy, 'No way,'" he said. "I mean, this man owes us several thousand dollars. I'll be damned if I'm going to give him back property that he signed over to me. . . . So I got on the phone and I said, 'I'm not giving them to you. I'm not. It ain't going to happen.' So we went back and forth a little bit, and it was, you know, 'Fuck you,' you know, 'Motherfucker.'"

The next time the pair met, Zaffino referred to himself in the third person: "You don't want to mess with John Zaffino. He's a bad dude. If you cross him, he'll get even."

Eventually, Forrest locked the helmets in a closet. When Zaffino next asked about them, he was told that they had been sold.

As for the motorcycle, it had arrived in Pennsylvania suddenly. Zaffino had covered up its identifiable stripes, with duct tape, and driven it in from Ohio at night, when few witnesses would be traveling on the roads. He'd apparently received it from a girlfriend, Forrest told detectives— a woman who'd also provided John with a hundred dollars to spend the night in a motel during the excursion. Now, the suspect "wanted to get rid of the bike," Forrest said, "and he wanted me to finance him a Jeep that I had on my lot . . . He asked me on the phone and pleaded with me, 'Hey, you got to finance this for me. I really need a vehicle.' He says, 'I can't use a bike. I need a Jeep. I need something I can put stuff in.' I said . . . 'I'm not helping you, pal . . . You haven't paid child support. I can't do it.'"

Zaffino decided to drop the bike off at Forrest Motors anyway. The date was June 18, 2001—two days after the murder.

Forrest remembered Zaffino asking for a ride back toward Ohio afterward. He said that a girlfriend named Cindy would pick him up at a midway point.

As detectives listened, Forrest recalled an unusual conversation he'd had with John the previous Friday, while dropping off Nancy's son at a Wellsville, Ohio, restaurant for a visit with Zaffino. The suspect had mentioned that Christine Todaro had informed him that the police were asking questions about his involvement in a homicide.

"I never killed nobody," Zaffino assured Forrest. "I didn't hurt nobody."

"Well, good for you," Forrest countered. "I hope you didn't."

Zaffino repeated this assertion several times. "Then," Forrest told detectives, "he asked me about the bike, and wanted to know if I had sold the bike yet. And I told him I had a potential buyer, because I didn't want him threatening me to get the bike back. And he said, 'Well, if you don't sell it, I have a friend that will buy it . . . I'll even have them call you direct.'"

In the past, Forrest had wondered whether Nancy's ex-husband had ever passed him stolen merchandise. Now, with Detectives Schaeffer and McFarland seated in front of him, Forrest realized that he'd become knotted in a homicide case.

"I'm a nervous wreck," he uttered. "I know I didn't do anything wrong. Yeah, worst-case scenario, I was thinking, maybe I possessed some stolen goods. But I have a clear title to the motorcycle, so . . ."

"You know where the focus of our investigation is," McFarland responded.

"Oh, clearly."

"Okay."

"Yeah, I know who you want."

McFarland's tone grew conspiratorial: "It's to our advantage to keep everything that we did here today quiet for as long as possible."

"Uh-hum."

"And we would ask for that in return."

"Oh, absolutely."

At no point did the detectives ever sense that the couple was hiding the truth. Their body language and facial expressions betrayed not even a trace of deception. Replies were natural, and completely un-choreographed. Because the police had appeared so suddenly, there was no way that the pair could have contrived their responses.

Nancy knew that if she suddenly withheld visitation from Zaffino, he'd become guarded. So, convinced that he'd never harm their child, she told police that she'd continue to let her son see his father.

In the future, though, police advised the pair to tell Zaffino that the motorcycle had been sold, keeping a pseudo-receipt on hand, in case he asked for proof.

The meeting ended successfully, with handshakes all around, as arrangements were made for the City of Akron service garage to send a flatbed truck to Forrest Motors, and haul the motorcycle back to Ohio.

EIGHT

STILL, THE TENSION between Felber and Daugherty never abated. Because of Christine's anxiety about working with other members of the department, Felber had purchased a cell phone so she could reach him at any hour of the day or night. She called him nearly every day, generally just to be assured that the police would keep her safe.

A week after learning that Christine had been outed by a fellow detective, Felber received a hysterical call from her. She wanted to meet at the police station right away, but Felber reminded her that it was the wrong place to discuss the case. Without time to think of a better meeting point, Felber gave her his home address.

It was not the procedural thing to do. But Christine wasn't a traditional "source" with a criminal past. She was a civilian, risking her life so police could catch a killer. Plus, Felber's home was currently on the market, so he wouldn't be at that address for much longer.

Felber contacted Lieutenant Whiddon and informed him of the situation. The supervisor declined an offer to join the pair at Felber's home. "Just call me later, and let me know what happened," he said.

Christine arrived at the house, irate. This time, she said, a man she knew had asked her if she was worried about getting murdered by Ed George. The man said that his boss was friendly with Captain Daugherty—who, in arranging follow-up interviews on the investigation, allegedly mentioned Chris' participation in a homicide case involving the restaurateur.

"I can't believe I let you talk me into helping you," she yelled between expletives.

"I'm going to take care of this," Felber pledged, aware that his vows to protect his source were beginning to sound tired.

As soon as Christine left, Felber called Lieutenant Whiddon. Both detectives were incensed by Christine's allegation. Unfortunately, there wasn't much that they could do—other than try to keep their captain out of the loop as much as possible.

IN THE MIDDLE of the investigation, Christine spotted the older man who she claimed had been following her around Akron. Instead of running in the opposite direction, she walked up to him and asked his name. He identified himself as Sal Cicerello.

The name sounded familiar to Felber, but he couldn't remember why. Later when he scanned the Georges' phone records, he noted that, several times a day, Cynthia had exchanged calls with a man of the same name. After some searching, he located a picture of Cicerello, then mixed it up with a few others to create a photo lineup. Christine pointed him out immediately.

Sal was a heavyset former Teamster, in his late sixties, whose evenly distributed weight lent an imposing air. Although he lived in a low-income housing project, his apartment seemed nicer than the higher-priced ones across the street. At his home, police showed Sal a photo of John Zaffino. Cicerello nervously denied knowing the suspect— or anything about him.

Felber nodded, allowing Sal to do most of the talking. It

was a tactic that the detective had successfully employed on hundreds of occasions: let the interviewee speak. Even if the information was false, Felber believed that there was truth hidden in every lie. The goal was to make the subject comfortable—feigning belief, as the words continued to flow. Then, little by little, Felber would unravel the false-hoods, shattering the interviewee's confidence until the lies were covered with more lies that were easier to splinter. By the end, the subject would become confused to the point that there was no choice but to tell the truth.

Sal did admit to his friendship with Cynthia George, saying they'd met five or six years earlier at the Tangier, and that he was well acquainted with Ed and her kids. He'd even been to their house to help set up Christmas decorations.

Felber looked back with a half-smirk. "We know you and Cindy are much closer than that," the detective stated. "And we have the phone records to prove it."

Sal began to fidget.

"By the way you're acting, I'm wondering if you're hiding something you know about Jeff Zack's murder."

Sal paused. Yes, he conceded he was well acquainted with Cynthia's problems; she often confided in him. About four years ago, he said, he'd seen her with a black eye. She'd claimed that Zack had punched her, and thrown her bicycle into a river. Yet Sal said that she couldn't contact authorities for a variety of reasons: she'd feared pulling the George family into a scandal, and believed a threat Zack had made about deforming her face and hurting her children.

When Jeff was found murdered, Sal told police, he assumed that God had answered his prayers, and relieved Cynthia of a burden that she didn't deserve.

"Did she ever tell you who might have committed the murder?"

"No," Sal insisted. "She didn't have anything to do with it."

Police were never able to prove that he knew more. During a second visit, Sal said that, after touching base with Cynthia, he was even more convinced of her innocence. "She's a sweet, kind Christian woman who'd never have an affair," he snapped before ordering detectives to leave.

Still, because of his connection to the Georges, it seemed more than a bit curious that he often turned up in the same location as Christine Todaro—the primary witness in the homicide probe. Now that Sal found himself in the authorities' radar, though, he was likely to change his habits.

SENSING THAT HE would soon be arrested, Zaffino was beginning to treat Christine like an enemy. To be safe, she'd relocated to a new address. But she maintained telephone contact with Zaffino and, during one conversation, he turned on her, threatening to kill both her and her son.

Once again, Felber allowed Christine—this time with her son—to come to his home to discuss the matter. The detective called Lieutenant Whiddon for approval, but was told that he wasn't home. So Felber phoned Sergeant Hudnall instead, and discovered that he was hosting a barbecue for the Persons Unit on his back porch. He immediately handed the phone to Whiddon, who mumbled a few "okays" without asking any questions. Major Callahan had recently retired to become the police chief at The University of Akron—and his replacement, Michael Madden, was now sitting inches away from the lieutenant.

"Anything I need to know about?" Madden asked Hudnall.

The sergeant smirked at his old friend, and muttered, "No."

At Felber's home, the detective led Christine's 16-year-old son to a bank of computers in the basement. As the boy played video games, Felber went upstairs, calmed Chris down, and contacted the Cuyahoga Falls police to check on her home throughout the night. He even drove around the town, searching for Zaffino's car.

He didn't see it.

On August 20, 2002, Captain Daugherty received news that Christine had been in Felber's house. She was soon engrossed in conversation with Major Michael Madden, who now realized that part of his new job would involve refereeing the enduring battle between the captain and her stubborn detective.

Whiddon and Hudnall were in the major's office with Daugherty when Felber arrived. "Do you know where Christine was on Saturday?" the captain asked.

"Yes," Felber replied calmly. "She was at my house. And she's been there before, too."

For the benefit of the new major, Felber explained that the department had placed the witness in jeopardy in the past. With Lieutenant Whiddon's approval, the detective had used his home as a refuge. The captain insinuated that there had to be more to the relationship, and vowed to call in internal affairs to investigate. If she hadn't found the motorcycle, she insisted, investigators might never solve the case, given Felber's poor judgment and overall ineptitude.

"If you hadn't threatened to arrest Chris," Felber retorted in anger, "if you hadn't accused her of taking part in the murder, if you hadn't negligently put her life in danger by outing her, maybe I wouldn't have to go to such extreme measures—inviting her to my home—to keep an informant's confidence."

The captain appeared staggered by the detective's accusations.

Both Whiddon and Hudnall spoke up on Felber's behalf, reinforcing his assertion that they'd endorsed Christine's visits to the detective's house. Still, the captain ordered Felber never to speak to the informant again. From this point forward, Detective Mike Schaeffer was going to be her handler.

Schaeffer already had a full caseload, and preferred working on his own assignments to wading into this mess. But he agreed to visit Christine with Whiddon, Hudnall and Felber to inform her about the change in plans. Determined to follow procedure, Felber said nothing to sway the witness. He simply listened as Christine went ballistic.

"Does Daugherty have something to do with this?"

"Yes, she does," Whiddon answered.

"Fuck her!" Christine screamed. "I'm out!"

The detectives exchanged knowing glances. Whiddon and Hudnall talked down the witness, then came up with an amended arrangement. Felber would remain Christine's main contact. But nobody could tell the captain on the assumption this would all blow over.

"YOU'VE GOT THE biggest balls in the department," Hudnall chuckled to Felber, extending a hand with a closed fist.

Felber declined the invitation to tap knuckles.

"I just have to warn you," Whiddon said, "you better watch yourself around here."

"Or what?" Felber replied. "The only way things can get any worse for me is if the captain has me arrested."

By the end of the summer, police had begun interviewing associates of the Georges again. Only now, they hoped to find a link between the couple and Zaffino.

Nanny Mary Ann Brewer was one of the names at the top of the detectives' list, but they had low expectations. Since she'd lived in the Georges' home, investigators expected to be told that the couple's attorney would handle all inquiries.

Instead, they discovered a woman with her own free will, residing in a duplex in the midst of a once-desirable neighborhood now speckled with sub-divided homes and drug houses. Mary Ann invited detectives into an apartment adorned with nostalgic doilies and knick-knacks, and offered them iced tea. Like Sal, she claimed to have also seen Cindy with a black eye. Zack had attacked her, Cynthia reportedly told Mary Ann.

In contrast to others with close ties to the family, Mary Ann expressed certainty that the relationship was far beyond platonic. She recounted the story of one of the George girls spotting the pair kissing. In the middle of the night, Mary Ann said, Zack would drive onto the property, park by the farm house, turn off the lights, and wait for Cindy to sneak out. Even when he'd tried disguising his voice, Mary Ann maintained, she recognized it on the phone. When one of the children answered, she continued, Jeff would often hang up.

The day after the homicide, Mary Ann said, Cynthia had decided to visit her onetime nanny with the kids. It seemed unusual, since they hadn't come by in about a year.

"I said, 'What's going on?'" Mary Ann recalled. "And she said, 'Oh, the children wanted to see you.' I said, 'Well, good. I'm so happy to see them.' And they wanted to play on the trampoline. So I said, 'Okay, fine, let's go outside.'

"We were standing there, and Cindy wasn't saying very much. She was just kind of quiet. So I said, 'Well, that's terrible what happened to Jeff. I can't believe that happened.' She didn't answer me. And I said, 'Well, now, he won't be bothering you anymore, will he?'

"She didn't say a thing."

A few days later, Mary Ann stated, Ed George told her specifically not to discuss the murder with police.

Detectives concluded that Mary Ann seemed to favor Ed over Cynthia. Nonetheless, the information helped paint a picture that could bolster a case—if the key elements fell into place.

John and Kimberly Ginley, the couple who'd lived in the Georges' farmhouse, had witnessed Zack's nocturnal visits onto the property. Once, when John approached the vehicle, Jeff drove off, but continued cruising up and down the road, in apparent anticipation of Cynthia's arrival.

Although they never had any evidence, the couple speculated that Ed had engineered the homicide. If they knew about the affair, they reasoned, Ed did, too.

Believing that they were on a roll, Whiddon and Felber decided to test their luck, contacting Ed's brother, David. A few years earlier, Felber had arrested an employee for stealing from Bell Music, the company David ran, across the street from the Tangier. Now, as the investigators waited in the office, David appeared, and graciously invited them into another room.

The investigators explained that they were close to making an arrest in the Zack homicide, and had reason to believe that Cynthia was involved. "Ed is between a rock and a hard place," David answered, and asked if his brother could be given immunity.

"No," Felber replied.

Shaking his head from side to side, David moaned, "What's Ed supposed to tell the kids?"

He indicated that he'd be more open to discussing the case if investigators promised to keep his identity secret. Unfortunately, the detectives could not accommodate this request. If David provided damning information, there was no question that he'd be asked to testify.

David exchanged handshakes with the pair, as they left his office. "It seems like he wants to help us," Felber observed in the car, after turning down the lieutenant's country music.

"He definitely seems sincere," Whiddon responded, turning the music back up.

"I get the feeling that he thinks Cindy really had something to do with this."

Whiddon nodded. "I know. But I'm not sure we're going to get anything more."

Knowing the nature of the Georges, neither detective could envision David doing something that could jeopardize the family or their businesses. "Their loyalty would be admirable," Felber said of the clan, "if we weren't trying to solve a murder."

MEANWHILE, POLICE CONTINUED revisiting the events of June 16, 2001, hoping to find that one clue they'd missed in the past. Had the Georges, Zaffino or some other close associate phoned Zack and arranged a meeting in front of BJ's? Detectives couldn't find a record of such a call.

At the same time, investigators theorized that there were phone numbers—for the Georges and Zaffino—that they'd yet to discover. Through their research, detectives learned that each major phone company was allotted a certain number of cell phone numbers. These were then divided among thousands of cell phone dealers, some operating out of corner stores that closed within months. Many of these dealers kept poor records—in some cases, deliberately— and failed to provide larger companies with customer lists. Additionally, it was close to impossible to trace temporary phones and calling cards to purchasers.

Police speculated that Zaffino relied on a more traditional way of concealing his identity: dialing associates from various pay phones.

REACHING OUT TO the Summit County authorities, Akron police proposed monitoring Cindy as she went about her daily chores. Both the narcotics unit and fugitive task force were willing to cooperate, but there was a problem: the street in front of her home was so wide open that there was no place to hide a surveillance vehicle.

As they pondered the possibility of obtaining a search warrant for Zaffino's home, Whiddon and Felber traveled some forty minutes outside of Akron to a countrified strip of empty lots dotted by patches of houses. The suspect lived in the town of Rittman, alongside a two-lane road without street lamps, with ditches instead of sidewalks. His duplex backed into an undeveloped wooded area. Before police barreled into a home with a warrant, they wanted to ensure that they'd targeted the proper location. So Whiddon drove back and forth in front of the duplex, never slowing to avoid arousing suspicion, as Felber took careful notes on the building's architecture.

"Do you have a good description yet?" Whiddon asked, as they swung by the duplex for the third time.

Felber shook his head from side to side, observing the yellow siding and white doors on the brick building.

"Why the hell not?"

"Because I flunked shorthand in college," Felber answered with characteristic sarcasm.

SOUTH OF AKRON, police began canvassing Zaffino's friends and neighbors. They found Chad Adkins at the firehouse where he volunteered. Very quickly, he mentioned that his father had also been a detective. Now, Chad was willing to do whatever he could to assist.

Chad lived in the same complex as John, and remembered a girlfriend who generally visited Zaffino between the hours of 11 PM and 2 AM. Zaffino boasted about their sexual exploits, specifically citing her "kinky" tastes. When shown a photo, Chad identified the woman as Cynthia George.

Even more telling was the fact that Chad had last seen Cynthia's car outside of Zaffino's house the night before: September 22, 2002. For whatever reason, the couple had stuck together for fifteen months since the homicide.

Chad's girlfriend, Jennifer, a former college cheerleader, also identified Cindy George from the photo. Jennifer maintained that Zaffino enjoyed speaking about sex and violence, once reminiscing about an arrest that transpired after he'd pummeled a man on the hood of a car.

At North Canton Transfer, the trucking company where John had met Christine Todaro—and worked at the time of the homicide—Larry Northrup remembered Zaffino mentioning a rich girlfriend being harassed by an ex-boyfriend. A week before the murder, Northrup added, Zaffino had quit the company because he claimed that his love interest was setting him up in business.

The last time that Zaffino had dropped in at North Canton Transfer, Northrup said, he spoke about becoming the subject of a homicide investigation. "Fuckin' Chris went to the cops, and said I killed somebody," he asserted, "and now I have to hire a lawyer to defend myself."

Truck driver Bob Cole told police about John's contention that he had a girlfriend who ran the Tangier restaurant—and had bought him a motorcycle. Cole had actually seen the bike himself once. He described it as a "crotch rocket."

"There's some guy bothering her," Zaffino allegedly stated. "I've told him a couple of times to stay away, and he just won't take no for an answer. I think I might have to do something about it."

"Don't do something you're going to regret," Cole warned. "It's not worth spending your life in prison."

Cole said that about a month before Zaffino left North Canton Transfer, he'd inquired about purchasing a handgun. Cole sold him a .357 chrome Smith & Wesson revolver with a four-inch barrel, as well as a Smith & Wesson Model 66 .32 chrome-plate pistol with a wooden handle.

According to Cole, Zaffino later claimed to have lost the .32 in a park in Akron.

Detectives practically kissed the witness on the lips. The news about the gun was one of the most significant pieces of information they'd discovered—ballistics tests had confirmed that a Smith & Wesson Model 66 was among the weapons capable of firing the .38-caliber slug recovered at the crime scene.

POLICE NOW DECIDED that they needed to contact Mike Frasher before John got to him. Around the time of the homicide, the two had become close friends. Zaffino didn't confide in many people. Detectives hoped that Frasher—whom John knew through his trucking connections—might be an exception.

"Lieutenant, I'm going to need you to pull over," Felber teased Whiddon, after he unwittingly drove through a red light.

"What?"

"You just blew a red light back there."

"You're crazy. There wasn't any light."

"Yes, there was. Check your rear-view mirror."

"It must have been green."

"No, it was red. Now, pull over so I can give you a ticket."

"If I pull over, it'll be to let you out, so you can walk back to Akron. Besides, we're not in your jurisdiction."

At Frasher's house, Zaffino's buddy remembered him being aggressively pursued by a wealthy woman who paid his bills, and subsidized his old apartment on Nine Iron Drive. Like Cole, Frasher claimed that the woman had bought John a motorcycle. But Mike added to the story by recalling how Zaffino had given it to an ex-wife in exchange for child support.

Afterward, Frasher was the one who'd driven his friend home. As they'd rolled down the highway, Zaffino claimed that he was sick, and needed his medication. Mike drove him to a pharmacy. Along the way, Frasher said, the girlfriend phoned Zaffino constantly.

Without any prompting from police, Mike at some point stopped referring to the woman as John's girlfriend, calling her "Cindy" instead. Frasher professed that Cindy was so possessive that she'd forced Zaffino to quit his job. This apparently enabled him to be available whenever she wanted.

THE NEXT DAY, detectives received an urgent phone call from Frasher. He was scared, and needed to come to the police station right away to report his recent encounters with Zaffino.

Twenty minutes later, he arrived with his wife, Kari. Both appeared frantic. Detective Bonnie Shenice had attended school with Kari, and took her into another room, while Frasher sat down with Whiddon and Felber.

After police had left his home the previous day, Frasher called Zaffino, friend to friend, and informed him about the visit. The two appeared to be getting along. Zaffino recalled stopping by Frasher's home and asking him to a car show on the day of the homicide. Then, without thinking much about it, Frasher mentioned that he'd told detectives about the motorcycle being dropped off in Pennsylvania.

"You just keep your fuckin' mouth shut," Zaffino snarled. "I'm being set up, and now *you're* fuckin' involved, too."

Mike claimed that he and his wife were both frightened by Zaffino's flare of anger. They had barely slept that night. In the morning, after Mike had left for work, an agitated Zaffino suddenly showed up at the Frashers' front door.

"I need to speak to Mike," he demanded.

The moment he left, Kari had grabbed the kids and dropped them off at a relative's house. Then, the couple called the police.

On the ride over to the station, though, Zaffino had managed to get Frasher on the phone, and calmly explained his predicament. Mike hung up, wondering if maybe he'd overreacted.

"I'm not really sure John's that dangerous," Frasher told detectives at the station.

"Oh yeah?" Felber answered. "Then why'd you drop off your kids, and rush over here to meet us?"

"I'm just not sure. I mean, John even remembered that he was standing on my porch on the day the murder happened."

"What time was this?"

"It had to be about four PM. He wanted me to go to a car show with him, but Kari and I were getting ready for a wedding that started at five."

Felber calculated the math. Zack had been killed about four hours before Zaffino's purported visit. If this was going to be his alibi, it was a bad one.

Kari emerged from her meeting, recalling a similar timeline. The difference was that she still believed that Zaffino wanted to kill her husband.

For the time being, Christine appeared out of Zaffino's reach. But now, detectives were concerned for the Frashers' safety. No matter what John said after his eruptions subsided, investigators viewed him as a cold-blooded killer with an uncontrollable temper.

When Whiddon and Felber were finished with the couple, they briefed Captain Daugherty on their interviews. This time, everybody was in agreement. There was definitely enough evidence to arrest John. Whether that information could convict him was another issue.

Daugherty called Sheri Bevan Walsh and Mary Ann Kovach at the Summit County Prosecutor's Office. In the past, the prosecutor's involvement in a case usually began after a suspect's arrest. But this was different. For the last several weeks, the two had been following the turns in the Zaffino investigation.

Despite their demanding schedules, Walsh and Kovach pushed their work aside, and crossed the access way from their building to police headquarters. There, they were joined by Tom Dicaudo, a police legal advisor who helped review facts before charges were signed.

Everyone feared the same thing: if Zaffino wasn't apprehended right away, he might seriously hurt someone. Because of the publicity surrounding Zack's murder—and the connection to the George family—Daugherty and the prosecutor's representatives understood that an arrest would make headlines. They also realized that if prosecutors were unable to obtain a conviction, their reputations could be compromised. But this was a secondary issue. People were in danger, and Zaffino needed to be taken off the streets.

Within an hour, a warrant was being prepared for Zaffino's arrest.

NINE

IT TOOK THREE hours to complete the paperwork for the arrest warrant, and the detectives involved in the case were tense. Concerned that someone in the station might tip off the wrong person, the investigators went about the task in the most discreet way possible. If Zaffino became aware of his impending arrest, it was feared that he'd become dangerous, as he readied himself for the confrontation.

On September 25, 2002, at approximately 3:20 PM, three unmarked police vehicles, as well as a cruiser, pulled into Zaffino's driveway, and, in order to avoid detection from the road, drove to the rear of the building. Detectives knocked on the back door, but received no response. As they were strategizing a way to survey the apartment until the suspect arrived, they heard tires rumbling over gravel in the driveway—and looked around a corner to see Zaffino pulling up in his pickup truck.

He alighted to meet eight pointing Glocks.

"What's going on?" he asked, calmly following police instructions to exit the vehicle.

"You're under arrest for murder," explained Detective Shawn Brown—borrowed from the narcotics division for the day—clamping the cuffs around John's wrists.

◆ ◆ ◆

ZAFFINO SAID LITTLE on the ride to Akron, and detectives made no attempt to engage him. No one wanted to blurt out the kind of comment that a defense lawyer could use to challenge the case. The interrogation would take place at the station.

Felber and Whiddon were anxiously waiting there when Zaffino arrived. Captain Daugherty had also stayed late to monitor developments. Felber's goal was to get John talking. If the suspect claimed to have been with his friend Mike Frasher at the time of the homicide, the interview would be successful. Detectives were fairly certain that the alibi was false. If this was his explanation for his whereabouts, the logic went, a jury would assume that he'd lie about anything.

Of course, no one was sure if Zaffino *would* talk to investigators. He was under no legal obligation to do so. And, over the last three months, the theme of virtually every conversation he'd conducted with Christine Todaro involved stonewalling the authorities. In Larry Whitney, Zaffino had one of the best attorneys in Akron. Detectives were all but certain that Whitney had urged his client to say nothing to the cops.

Still, a loose cannon like Zaffino was capable of anything. Felber had urged the detectives who'd apprehended John to treat him nicely. Despite the circumstances, it was better for Zaffino to feel relatively relaxed. A jacked-up suspect was likely to howl for his lawyer immediately. If he felt unruffled, he might be a little more generous.

"What's his demeanor like?" Felber asked Detective Brown, minutes after Zaffino was deposited into an eight-by-eight cell.

"Calm. Even a little cocky."

Felber managed a grin. "That's what we like to hear. A cocky suspect is a talking suspect."

The detective had been imagining the interview for months. He wouldn't use a recorder to keep the suspect as comfortable as possible. The plan was to act dumb and agreeable, as Zaffino tangled himself up in a series of lies. First, though, the investigators would have to convince the suspect of their gullibility.

Felber and Whiddon entered the holding cell. Two metal chairs were welded to a table screwed into the back wall. Felber sat down across from Zaffino, while the lieutenant dragged in his own chair, and placed it against the door.

"This is your chance to tell your side of the story," Felber began. "We're really not sure what's going on here. There's a lot of things we don't know about. Only you can give us the answers."

Zaffino contemplated the words.

"But first, I have to read you your rights." Felber removed a card from his pocket, and looked down at it. "You have the right to remain silent. Do you understand that right?"

"Yes."

"Anything you say can and will be used against you in a court of law." Because of the Supreme Court's 1966 *Miranda v. Arizona* ruling, the detectives were obligated to inform Zaffino that he'd be an idiot to talk. "Do you understand that right?"

"Yes."

"You have the right to talk to an attorney, and have him present with you while you are being questioned. Do you understand that right?"

"Yes."

"If you cannot afford to hire a lawyer, one will be appointed to represent you before any questioning, if you wish. Do you understand that right?"

"Yes."

"You can decide at any time to exercise these rights, and not answer any questions, or make any statements. Do you understand that right?"

"Yes."

Felber turned over the card to begin the section he most dreaded: "Do you understand each of these rights I have explained to you?"

"Yes."

"Having these rights in mind, do you wish to talk to us now?"

"Sure."

Then, suddenly, Zaffino produced a business card, and placed it on the table: "This is my attorney, Larry Whitney."

Felber made sure that his voice was free of anxiety when he asked, "Are you telling me that you want your attorney?"

"No. I just want you to know I hired Larry Whitney to represent me. But I don't feel I need him here, because I didn't do anything. I even asked him this morning—before you guys showed up—if I should go down to the station and talk to you. I was willing to go and everything. But he said, 'Wait for them to come to you.'"

"I guess that's what you did."

Zaffino nodded with satisfaction.

"How do you know Cindy George?"

Zaffino shrugged. "I just know her a little—'cause I went to her house to do some work on her car. Other than that, I don't really know her at all."

Both Felber and Whiddon felt hopeful. It wouldn't be hard to prove this guy's dishonesty to a jury.

"You know, Larry Whitney told me I should try to account for my whereabouts on the day of the murder. So I thought about it, and remembered I was at a car show. I went to my friend Mike Frasher's house, at maybe ten o'clock in the morning. But the rest of the day, I was at the car show."

Generally, wealthy suspects had an advantage over those from different social backgrounds because they could hide behind their attorneys. Because middle- and lower-income arrestees often could not, they tried outsmarting their interrogators by lying. This wasn't something Zaffino had to do; he'd been bestowed a gift in the form of Larry Whitney. Still, John couldn't restrain himself from behaving like a low-rent hustler.

Zaffino claimed that he didn't know the time that the homicide had occurred. In fact, he continued, he didn't even know about the murder until he'd read about it approximately two months before his arrest.

"Did you know Jeff Zack?"

"I never met Jeff Zack, never even talked to Jeff Zack . . ."

"And what about his relationship with Cynthia George?"

"I don't know anything about that."

Zaffino was feeling loose now, his confidence growing. He sat straight in his chair, never hesitating when questioned, convinced that he was hitting every pitch out of the ballpark.

"How many times would you say Cindy visited your apartment on Nine Iron Drive?" Whiddon asked.

"I can't really say she was ever there."

"How often would she call you on your cell phone?"

"Sporadically." The majority of the discussions, he added, involved bike riding.

Felber asked about the conversations that the suspect had with Cynthia about the homicide. Zaffino had his answer ready: "Cindy doesn't talk about the murder to me."

"Have you ever owned any motorcycles?"

"I've owned tons of motorcycles. I figured you guys would know that, just looking at the motorcycle endorsement on my driving record."

"What kind of motorcycle do you own now?"

"Honda—what other kind is there? You should know. I still have it in my garage."

The detectives estimated that Zaffino had already lied at least ten times. And he actually seemed to be enjoying himself. Now, it was time to crush his confidence.

Felber straightened his shoulders, maneuvering his

six-foot-three-inch frame to tower above the small table in the jail cell, switching the tone of his soft, understanding voice to loud and agitated.

"This is the biggest bunch of shit I ever heard. If you think anybody is ever going to buy this crap, you're nuts. You've been fucking Cindy for years. Frasher, Cole, Todaro, your neighbors—everybody told us that. You have a big mouth, John. And you've bragged to a lot of people."

Zaffino seemed stunned.

"And what's that bullshit about the car show being your alibi? I talked to the Coles and I talked to the Frashers. You didn't get to the car show until after three. You killed Zack at noon. Your alibi is shit."

The suspect appeared deflated. His posture slumped.

"The motorcycle you used to kill Zack—the motorcycle that Cindy bought you—it's not in your garage. It's in *our* garage. You drove the motorcycle to Pennsylvania after the murder. Your ex-wife told us. You even covered the stripes with duct tape."

Zaffino bowed his head, and shook back and forth.

"If you think you're going to get away with murder, based on the stupid shit you just told us, you're screwed. I can guarantee that you're going to spend the rest of your life locked up. If you have any hope, it's to start telling the truth right now and pray we feel sorry for you."

Disheartened, John raised his head to look at his interrogator. "What's going to happen to me?"

"You're gonna spend the rest of your life getting butt-fucked by some guy named Bubba—unless you start telling the truth."

It had all gone as planned. Now, the detectives anticipated that all they had to do was wait for the confession to start spewing. As Zaffino opened his mouth to speak, though, a loud pounding noise snapped him out of his stupor. Somebody was knocking on the cell door. Not just tapping—knocking, as if there was an emergency outside.

Worried that Zaffino was about to regain his senses, Felber kept going: "While you're rotting in jail, Cindy's gonna be out fucking every guy she can get her hands on—just like she was when she was seeing you. I hope you're not dumb enough to think you were the only guy she was fucking. She was fucking Zack right up until the time you killed him."

Felber had no idea if the statement was true. He just wanted to take advantage of the suspect's weakened state.

"I didn't think you were such a pussy. You want to spend the rest of your life petting some guy's hairy ass because you let some rich whore play you?"

Zaffino's head was practically touching the table. He looked like he was about to cry. For a second or two, even Felber felt sorry for him.

"If you want to help yourself, you better tell us how she helped you plan this murder, and you better do it now."

Zaffino looked up. He seemed to realize that it was finally over. Had Cindy used him all along?

He mumbled something that the detectives couldn't hear.

Then, it started again, even louder than before—the panicked pounding at the door. Felber imagined that Larry Whitney had swept into the station and demanded to see his client. The artful lawyer had probably created a new law to interrupt the interview. It had happened to Felber before.

The disruption allowed Zaffino to gather his wits. He was calculating again. "I want to speak to my attorney," he stated. "You guys obviously have one up on me."

The man was exercising his rights, and there was nothing the investigators could do about it. The interview was officially terminated.

When the cell door opened, though, the lawyer was nowhere to be seen. Instead, Captain Daugherty stood in the entranceway, exchanging dirty looks with Felber. Felber stalked past her, and walked down the hall, trying to come up with some legitimate reason why she'd intruded on the proceedings. Every seasoned police officer understood that you never interrupted an interview. An interview was sacrosanct.

By the time Felber calmed down, nearly an hour had passed. Whiddon and Hudnall had entered and departed from the captain's office. They left Felber alone until he was ready to talk.

"*Why?*" Felber demanded, entering Whiddon's office.

"She was listening to the interview on the intercom. She thought you screwed it up because you let him lie. She was going to save the interview."

Felber was beyond anger. Whiddon spoke to him sympathetically. During their most frustrating moments, the lieutenant was apt to mention his wife's work with terminally ill children. "Whenever you start feeling sorry for yourself," he'd remind the detective, "whenever you think life isn't fair, just imagine about what it's like for them."

But today, Whiddon understood, words and concepts were not going to pacify his friend.

"Look, let's just finish up the paperwork," the lieutenant said, "and get Zaffino off to jail. I'd like to be home in time to say goodnight to my kids."

AS DETECTIVES PREPARED a search warrant for Zaffino's home, Lieutenant Whiddon fielded calls from the press. He kept his comments simple—having been warned by the Akron P.D.'s legal department that he risked a lawsuit if he dared mention Cynthia George's name. When reporters brought it up instead—asking about the rumors concerning Zack's parentage of Cynthia's youngest daughter— Whiddon had no choice but to reply, "No comment."

Major Michael Madden was slightly less circumspect. "We are confident that Zaffino is our shooter," he told Cleveland *Plain Dealer* reporter Karen Farkas. "There are other persons who aided and abetted in this, either before or after the fact. But this was not a murder for hire, or related to Zack's business dealings."

The motive, the major emphasized, was personal.

AT ZAFFINO'S HOME, investigators found an eviction notice on the door. Inside, they were uncertain about what to confiscate. The gun used to kill Zack was, obviously, the goal, but no one believed that this suspect was stupid enough to leave it lying around his house. The other objective was finding anything linking John to Cindy: photos, letters, keepsakes.

John's apartment was neat. A home gym in the basement barely fit between the furniture lining the walls. Investigators walked through the workout area to reach the rest of the basement, zoning in on a set of metal filing cabinets. In one drawer, Felber discovered a collection of phone bills, neatly arranged in folders by month.

As Felber and Whiddon examined Zaffino's bills, they noted that there were several numbers that they hadn't seen before. One set of records contained numbers ending in 2791 and 2793, another 0132 and 0133. Zaffino's friends had disclosed that John had been using 2791, then changed the number to 0133. But who was using 2793 and 0132?

It seemed obvious that these were the private lines reserved exclusively for Zaffino and Cynthia. And the pair seemed to talk to each other a lot—even more than the 100 times a month Zack had communicated with her. In April 2001, for instance, Cynthia and Zaffino had shared approximately 2,700 cell phone minutes together.

On the day of the homicide, the records showed that Cindy had called John at 11:49 AM, chatting with him as he drove around the BJ's parking lot. Four minutes before noon, the conversation had ended. After Zack's 12:07 PM murder, there weren't any calls until 12:29 PM, when Zaffino had called Cynthia. The two stayed on the line for six minutes.

Of course, there was no way to know the content of the conversations. But, detectives concluded, it was easy to infer. For example, if a person wakes up in the morning, and finds snow in the driveway, the circumstantial evidence suggests that it snowed overnight—even though, technically, nobody witnessed the flurry. Police hoped that, ultimately, a jury would apply the same type of logic in this case.

TWO DAYS AFTER the arrest, detectives revisited several witnesses to re-confirm information that authorities hoped to use against Zaffino. Previously, Mike Frasher's wife Kari had told investigators that they'd attended a wedding at 5 PM on the day of the homicide. But when Kari called the bride and groom to verify this, she said, she learned that the event had actually begun at 3 PM. This meant that John Zaffino had shown up at the Frasher home at about 1 PM— possibly fifty-three minutes after the murder. Suddenly, John's alibi seemed to carry greater weight.

Or did it?

Whiddon and Felber decided to conduct a time study. Had Zaffino traveled at a legal speed, it would have taken him twenty minutes to flee from the murder scene to his home. After dropping off the motorcycle, it would have taken another twenty minutes to reach the Frashers'. In between, Zaffino could have called Cindy, changed clothes and switched vehicles.

Later, detectives would also interview the Frashers' babysitter, 19-year-old Danielle Watson. She'd arrived at the family's home early on June 16, 2001, at about 11 AM, because she enjoyed playing with the Frasher kids. Kari was in the shower at 1:30 PM, Danielle remembered, when Zaffino first showed up on the porch. Mike was already dressed for the wedding, and went out to talk to his friend.

"How positive are you about the times?" she was asked.

"Very positive."

Detectives studied Danielle closely. Her answers were matter-of-fact; she was nonchalant about discussing a murder investigation with two cops. They concluded that she was telling the truth.

METRO PARK RANGER Beverly Haywood was the one who initially reached out to the Akron police, contacting Detective James Pasheilich. Haywood's department had encountered Zaffino a month before the murder. She'd never thought much about it until she read about his arrest in the newspaper.

At approximately 9:25 PM on May 8, 2001, Ranger Lois Neff noticed a single car parked in the lot off the Everett Covered Bridge. The vehicle, an unoccupied green Ford Contour, was registered to John Zaffino. An empty, triangular-shaped gun case was resting on the floorboard on the passenger side of the car.

The ranger called for backup, and asked the Akron police to do a welfare check at Zaffino's home on Nine Iron Drive. She was concerned that John might be suicidal or dangerous. After a second ranger arrived, Zaffino was sighted returning to the Ford.

Yes, that was his gun case, he conceded. He was a truck driver, he explained, and needed a weapon for protection. But on this night, he added, he'd left his gun at home.

Ranger Neff patted down Zaffino, and confirmed that he wasn't carrying a weapon. The reason he was all alone in the park, he explained, was that he was having an affair with a married woman. They were supposed to have a rendezvous, he said, but she'd just called to tell him that she couldn't make it.

"Next time, please store your gun case in the trunk," Neff cautioned.

"I will."

Eight days later, on May 16, another ranger was responding to an unrelated call in the same park, when a citizen approached. He'd been picking mushrooms and found a loaded, semi-automatic .32 in some underbrush, next to a trail in the woods.

Most likely, this was the .32 that Zaffino had purchased from his friend Bob Cole—the gun that the suspect claimed to have lost in some park in Akron.

The gun was photographed, and turned over to the Bureau of Criminal Identification and Investigation (BCI), the state crime lab. A short time later, BCI changed locations and, apparently, the gun was lost in the move—an unfortunate, unusual occurrence for an organization renowned for its professionalism and strict protocols.

Phone records would later reveal that Cynthia George was communicating with both Zaffino and Jeff Zack, as the suspect waited in the park—talking to each man on a different cell phone simultaneously on a few occasions. Could Zaffino and Cynthia have been trying to set up Zack that night? It seemed highly likely.

Three days later, John would get a quote on a motorcycle from Midwest Motors. It was around this time that the phone calls between Zack and Cindy seemed to permanently stop. And, it also appeared, Jeff had sensed his impending demise, and made a trip to his mother's house in Arizona, apparently to say goodbye.

"He said, 'I can't speak to Cindy anymore, and I'm very unhappy,'" remembered his mother, Elayne. "His demeanor was very different . . . very quiet. He wanted to see everybody."

Jeff had even made amends with his estranged brother, Marc Zack, and his wife, apologizing for past eruptions. During a Mother's Day meal at a restaurant with Elayne, Jeff had held the couple's 3-year-old child closely. The open display of affection seemed so out of character for Jeff that Marc and his wife had discussed it later—theorizing that Jeff and Cynthia had had a baby together. Now that Jeff could no longer see the child, they'd concluded, cuddling with another youngster filled a void in his life.

Yet Marc also theorized that Jeff was running away from something dangerous. "He acted strange and peculiar," Marc told police. "His eyes looked like he was afraid of something. He seemed extra nervous."

Three weeks before his death, Jeff had taken his wife, Bonnie, into their basement, and shown her his financial files and other important documents—in case he wasn't around to provide for his family in the near future.

Bonnie's brother noted that his sister had commented on a recent change in Jeff's behavior. He seemed nice— *unusually* nice. It appeared that he was trying to compensate for past indiscretions.

Nonetheless, Jeff *did* embark on a long-distance affair with the woman he'd met on the flight to Arizona. Even with the best intentions, there were limits to the degree that he could transform himself.

Detectives would note that from the time of the incident in the park to three days before the murder, Jeff had spent the majority of his time outside the state.

ON OCTOBER 2, Felber and Whiddon interviewed a jailhouse snitch who claimed to have elicited a confession from John Zaffino while both were confined to a holding cell. The man said that the two had been awaiting a court appearance, when he noticed a jittery Zaffino.

"I've been to jail before," the snitch allegedly said. "It's no big deal."

At that point, Zaffino apparently relaxed, and described murdering a man, then riding off on a motorcycle.

Since the charges against Zaffino had been reported by the media at this point, the snitch's statement was not as significant as it appeared.

"Why did Zaffino say he killed Zack?" Felber asked, while interrogating the inmate.

"Because Zack owed him some money for drugs?" The response was delivered in a weak voice—and inflected like a question.

"But Zaffino didn't sell drugs."

"Oh, then it was because the girl he was fucking wanted to collect some insurance money."

Whiddon and Felber stood up, and said goodbye.

TWO DAYS LATER, the same detectives appeared at the suspect's grand jury hearing. It was deliberately slated to be the last proceeding of the day because prosecutors understood that, given the quantity of circumstantial evidence from which they'd weave their case, it would last a long time.

When Felber had testified in front of the grand jury considering Richard "The Curley Monster" Curley's break-ins, the entire proceeding had lasted a half hour. The Zaffino hearing took two hours—as opposed to the normal forty minutes or so for an equivalent homicide case.

Bob Cole and his brother, Randy, were in the waiting room, as well as Mike Frasher and Sal Cicerello. As soon as they spotted Felber, Frasher and the Coles pulled him aside.

"What's going on?" the detective asked.

"Who is that guy?" Bob Cole whispered, gesturing at Cicerello.

"A friend of Cindy's."

"He seems kind of dangerous," Randy observed. "Is he in the mob?"

"Not as far as we know. But even if he was, none of you guys are worth knocking off. You're not valuable enough to the case. You think the mob would take a chance—drawing police attention, drawing media attention—just to kill you?"

That seemed to calm them down.

"Let me show you something," Felber said, pulling out a Polaroid of the gun the rangers had found in the park, and displaying it to the Coles and Frasher. Bob agreed that the weapon resembled the pistol that he'd sold Zaffino.

ON THE MORNING of November 12, Zaffino was escorted from the Summit County Jail to Akron police headquarters. There, he met his lawyer, who cautioned the suspect against discussing anything related to the case. Instead, Zaffino was introduced to an audio technician, who handed him a script, and instructed him to read. The goal: affirming that the threatening message left on Jeff Zack's answering machine had come from John Zaffino.

THE NEXT DAY, another inmate from the county jail was a guest of the Akron police. "Oscar" asserted that he'd personally assisted Zaffino in his efforts to subvert the upcoming trial.

Several weeks earlier, Oscar claimed, he'd been approached by a prisoner called "Joe," and informed that John Zaffino needed their help. Zaffino hoped to find a person to claim that he or she had been at the scene of the homicide, and noticed both the motorcycle and its driver. The conclusion of the "witness": neither the bike nor the perp matched the descriptions that police intended to present.

Oscar was willing to have his girlfriend come forward—for the right price. After some negotiating, it was apparently determined that the woman would receive $5,000. Oscar and Joe would be paid another $5,000 and split it down the middle.

"Just get it done," Zaffino allegedly said.

According to Oscar, he then wrote a draft of a letter that he intended to send his girlfriend, outlining the alibi. But when Joe saw the document, he ripped it up and threw it away.

"Too detailed," he purportedly maintained.

With Zaffino sitting on his bed, and the others hovering

above him in his cell, the three crafted a second letter, featuring a suspect bearing absolutely no resemblance to the defendant. But before Oscar could mail it, he got into a fight, and was sent to another pod in the jail. A distressed-looking Zaffino apparently watched his associate pack up.

"Don't worry," Oscar claimed to have said. "Things are being taken care of."

FELBER NODDED INEXPRESSIBLY, taking in the tale. "Why are you telling me this?" he asked Oscar.

"I don't think it's right for a rich white woman and her boyfriend to get away with murder—when so many of *my* friends are in jail."

When the interview was over, Felber discussed the exchange with Whiddon. If Oscar was even telling a half truth, it was worth trying to enlist the inmate to capture Zaffino on tape. They recommended that Oscar get ahold of Zaffino, and urge him to contact the girlfriend personally. An undercover officer, borrowed from the narcotics division, would pose as the woman when the suspect called between 1 and 2 PM on November 18.

Narcotics would provide a special phone number for this purpose.

"Do you really think Zaffino's dumb enough to fall into a trap like that?" Whiddon said.

"Yeah," Felber answered. "I think he is."

Whiddon shook his head. "It's not going to happen."

"What do we have to lose? And if he wants to pay this girl, where's he going to get the money from? Cindy? This is our chance to get *her* into the mix, too."

Whiddon remained incredulous.

On the afternoon of November 18, Felber waited until 3 PM to phone Whiddon to learn if the call had taken place. "No," the lieutenant gloated, "you were wrong."

"Maybe I was," Felber retorted, "but this is the first time."

A day later, when the two passed each other on the sixth floor of police headquarters, Felber noticed that Whiddon looked down at the ground, and refused to make eye contact.

"What's going on?" Felber asked.

"I got a call from Narcotics this morning. They gave me the wrong number."

In other words, even if Zaffino *did* make the call, the number on the other end would have been out of service.

Both men chuckled. "Well, we tried," Felber said. "Shit happens. And, by the way, I wasn't wrong."

Two months before John Zaffino's trial started, detectives began meeting with Summit County Assistant Prosecutor Mike Carroll. This was rare; before trials, detectives and prosecutors might assemble for an hour, then let the litigators take over the case. But the Zack murder was different.

Felber and Carroll played in the same golf league, yet barely knew each other. But Felber noted that Carroll was a scratch golfer with a smooth, effortless swing. He never lost his temper, or showed signs of nervousness. Six-foot-three, gray-haired and svelte, Carroll could have portrayed a prosecutor in any TV drama.

Had he chosen, Carroll could have been a millionaire, defending moneyed criminals. But for some thirty years, he instead labored in the prosecutor's office, doing what he felt was right, fighting for justice. He was truly one of a kind—a storybook hero in the Jimmy Stewart mold.

Unfortunately, Carroll was going to be tied up for the eight weeks leading into the trial. There was no other choice. Two other homicide trials were scheduled, and his fellow prosecutors were overbooked. Felber and Whiddon tried to persuade him to change his mind. This was an unconventional case. Law enforcement had neither a key witness nor a decisive piece of evidence; the trial would be decided by small details. What made matters worse was that neither Whiddon nor Felber had ever been involved in a case of this magnitude. They needed Carroll to poke holes in their arguments, so they could find supporting evidence to seal up the flaws. If the prosecutor could not free up his schedule to prepare, Zaffino would go free.

"I'll meet with you whenever I can squeeze you in," the prosecutor told the detectives. It would be a day-by-day, hour-by-hour effort.

A month before the trial, Felber and Whiddon came to Carroll's office to once again press him to rearrange his plans. Suddenly, two other assistant prosecutors, Becky Doherty and Greta Johnson, stuck their heads into the room. Like everyone else in the Akron area, they'd been following the Cindy George saga in the press, and understood the effort it would take to get it right. As they listened to the detectives' pleas, both spoke up, volunteering to help Mike with his other cases.

The two women left the room but, a few minutes later, a number of other prosecutors filed in. They'd also assist to relieve the burden. Now, Carroll would be able to meet with the detectives daily.

EVERY MORNING, WHIDDON and Felber would stop at the police station between 7 and 7:30 AM, then walk over to the prosecutor's office at 9. Like every visitor, they had to sign in at the front desk, while the receptionist called Carroll to ensure that the pair had an appointment. After a few days, though, they no longer had to wait. After exchanging greetings, the receptionist automatically buzzed open the electric lock to the prosecutor's office.

The two were more than eager to double as secretaries, calling witnesses, scheduling appointments, making copies, arranging documents in chronological order. More importantly, they had to explain all their evidence—and the nuances contained within—to the prosecutor.

The office was staffed with twenty-nine assistant prosecutors for felony cases. Each had an assistant. With more than 5,000 cases a year, no one had any time to waste. Felber preferred working there to the police station, mainly because it seemed like three-quarters of the employees were female, the vast majority of them attractive. The style of communicating was different, as well. At headquarters, a typical salutation would begin, "Hey, I like your tie." Then, after a pause, "Too bad it doesn't go with your shirt."

"It's nice to get a 'Hi' in the morning, followed by a beautiful smile," Felber commented to Whiddon one day.

The lieutenant made his subordinate feel like they were still in the station by responding, "That'll change as soon as they get to know you."

FOR YEARS, CARROLL had been coming to work on Sundays to catch up on paperwork. After reading the documents related to the Zack case, he compiled a list of potential witnesses—a huge roster consisting of some thirty names. Whiddon and Felber were amazed and relieved that the prosecutor could grasp so much information—and the roles of the various players—so quickly. Sometimes, they even lost track themselves. But now, Carroll uttered something that frightened the detectives.

"We need to contact each of these people and have them come to my office so I can talk to them in person. I need to make sure they remember what they told you guys. And I need for them to get to know me, so they feel comfortable when they take the stand."

There were twenty working days until the trial—twenty days for detectives, first, to reach the witnesses, then for those people to take time away from their complicated lives and jobs to visit the prosecutor's office. But what choice did Felber or Whiddon have? They had to complete the assignment.

To their surprise, nearly every witness agreed to assist. These were mostly middle-class Americans who were proud to exercise their civil duty. Some asked if their lives would be imperiled. But no one said no.

Bob Cole, the man who'd allegedly sold Zaffino the gun, lived a half hour outside of Akron, and Carroll didn't want to risk losing him. So the prosecutor, along with Whiddon and Felber, drove to Cole's town, and met with him in a public library near his home. They even allowed him to bring along his brother Randy, to increase the comfort level. Whatever misgivings Bob harbored were allayed by Carroll's matter-of-fact attitude and ability to make a traumatic event seem casual.

BEFORE MOST HOMICIDE trials, the more competent defense attorneys search for ways to handicap the proceedings in a client's favor, finding loopholes in the law to block the amount of material that the prosecutor can present. It would be up to Summit County Common Pleas Court Judge James E. Murphy to decide whether to indulge or hinder these efforts. As the Zaffino trial drew close, detectives began hearing rumors that Murphy was friendly with Ed George's attorney, Robert Meeker. Many in law enforcement complained that Murphy exhibited something of a superior attitude in the courtroom, and made decisions that seemed based more on whimsy than on law.

At a precursor to the trial, the various sides met at a suppression hearing that the defense had initiated to limit the amount of evidence that the prosecution could introduce. Zaffino's admissions to police weren't valid, his lawyer argued, because, even after he'd mentioned that he had an attorney, detectives failed to halt their questioning and contact the lawyer. The prosecution countered that Zaffino explicitly stated that he was willing to talk without the aid of counsel.

In addition, the defense contended that the paternity tests involving Cynthia George's youngest child were not only irrelevant, but prejudicial. It was an issue detectives had struggled with from the beginning of the investigation. Since the girl had been raised to believe that her father was

Ed George, it seemed incredibly cruel to pronounce the test results in a media-saturated courtroom. But police determined that a jury needed to understand this issue in order to grasp the motivation Cynthia might have had for participating in the murder plot.

The judge considered the arguments carefully, then ruled in favor of the prosecution.

Ever skillful, Zaffino's attorney, Larry Whitney, also challenged the voice analysis taken to prove that the suspect was the same man who'd left the threatening message on Jeff Zack's answering machine. The test had not been properly administered, Whitney said, and the voice analysis company was less than credible.

This was a fallacy, of course. The company's clients included the FBI, among a catalogue of law enforcement agencies. But the game was in motion. Before the suppression hearing, Mike Carroll thought he had asked the judge about the information he'd need to bolster his cause. To this day, the prosecutor believes that he heard the magistrate say that he wanted to see documentation affirming the outfit's credentials. This was good news, as the prosecutor's office hoped to avoid the cost of flying in the company's officials, and paying for their room and board.

But when the hearing actually took place, and Whitney questioned the authority of the test, Judge Murphy asked Carroll to produce a company representative. The prosecutor approached the bench, and explained that he'd been led to believe that he simply needed the proper citations. The judge vehemently denied ever making such a statement, and ordered Carroll to present a witness. Carroll could not.

"We can arrange to have a representative here within a few days," the prosecutor pleaded.

The judge declined to delay the hearing to make this accommodation—and barred any mention of the voice analysis from the trial.

It was an unanticipated blow—one that the detectives had difficulty grasping. It seemed just because the magistrate was in the wrong mood, a vital piece of evidence had been expunged. They wondered how many cases were blown because of snap decisions.

The experience raised the whole issue surrounding the way that judges were appointed to the bench. Some were literally senile, but continued to serve because they were part of the political machine. While others were elected by popular vote, local political hacks filled seats that became vacant between elections. Any time certain judges ran for a particular seat and lost, they'd be placed on another bench by their benefactors. As a result, these magistrates were more beholden to their political bosses than the rule of law.

The wrong judge meant the wrong rulings. The wrong rulings meant that a murderer could easily walk free.

To offset this possibility, the prosecution team trained for a number of scenarios. If the judge refused to consider one piece of evidence, there had to be other material to make the same point. For example, Carroll planned to bring the motorcycle into the courtroom to show to jurors. Thus, when a witness described the lime green, black and white motorcycle at the crime scene, the presence of Zaffino's lime green, black and white motorcycle would make a powerful statement. Yet, even after the custodial staff at the county courthouse affirmed that it was physically possible to wheel the bike into a third-floor courtroom, prosecutors and detectives had to have an alternative plan—just in case the judge barred the vehicle.

Detectives had the Crime Scene Unit photograph the motorcycle. Then, confident that they'd covered the angles, the team shifted to other issues. But when Felber actually looked at the photographs, his heart jumped. For some reason, the lime green color came out yellow in the pictures. Felber rushed out to the storage garage to ensure that the bike actually *was* lime green. When he substantiated this, he took his own photos—assuming that the Crime Scene Unit camera had been defective. Much to his dismay, the motorcycle also looked yellow on his digital camera.

Since the motorcycle was no longer in production, no one seemed to be able to find any old brochures highlighting the bike's actual color. But a Honda representative did give Felber the name of the company that manufactured the motorcycle's fluorescent paint. After several phone calls, the detectives located an engineer who confirmed that, for some reason, the company's lime green paint often looked different in photographs. But what was the prosecution supposed to do now? Subpoena the engineer to tell jurors, "What you see isn't really what you're seeing"?

Fortunately, in this instance, the judge again ruled in the prosecution's favor. Felber, dressed in a brand new suit, and a couple of sheriff's department deputies were allowed to wheel the large, heavy motorcycle into a small elevator, and park it in front of the judge's bench.

BY NOW, THE team had taken over the library in the prosecutor's office. Because the space also doubled as a lunch room, other prosecutors were constantly passing through, and smirking, "Sorry to interrupt your very important work."

Once, a public advocate contemplated the sight of Felber and Whiddon hunched over a collection of documents, and asked Carroll, "Did we hire these guys? Or are they just political appointees?"

It was during these meetings that the team debated the way to present the incident in the park by the Everett Covered Bridge. On the surface, Zaffino was simply stopped by some rangers, and hadn't broken any laws. Because the gun was found, police were certain that John had been hiding in the woods, waiting to shoot Jeff. But prosecutors were unsure of the way to convince a jury of the same thing. The last thing they wanted was for jurors to think that the prosecution team was standing there, grasping at straws.

The phone records told a powerful story. While John

was in the woods with the gun, he and Cindy were on the phone almost continually for three hours. During this period, Cynthia was also on her other phone with Jeff. One call with Zack lasted seven minutes. Another went on for five, and ended just before Zaffino emerged from the woods for his encounter with the rangers. As soon as he drove away, Cindy called Jeff another time. Then, an hour later, Cynthia and John were on the phone again—for more than two hours, until 1:30 AM.

It wasn't until ten days before the trial that Felber finally tracked down a phone number for David Amstutz, the kindly old mushroom hunter who'd found the gun. Dressed in coveralls and a flannel shirt, Amstutz visited the prosecutor's office, telling his story with meticulous honesty. Amstutz was an amiable family man who seemed able to divorce himself from the obstructions of the modern world, and value what was truly important. He was envied by the entire team. With Amstutz on the witness stand, Carroll decided, it was worth telling jurors about the episode in the park.

OF THE SIX hours of recorded conversations between Christine Todaro and John Zaffino, the team found twenty clips that they wanted to use in court. The hope was that the judge would allow the prosecution to play the highlighted sections. If jurors were forced to listen to a thirty-minute discussion simply because there were sixty seconds of relevant material somewhere, they might become impatient, if not outright hostile.

While Carrie Stoll, the Persons Unit secretary, worked overtime, transcribing the conversations, Felber digitized the exchanges from cassette tapes to computerized audio files. But Carroll had always used cassettes in the courtroom, and seemed in no rush to change. When Felber explained that the CDs could be played on a computer, rather than a compact disc player, the prosecutor seemed unmoved. As a result, the CDs were handed over to an audio studio, where the relevant excerpts were transferred back to cassettes.

Because of their naiveté about trial procedure, Whiddon and Felber were discouraged to learn that, under the law, defense attorneys were allowed to visit the prosecutor's office, and examine every report, document, transcript, recording and phone record. Only personal notes about trial strategy were off-limits. And the defense was not required to reciprocate—at least until the trial was about to start.

This meant that Larry Whitney had the names, addresses, phone numbers and statements of all the witnesses, an advantage he used to pass some of the information on to one of John Zaffino's sisters. She then apparently contacted a number of witnesses by mail, claiming that she'd read the statements they'd made to police. Later, Felber would be told that the Coles had been informed that he'd described them as stupid in a police report. He had to show them the actual report to prove that the allegation was false.

When Felber found out that Whitney was planning to call Mike Frasher to the stand, the detective phoned the man himself. What he next discovered forced the prosecution team to change their tactics, and mobilize for a hostile witness. It seemed that Frasher had been visiting Zaffino in jail, and was now completely convinced that they'd been chatting on his porch while the homicide took place.

Previously, the team had told the Frashers' babysitter, Danielle Watson, that they didn't need her for the trial. But now, John had an alibi. When questioned again, she repeated her assertion that Zaffino had not arrived at the home until more than an hour after the murder. That's what the prosecution wanted to hear.

"There's going to be a change of plans," she was advised.

She would now be an important witness.

At the suppression hearing, Carroll had been informed that Whitney was planning to call a witness who maintained that she'd seen someone other than Zaffino fleeing the BJ's parking area. As soon as Felber read the woman's statement, it seemed strangely familiar—like the letter Zaffino's fellow inmates had been planning to write on his behalf.

As it turned out, the woman was the mother of yet another prisoner. But the inmate—serving 43 days on a contempt charge for theft and various alcohol-related offenses—asserted that he'd never met the suspect, and knew nothing about Zack's murder. When his mother was summoned to the prosecutor's office two days later, she claimed that no one had approached her to speak about the murder. She'd simply seen Zaffino's photo in the newspaper, and called Larry Whitney because she didn't want to see an innocent man go to prison.

The woman said that she'd been at a red light when she saw the motorcyclist racing away from the crime scene. The motorcycle was lime green and cream-colored, she recalled, and the killer was wearing a brown, silk-like jacket, brown slacks and socks, and strange-looking shoes. That's how she remembered him so vividly, she asserted—his shoes.

The man was also wearing a black helmet with only a partial visor, she continued, and—through the hole—she'd spotted his cheeks and his brown eyes. From her point of view, he appeared to be Iranian.

Neither Whiddon nor Felber asked any questions, as Carroll methodically questioned the woman; they were trying not to laugh. Felber was particularly amused that this woman—who seemed like she'd grown up in the hills of West Virginia—was adept enough at distinguishing nationalities to conclude that the suspect looked Iranian. Like Zaffino, Felber was of Italian ancestry, and knew that it wasn't that difficult to mistake a person from Bari or Naples for an ethnic Persian; the detective was regularly taken for Middle Eastern himself. If the woman wanted to throw off investigators, Felber concluded, she could have said that the murderer looked Swedish. And if the man flew by her vehicle so quickly, how had she managed to observe his eyes, his shoes and his socks?

Later, Felber and Whiddon told Carroll they hoped that Whitney would call the woman to testify. "She's so unbelievable," Felber said, "she might be our best witness."

As she spoke, a daughter sat beside her, nodding at some of the statements. When the interview ended, the detectives thanked the women for their time. Then, grinning at Whiddon, he remarked, "I bet you like country music?"

"Yes," they replied.

It was the same question that Felber had asked the woman's son during his interview. And the lieutenant didn't seem the slightest bit amused.

TEN

TWO WEEKS BEFORE the trial, Brad Gessner joined the prosecution team. Like Carroll, he amazed detectives by instantly absorbing information. But that's where the similarity ended. Gessner was young and more aggressive. In the courtroom, he loved to attack. Although the two barely knew each other—Gessner was relatively new to the Summit County Prosecutor's Office—it was clear how their personalities could be used at the trial. The pair would play good cop/bad cop. Carroll's charm and relaxed demeanor could soothe nervous witnesses. Gessner would go after anyone whom prosecutors deemed hostile.

The days leading up to the trial would often stretch as long as twelve hours. This was particularly difficult for Whiddon, who had two children in grade school and a wife busy with a career of her own. There were scheduling conflicts and emergencies, and the lieutenant was constantly trying to achieve the right sense of balance between his personal and professional personas. When he'd have to dart out of a strategy session for a few hours, Whiddon often felt guilty. But the rest of the team always supported his decision. He'd come through in the investigation, and they knew that he'd display the same sense of character during the trial.

Everyone understood the importance of picking the right jury. A few times, the topic came up of hiring a specialist who could present scientific data about how different demographic groups viewed certain types of defendants. But Carroll and Gessner weren't interested. Their experiences told them to seek out jurors who could analyze and compare different types of evidence. The preference was anyone with a college degree, or simply an independent thinker, regardless of race or background.

At every major criminal trial in Ohio, the lead detective is invited to sit alongside the prosecutors. It's an incredible advantage, since this is the only witness who can listen to others testify before taking the stand himself. The day before the trial began, Carroll and Gessner decided to bestow this honor on Lieutenant Whiddon. Felber felt disappointed and relieved at the same time. The banishment from the courtroom would cause a great deal of frustration. But Felber also had more time to prepare his testimony. He'd already rehearsed twice—once in front of a group of prosecutors and assistants, another time in front of his sister—and stammered and stuttered his way through the descriptions of the phone records. In Larry Whitney, Felber had an adversary renowned for making detectives look stupid. The practice sessions would be invaluable.

Despite his own apprehension, though, one of Felber's courthouse tasks became maneuvering the prosecution witnesses to an alcove to calm them down before testifying.

"What happens if I make a mistake?" he'd be asked.

"We all make mistakes. It's up to Mike Carroll and Brad Gessner to help you correct it."

"But could I get arrested for making a mistake?"

"Not if it isn't intentional."

"What happens if I don't understand a question?"

"Say you don't understand it. They'll ask it again."

Because of television, the majority of witnesses seemed convinced that their answers had to sound scripted.

"**CINDY GEORGE HAD** a problem," Mike Carroll declared in his opening statement on February 26, 2003. "That problem was Jeff Zack. The solution to the problem was John Zaffino."

Slowly and clearly, the prosecutor explained the case in almost affable terms. Jurors would learn about Cynthia and Jeff's relationship, their secret child, Zack's persistence as his lover began to pull away and, ultimately, the affair with Zaffino and the murder plot. Jeff's mother and wife would testify, as well as two of Zaffino's ex-wives, and Ed and Cynthia George. There would be details like the $5,300 Cindy had withdrawn from the bank three hours before John paid $5,267.98 for a 1995 Honda with lime green highlights. Piece by piece, Carroll planned to build a cell around Zaffino, from which he'd have no chance of extricating himself.

"This is a case where we're proving things, rather than directly, proving them indirectly," he said. "But we will prove them just the same."

Whitney came across as equally genial, a style he'd maintain throughout the entire process. Even when it seemed like Zaffino was backed into a corner, Whitney never lashed out and attacked the witnesses. He simply allowed them to tell their stories, and only cross-examined them on a few details. The message he conveyed was that none of the evidence was really that relevant. Why inflate its value by making it appear more important?

Zaffino, the lawyer stressed, didn't deny buying a motorcycle or gun, or knowing Cynthia George. "But," Whitney added, "that does not amount to him being a murderer."

He left the courthouse with the gait of a man who knew that he'd won the first round.

> The trial of John Zaffino, who is charged with killing Jeff Zack while he sat in his vehicle at a gas station in June, 2001 has been postponed because Zaffino's attorney, Larry Whitney, had a heart attack Wednesday night. Whitney, who did not have another attorney assisting him, is in Akron General Medical Center, according to the court . . . Jurors had heard one day of testimony, If the trial is delayed too long, they may be dismissed and the trial rescheduled.
>
> —*Cleveland* Plain Dealer *staff reports*

As jurors shuffled into the courtroom, they were greeted by a dour-faced Judge Murphy, who addressed them in an even, paternal voice:

"Ladies and gentlemen, as all best-laid plans of mice and men, I think the expression goes, Mr. Whitney had an extreme medical emergency last night, and he's in the hospital in Akron General. It's anticipated he'll be in the hospital for at least two or three days—at least over the weekend . . . Obviously, he's in no condition to talk to us, nor do I demand it."

The prosecution team left the courtroom, and convened back at the office, stunned by the news. Whitney was one of the rare defense attorneys who even police officers liked. No matter how reprehensible his client, Whitney played fair, never resorting to unsavory gimmicks to score points. Once they realized that he was recuperating quickly, prosecutors joked that, burdened with a completely offensive client, Whitney had faked his heart attack to elicit sympathy for himself.

The unscheduled delay allowed prosecutors to better prepare their case. The next several days felt chaotic, but in a good way. By the time Whitney was healthy enough to return to the courtroom, prosecutors had plugged holes in the case that they hadn't had the opportunity to repair before.

BY MARCH 5, it seemed as if Whitney had regained his stamina. Zaffino's ex-wife, Nancy Bonodio, and her fiancé, Russell Forrest, recounted the night the defendant had suddenly shown up at their home with his motorcycle. Bob Cole's brother, Randy, testified, but became so confused that he inadvertently gave Zaffino an alibi—claiming that they'd met at a car show on June 16, 2001, sometime between 12 and 12:30 PM. Carroll produced the three interviews that Randy had given police, indicating otherwise. But Randy appeared overwhelmed by the responsibility of testifying, and couldn't seem to sort out the facts. Jurors may have detected his puzzlement, however, because the testimony had little impact on the trial.

When Bob Cole took the stand, he affirmed that he'd run into Zaffino at the car show after 1 PM, but he wasn't sure of the exact time. He also spoke about selling Zaffino two handguns—one matching the description of the pistol found in the park, the other identical to the type that had killed Jeff Zack—and worrying that his friend might use the weapons to hurt somebody. Then, David Amstutz, the mushroom hunter who'd handed over the gun in the park, as well as two rangers, testified.

Whitney's cross-examination was consistent with the theme he'd already established. Sure, Bob Cole had sold Zaffino two guns, but so what? There were thousands of similar weapons in circulation all over the United States. And waiting for a girlfriend in the park at night did not make a man a murderer.

MARCH 6 WAS supposed to be the highlight of the trial. As media members slid between family and friends of the parties in the spectators' gallery, a demure-looking Cynthia George entered the courtroom, hair pushed back into a bun, a pair of wire-rimmed glasses perched on her nose. Once on the stand, she was asked some rudimentary questions—her name, the name of her husband, the number of children in the George family—and answered in a voice so soft that it was almost impossible to hear.

Some observers wondered whether she was heavily sedated.

Suddenly, her attorney, Mike Bowler, interrupted, and asked the judge to clear the courtroom. As the jurors repaired to the jury room, Bowler approached the bench.

"Your Honor, my client intends to assert her Fifth Amendment rights at this time to any further questions with regard to this matter," Bowler said.

Judge Murphy turned to Cindy: "You know the subject of this inquiry here regarding the death of Jeff Zack? That's why you're here?"

"Yes," Cynthia responded in a near-whisper, looking only at her attorney and no one else.

"And you understand the nature of what is called the Fifth Amendment privilege, do you not?"

"Yes, I do."

"All right, do you wish to assert that privilege?"

"Yes, I do."

Murphy looked away from Cynthia. "The witness has answered the subpoena," he stated. "She is not available to testify."

As the press watched closely, vainly waiting for a gesture that would reveal a peek into the soul of a woman who, if guilty, was capable of tempting one extra-marital lover to slay another, Cynthia stood—her beauty masked in a sexless costume—and left the building. Her lawyer trailed closely behind.

SHE WAS FOLLOWED on the stand by Jeff's mother, as well as onetime romantic rival Bonnie Zack—who'd since remarried and changed her name to Bonnie Cook. Exuding the candor that detectives had come to respect, Bonnie told jurors what she knew about Jeff's relationship with Cynthia George, as well as the June 13, 2001, phone message that had apparently demoralized her husband.

"He got very frantic and upset, and started pacing around the kitchen," Bonnie recalled.

But it was Mary Ann Brewer, the nanny, who took jurors into the George home, where Jeff had apparently transformed from a welcome guest to a persistent tormentor—one who seemed to have a hold over Cindy for life because he'd allegedly threatened to whisk their love child away to Israel.

AS ZAFFINO FOUGHT for his freedom, Cynthia and Ed united on an unrelated project, altering the image and cuisine of the Tangier to reconcile the storied eatery with the new millennium. Since July, Ed had spent an estimated $2.5 million on the restaurant—$1 million on the main dining room alone. The city of Akron was kicking in another $30,000 to preserve the West Market Street icon.

Cynthia was quoted in the *Akron Beacon Journal*, describing her hesitance to discard familiar decorative items "or it wouldn't be Tangier anymore."

Ed spoke about the restaurant's three new chefs, and their penchant for nouvelle dishes like cutefish, and pan-roasted lobster over red-pepper grits with a tomato concasse and brown butter-cognac sauce.

"I haven't spent as much putting the lawn in my house as they spent on asparagus," he said.

But it was a different Ed George who appeared in court several hours after his wife. Once again, there was a stipulation attached to his testimony: invoking marital privilege, Ed would not divulge anything that his wife of eighteen years had told him in private.

Still, he disclosed quite a bit more than the former

pageant queen. He and Jeff Zack initially had a "customer relationship," the restaurateur said, then became "casual" friends.

"He was at our house," Ed maintained, "I can't recall, once or at a communion or some function some time."

Queried Carroll, "How about you going to the Zack household? Did you ever do that?"

"No."

"How about your wife? Did she go there socially that you're aware of?"

George's attorney, Robert Meeker, rose to object, but was overruled.

"I don't recall," Ed answered. "I don't know if she went there."

Still, he did remember a series of telephone hang-ups that had occurred with such frequency, he'd felt compelled to contact his friend Major Paul Callahan, in January 2001. After the murder, Ed said, he told the major that the caller was Jeff Zack.

"Mr. George, if I use the name John Zaffino," Carroll asked, motioning a toward the defendant's table, "—that's actually this fellow right here, sitting behind his attorney—have you heard the name before?"

"Recently, I have heard it."

"In connection with this case?"

"Yeah."

"Did you ever know the man?"

"No."

"Before this case?"

Ed shook his head. "Uh-uh."

Whitney picked up on the exchange during cross-examination:

"Mr. George, you've already said that you don't know this man right here?"

"Correct."

"I assume that you're going to tell the jury that you didn't hire this man to kill this Jeff Zack? Is that correct?"

"Yes."

". . . Whatever problem you were having with Jeff Zack, you decided to deal with it with the police, by calling the major of the Akron Police Department? Is that correct?"

"Who else is better?"

For the prosecution, it was another day of background information, linking Cynthia to John and setting up motive. Whitney was never thrown off-course, though. When members of the media filed their stories, they questioned whether prosecutors really had enough to make a case.

THE NEXT DAY was going to be crucial. That's when Christine Todaro was scheduled to testify, and her covertly recorded tapes of Zaffino would be played. Since Zaffino refused to take the stand, this would be the only opportunity for jurors to hear the suspect's own voice, as he was questioned about his possible role in the murder.

The plans also called for Felber to testify later in the day, and the detective was nervous. Twenty years earlier, he'd developed laryngitis before a speech in college. But being on the job had changed him. He only hoped that it had changed him enough that he wouldn't choke this time around.

The detective arrived home at about 7 PM, his mind cluttered with details about the phone records. Would he be able to convey the information clearly, or would he freeze on the stand? It seemed like he'd be possessed by these questions all night—until he realized that a group of cops were going to be practicing for a charity basketball game in about an hour. Felber loved basketball. It provided an escape from the rigors of the job, and he wasn't bad for a guy in his forties. So he ate quickly, and drove over to the gym.

There were about twenty officers on the court when he arrived. Average age: 28. But Felber didn't mind at all. Over the past few years, he'd learned to use height and technique to overcome opponents' speed. He played two games, then volunteered for a third. In the midst of it, he found himself guarding a much quicker rival. As the man drove down the lane toward the basket, he tried sidestepping around Felber. The detective followed him, move for move, leaping up in the air as the man jumped to take his shot. Suddenly, another officer accidentally barged into Felber, taking his legs out from under him. Attempting to break his fall, Felber stuck out his left arm, but it became entangled around another player's body. Felber fell, his elbow taking the full force of the blow on the hardwood floor.

The ball bounced off the backboard, and Felber quickly rose to grab the rebound. But when he raised his left arm, pain coursed through his body. He took himself out of the game, and waited for the throbbing to subside. When it didn't—a half hour later—he went home.

By 5 AM, he realized that the pain was getting worse instead of better. He hadn't slept, and needed to make a decision. Should he go to the hospital and have his broken arm set in a cast? He was due in court in three hours, and there didn't seem to be enough time. But as an Akron police officer, he knew which hospital had the shortest emergency room wait.

So at 8 AM, after returning home and showering, Felber walked into the courthouse with an ostentatious white cast. Whiddon, Gessner and Carroll were flabbergasted. How could Felber have been so stupid, playing basketball before the biggest trial of his life?

"You're making a big deal out of nothing," Felber responded. "My arm's broke. Not my mind." To keep his wits, he'd opted to forsake the prescribed pain medication. His only disadvantage was the fact that somebody else would have to lift the enlarged phone record boards onto the easels in the courtroom. In fact, in some ways, the broken arm was a blessing. It had prevented Felber from worrying and second-guessing himself about his upcoming testimony. Either way, he wouldn't have been able to get a decent night's sleep.

"Let's look at it this way," he began. "Whitney won everybody over by having a heart attack, then coming back in less than a week. The jurors'll take one look at my cast, and we'll get them back on our side."

There was no time to debate the matter; Christine was minutes away from the courthouse.

"John's not going to be in the courtroom, is he?"

Christine Todaro knew the answer, but somehow hoped that by asking the question, she'd receive the reassuring response she wanted.

"Yes, he will," Felber replied. "You know that, Chris."

"I don't have to look at him, though? Right?"

"Right. Just look at Mike Carroll—and tell the truth. We've been going over this for months. That's all you have to do—tell the truth."

Christine was actually shaking when she entered the courtroom. But when she was called to testify, she exhibited the same coolness that had confounded police during those frightening sessions in the suspect's car. Every question was answered with certainty and confidence. And when the tapes of her conversations with Zaffino were played for the jurors, they could hear the sarcastic tone in the defendant's voice when he claimed to know nothing about Zack's homicide.

They also heard Zaffino become progressively more anxious as the investigation continued—and menacing when his temper flared and he threatened Christine's boyfriend. Although the transcripts of the discussions were adequate evidence, the inflections he used were damning. Zaffino emitted the types of sounds that simply didn't come from an innocent person.

While Christine testified, Felber stood outside the courtroom, once again reviewing the phone records. Finally, he stopped. There was simply too much data in his brain to absorb any more. Now, it was time to go in front of the jury and take his shot. One thing was certain: his composure was as important as the information contained in the evidence.

If the detective wasn't relaxed, the jurors would become uncomfortable watching him.

At noon, the courtroom doors finally swung open. But instead of Brad Gessner coming out to usher in the detective, a swarm of people streamed into the hallway. It was lunchtime. The testimony would have to wait.

Felber nibbled on a sandwich, listening to the team describe Christine's appearance in glowing terms. The detective had to admit that he felt proud of this woman who'd stuck with law enforcement, even when law enforcement had treated *her* like the criminal. She'd performed heroically from the very beginning. He only wished that she could have eavesdropped on the team's conversation, listening to every accolade.

"Don't let Murphy get to you." Gessner was looking across the table at Felber, switching the subject to the daunting presence the judge brought to the courtroom. "He sometimes loses patience, especially with cops. He'll probably yell at you at least once."

Now, Felber was the witness who needed reassurance. "So what happens if I screw up? Should I apologize?"

Both Gessner and Carroll shook their heads. "It'll give him an excuse to vent some more," Gessner said.

Generally, judges don't expect witnesses to understand courtroom procedure. But the concession is waived for police officers. Cops know that they're not supposed to repeat information received from a third party, or facts that the jury shouldn't hear. If Felber mentioned the sound lab results, for instance, the defense would be entitled to demand that the case be thrown out of court.

Now, the detective put his faith in Mike Carroll's hands. The prosecutor did not disappoint, starting off with easy questions, like Felber's background, then proceeding to findings at the crime scene, the way certain witnesses had been located, and so on. Some of these exchanges should have been relatively simple. But Felber realized that, in investing so much time on the phone records, he hadn't reviewed other important aspects of the case. Still, his brain didn't fail him.

Eventually, the phone records were introduced—some forty-five minutes after Felber began testifying—and complications set in. He'd hoped that the judge would accept the assumption that numbers 0132 and 0133 belonged to Cynthia and Zaffino. But when Felber said "Cindy called John," Larry Whitney objected. There was no definitive proof that Cynthia was on one phone, and Zaffino on the other, he argued.

The judge sustained the objection. This meant that Felber would have to use numbers—as in "0132 called 0133"—rather than names, and manage to maintain the jury's attention.

Gessner handed Felber a pointer, and the detective rose, taking the object with his right hand, while he held his plaster-coated left arm at his side. Standing in front of the easel, Felber began describing the phone calls. To his surprise, he felt relatively comfortable. At one stage, he lost his place, and smiled embarrassingly at the jurors. But they were paying attention. Without hesitation, several pointed at the proper spot on the chart.

The detective playfully chided himself, telling the jury, "You're better at this than I am." The rapport was cemented. The jurors smiled back and, from that point forward, their eyes remained on the boards.

It took the team three hours to cover the phone records. The information was dry, but critical—or, as Phil Trexler of the *Akron Beacon Journal* described it, "mundane, yet telling."

Felber returned to the witness booth, ready for whatever Larry Whitney could deliver in his cross-examination. But then Judge Murphy made a decision that the detective didn't want to hear. It was 4 PM, and the trial was adjourned for the weekend. Felber's stomach churned. For the next two days, he'd have nothing to do but imagine one of the brightest attorneys in Summit County embarrassing him on

Monday. At the same time, Whitney was going to have the entire weekend to prepare for Felber. There were some 500 pages of reports that the detective had written, along with more than 1,000 pages of phone documents. Whitney would have the luxury of picking a random section, throwing it back at Felber, and turning him into a fool or liar on the witness stand.

Even worse, the detective had been subpoenaed to testify against the leader of the cigarette bandits in another courtroom on Monday. This involved ten different suspects in ten separate break-ins. But Felber hadn't crammed for the case yet. He'd hoped to finish up with Zaffino, then switch gears.

As the detective left the courtroom, he passed Larry Whitney in the hallway. "Monday," the attorney said with a friendly, yet challenging grin, "you are *mine*."

All this, and only one arm. It didn't seem fair.

UNDER DIFFERENT CIRCUMSTANCES, the team would have met over the weekend, and prepped Felber for the confrontation with Whitney. But everybody was burned out. Felber instead spent Saturday and Sunday at his sister's house, playing with her two kids. They took him as far away as he could get from work—so far, in fact, that he actually slept well on Sunday night.

There was no pep talk awaiting him when he turned up at the courthouse on Monday. Carroll and Gessner were busy formulating their closing arguments. Only Whiddon walked over to Felber and asked if he was ready. The lieutenant seemed as nervous as the detective—maybe more so. At least Felber had some control over what would transpire in the box—the term insiders used for the witness stand. All Whiddon could do was sit there and watch.

"Do you want to go over some stuff?" the lieutenant offered.

"It's too late. If I'm not ready now, I won't be in an

hour. At this point, the less I think about it, the better off I'll be."

Felber knew that Whitney's attack would be cerebral, and it was. Aware that the police had subpoenaed financial records for the Georges, Whitney asked about notations regarding payment to John Zaffino. Felber replied that he hadn't found any.

Whitney also grilled the detective on aspects of the case that other investigators had handled. A few times, Felber was uncertain about a minor detail, and the attorney corrected him. The detective didn't argue—Whitney wouldn't bring up a topic if he didn't know the answer, so it made no sense to debate him. There were questions about leads that had never panned out. But Felber never took the bait and became defensive. And when the judge yelled at him, as predicted, he followed the advice not to apologize. He was confident in the investigation.

Slowly, Felber began to feel like he was winning the encounter. When the lawyer brought up the phone records, the detective listened closely, and corrected Whitney about certain details. Whitney apologized, and tried again. But all the time spent examining the tedious documents was paying off. This was now Felber's area of expertise, and he maintained the edge.

Whitney paused, and looked as if he were about to ask another question. Then, he concluded the cross-examination, and took his seat. The team had one more opportunity to clear up whatever errors the detective had made. But when Judge Murphy asked Carroll if he wanted to question Felber another time, the prosecutor declined. Felber was excused.

AS HE LEFT the courtroom, he saw Mike Frasher, now a defense witness, waiting in the hall. Despite his friendship with Zaffino, Mike didn't seem like a bad guy. To Felber, Frasher was allowing himself to be misled because he didn't want to believe the worst about a friend. Without pausing, the detective approached Mike, and beseeched him to look at Zaffino's phone records one more time.

The two sat down. Frasher now claimed that Zaffino had shown up at his house at about 12:30 PM, less than a half hour after the homicide. Felber noted that Zaffino had phoned Mike at 12:41, and then at 12:56. "Why would he call you if he was already at your house?" Felber asked.

Frasher shook his head. "Could the records be wrong?" he wondered.

Ten minutes later, Frasher sat in the witness box, telling jurors that Zaffino had come to his home at 12:30. Gessner was prepared for this statement, and motioned at the phone records. Frasher pondered the documents, then admitted that Zaffino could not have been on his porch at that time.

It was a coup for the team. After all, it was always better to have a defense witness damn a defendant than somebody picked by the prosecution.

WHITNEY'S CLOSING ARGUMENT emphasized that John Zaffino could go to prison because of a seemingly random jumble of circumstantial evidence. There wasn't one item, the lawyer emphasized, linking the defendant directly to the murder. No one could identify the killer. The murder weapon had never been found. There was no proof that the motorcycle that had been wheeled into the courtroom was the one used in the homicide. Therefore, there was no way to conclude with absolute certainty that Zaffino was guilty.

During his closing statement, Gessner agreed that no individual piece of evidence confirmed John's guilt. But, taken together, the pieces of the puzzle created a picture that established the defendant as the murderer of Jeff Zack.

Underscoring the point Carroll made in his opening remarks, Gessner declared, "Ladies and gentlemen, Cindy George had a problem. Jeff Zack was that problem. Cindy

George had a solution, and we ask you to find that solution guilty beyond a reasonable doubt."

WITH SO MANY minute portions of evidence presented, prosecutors theorized that it would take days for jurors to agree on a verdict.

They were wrong.

It took less than four hours for the judge to learn that the jury had reached a consensus. Zaffino returned to the courtroom, apparently unconcerned. Turning in his chair, he made eye contact with his sister in the gallery, loudly prognosticating, "I'll meet you for dinner at four o'clock."

He never made the dinner date. Zaffino was found guilty of aggravated murder.

His arrogance now melted into tears; deputies noted that the suspect was crying as he was led from the courtroom.

"There was an overwhelming amount of evidence, a lot of it circumstantial, but a mountain of evidence against John Zaffino," juror Kimberly Cefalu told the Cleveland *Plain Dealer*.

Jurors said that it had only taken an hour to determine Zaffino's guilt. But they didn't want to rush to judgment so quickly. So for the next three hours, they sat around, discussing the person who *wasn't* on trial. Why, they asked, hadn't Cynthia George been arrested?

"From the evidence I heard, she definitely had knowledge of what was going on," juror Deborah Dorsey told the press. "I think it's a shame that, in our system, someone who, in my opinion, played a key role in a homicide couldn't be questioned. Her [lack of cooperation] was evidence to me."

IT WAS A premise that lingered in the air for a week, until Zaffino's sentencing hearing. Zack's widow and son both addressed the court, and each pointedly mentioned Cynthia George.

"If it wasn't for Cindy George," Bonnie Cook asserted, fixing her gaze on Zaffino, "my husband wouldn't have been shot, my son wouldn't have lost his father, and you wouldn't be looking forward to spending the rest of your life in jail. You are just the fall guy. Do you think she cares about you? Are you willing to take all the heat for this, and let her continue to live her extravagant lifestyle?"

As his mother held his hand, 14-year-old Brian Zack said that he regretted quarrelling with his father on the day he died, and not saying goodbye before Jeff had left for the gas station. "I know my dad did not always do the right thing," the boy stated. "But he did not deserve to be killed."

Brian also asked Zaffino if he regretted making a decision that would keep him apart from his own son: "Was it worth killing my dad for Cindy?"

When the judge asked if he wished to speak, a contrite Zaffino replied, "No, sir." Then, he was sentenced to the mandatory term for murder and using a gun: 23 years to life.

This time, Zaffino was expressionless. But his sister, Judy Diggelman, turned to Felber in the gallery, her long black hair hanging on each side of her puckered face. "You fuckin' liar," she hissed. "You'll pay for this."

The press was waiting for the victorious prosecutors as they left the courtroom. Zack's relatives tried to reach the group, as well, but they couldn't break through the huddle of reporters and cameramen. Only when the chaos subsided did the Zacks manage to express their gratitude. Yet no one was elated. A husband and father had been murdered, and another father would be spending at least a generation locked up.

Everyone understood that the case was incomplete. Carroll confirmed this by telling the press that his work had just begun.

"It's not over," he promised.

ELEVEN

ALL THROUGH THE trial, detectives wondered how a man in the process of being evicted had found the money to pay for one of the highest-priced attorneys in the city. They had their suspicions, but couldn't prove anything. Yet, even without proof, it was fairly obvious that the Georges had paid the bill. What made this more infuriating was the fact that the city had donated $30,000 toward the Tangier's renovation. As far as Felber and Whiddon were concerned, this meant that taxpayer dollars had been used to subsidize Zaffino's defense.

The challenge now was establishing the link that would bring the palace tumbling down on Cynthia George.

Prosecutors agreed that Cindy seemed culpable. But Gessner didn't want police arresting her prematurely. He suggested that investigators wait until Zaffino was transferred to a state prison, where his phone calls would be recorded. Maybe he would say something stupid.

The Akron Police Department had never used this tactic before. But detectives wanted to reinforce their case in other ways. Felber contacted a sheriff's deputy assigned to the Summit County Jail, and asked about the associates the convicted killer kept during his confinement there. The deputy mentioned three inmates, all violent offenders with no love of law enforcement. The possibility of inducing these guys to talk was about as likely as Lieutenant Whiddon forsaking country music for hip hop—the chance of them giving up Zaffino even smaller. But it never hurt to try.

One inmate regularly played cards with Zaffino in the jailhouse. During their early encounters, John had apparently insisted that he was innocent. But, his new poker buddy claimed, as time went on, the position changed. The man maintained that Zaffino had told him about the plan to set up Zack in the park: Cynthia was doing everything she could to persuade Jeff to show up, but he wasn't interested. Perhaps he sensed impending danger. So Cindy continued to phone her ex-lover. Before the scheme could be realized, though, Zaffino said that "the fuckin' rangers screwed it up."

Felber excitedly drove back to the police station, and looked for Whiddon. But the lieutenant had left for home. Felber's policy was never to disturb the lieutenant's family time, so the news had to wait until the next work day.

When Whiddon at last heard the details, he burst into a wide smile.

The pair phoned Carroll and Gessner, and arranged a meeting. The prosecutors listened intently. Much to the investigators' dismay, the prosecutors still did not want police to arrest Cynthia.

The latest information, after all, had come from a criminal. If the prosecution dared put him on the stand, a defense attorney would attack his credibility, neutralizing the revelation. Nonetheless, the interview was valuable.

An inmate named Raymond had also participated in the jailhouse card games. His record read like the Ohio Revised Code; he'd been arrested for every misdemeanor Felber could imagine, and a few crimes that the detective didn't know existed. He'd since been transferred to the Lorain Correctional Institution, and Felber and Whiddon made the forty-five-minute trek there. According to Ray-

mond, he and Zaffino had become "close friends" behind
bars, and John confided secrets that he wouldn't normally
disclose.

For example, Zaffino apparently said that his lawyer
had talked to him about offers ranging from 5 to 15 years,
if John "rolled" and divulged Cynthia's role in the murder.
But Zaffino had chosen to "stick" with Cindy. While John
may have suffered for his decision, Raymond said, his
stature rose among the inmates for rejecting a deal with
law enforcement.

Like his other poker-playing jailmate, Raymond asserted that Zaffino had admitted to the assassination attempt in the park. Raymond also claimed that John had
confessed to murdering Zack. And there was more. Cynthia had orchestrated the homicide, Raymond said, luring
Zack to the gas station for Zaffino to pick off.

Raymond theorized that Zaffino was paid with either
"money or pussy" for the killing. But, he added, John legitimately loved his co-conspirator, and desperately missed
her company. Because prison officials were watching to
see if Zaffino and Cynthia made contact, the pair were unable to speak. As a result, one of John's most valued possessions in prison was a Bible that he'd been sent by Cindy.

Zaffino's former cellmate at Lorain was a hardcore
gang member. Although the two didn't get along—Zaffino
complained about the guy smoking—they apparently spent
a great deal of time talking. And Zaffino seemed to enjoy
talking a lot. He bragged about shaking down bar owners
for protection money, and manufacturing counterfeit
credit cards. There were boasts about killing people in
Pennsylvania, and dumping their bodies in a lake. And,
Zaffino allegedly added, he'd been paid by the Georges to
carry out a hit on Jeff Zack—funds John later used to hire
Larry Whitney.

According to the gangbanger, Zaffino said that Zack
had been stalking Cynthia "at all hours of the day and

night." And, the inmate said, John had made painstaking arrangements to avoid conviction: wearing a full-face helmet, driving the motorcycle to Pennsylvania, and disposing of the gun there in a spot police would never discover.

Zaffino fully expected to be released on appeal. He bragged that the Georges would take care of everything. If he ever turned them in, though, Zaffino expected to be whacked himself. In the meantime, he'd apparently worked out a clandestine system of communication with the couple. The former cellmate claimed that Cindy had sent John a letter disguised as a missive from one of his sisters.

The source promised to tell the police whatever they needed to know. But he'd never testify about anything in court. That's what snitches did, and snitches got killed in jail. Since the inmate was serving time for murder—and, police assumed, probably was guilty of a few more—a deal couldn't be cut to lessen his sentence. Essentially, this guy was talking to break up the monotony of life behind bars.

Still, Felber and Whiddon passed on their intelligence to Carroll and Gessner. The prosecutors were intrigued by some of the information, but the sources weren't plausible enough to take the next step.

Once Zaffino was transferred to the Lorain Correctional Institution, Felber contacted authorities there about gaining access to the prisoner's recorded phone calls. It took four weeks for the request to be granted. However, because the prison was short-staffed and the employees overworked, acquiring the actual recordings became another drama. Felber would call the prison to be told that equipment was faulty, or the person charged with teaching the deputies to retrieve the audio communication had never shown up.

Eventually, Felber drove out to the prison to pick up the discs containing the recorded calls. Back in Akron, after twenty minutes of searching for the proper program on the police department computer, the detective finally heard

Zaffino's voice on the other end of the headphones—in its familiar, agitated state.

AT THE BEGINNING of each call, a recorded phone message would be heard, reminding the inmate that the conversation was being recorded. Every five minutes, the call would be interrupted with the same warning. To detectives, this was one of those legal hurdles created by lawyers somewhere to undermine the police. In Zaffino's case, investigators hoped that the inmate's human need to talk about his problems would outweigh his common sense, compelling him to say something indictable.

The first call that Felber monitored had taken place on April 5, 2003, between Zaffino and his sister, Judy Diggelman. The overriding topic was John's appeal. He claimed to have written a letter to Larry Whitney, asking for assistance.

"I said, 'Larry, I want you to hire somebody like Johnnie Cochran or F. Lee Bailey or somebody very famous,' " John stated. "And I said, 'Call my friends and you tell them that they will pay for it.' " He was careful to use the term "friends," rather than particular names. " 'Get the checkbook out and not worry about it. This is the way it's going to be, or they're going to lose their freedom.' "

Whoever those "friends" were, Zaffino was urging Judy to contact them: "Call over there and talk to him or her directly. Say, 'Look, see, there's a lot of choices you can make in this world. But one of them is going to be, "Do you want to keep your freedom?" And the other one is "Get my brother the fuck out of prison." ' "

Judy lent a supportive voice to the exchange: "Well, I think they're not keeping their end of the deal."

". . . I want Larry and a couple more or a whole firm working on this. I shouldn't even be here, you know."

"I know it."

Felber noticed that Zaffino never came out and said that

he was innocent—just that authorities hadn't had enough proof to convict him: "There's no physical evidence. He [Whitney] let me down, but I'm not going to tell him that . . . because I need him."

"I know."

"But I want you to tell him, 'Larry, you're going to have to hire somebody. It's gong to have to be somebody like Johnnie Cochran or F. Lee Bailey or somebody big.'"

"Okay."

"'Cause that way, when we put their name on stuff, it's going to get a lot of attention, and people are going to know that we're real serious about winning this."

"That's right."

". . . I want more lawyers, and I want them right now."

"All right."

"I mean *right* now."

"Okay."

"Next week. And I think if we do it this way, I'll be out of here in less than a year or two . . . See, once the appeal gets accepted, I can get bond. Now, they better bond me the fuck out of here. I don't care if it is ten million, they better bond me out."

"Absolutely."

"They just put two and a half in their restaurant there."

"Yeah, well . . ."

"While I've been in jail. So the partying days are over."

He continued self-righteously, "I went through with my deal. Now, it's their turn, you know? Now, I'm pissed, so they don't have a choice now. They have no choice."

Felber put down his headphones, and tried to absorb what he'd just heard. Zaffino was doing a pretty poor job of speaking in code. "Two and a half in their restaurant"? How many other eateries recently had a $2.5 million renovation? The problem was that prosecutors would want the inmate to identify his "friends" by name, leaving no question in jurors' minds about his apparent co-conspirators.

When the detective returned to the recording, the prison

had just sent a warning that there were only sixty seconds left on the call.

"I want lawyers this week," Zaffino demanded again. "Big lawyers. Big ones. Firms. And they're going to pay for it. Just tell them they're going to pay for it. Call them. Get the price and tell them. Tell the Georges, 'Write a check.' All right?"

"Yep, I'll do that."

"All right. Love you."

"Love you, too. Bye-bye."

"Bye-bye."

Felber again removed the headphones. "I love you, too," he mouthed to himself. Leave it to Zaffino to show his hand in the last minute of conversation. He'd just admitted that he had some kind of deal with the Georges. It wasn't exactly a confession, but it came awfully close.

The detective began listening to another call—this one between Zaffino and his other sister, Laura Henry. Laura began the discussion by trying to keep John apprised about her kids and general family life. After a while, John appeared to become exasperated, and shifted the talk back to his circumstances—and his needs.

"I want somebody famous, big-time lawyer firm, to handle this, 'cause I shouldn't be here . . . And I told him [Larry Whitney] to tell them they're paying for it."

"Who's going to pay?"

"You know."

"Who?"

"No, Jesus Christ, who am I sitting here for? My friends."

"Oh yeah."

". . . I've had it now. That's it. So they're either going to help me or else."

"Okay."

"'Cause if I start making phone calls, shit's going to happen. They just spent two and a half million on something, you know?"

"Right."

"So they better spend another two and a half on me."

In a subsequent call to Judy, Zaffino suggested sending a letter to his friends to urge them to assist with fees for the appeal: "Their address is somewhere on Allard Road in Medina."

It was the street where the Georges lived.

Felber met with Gessner, and asked when the prosecutor thought that it was best to arrest Cynthia. "I'm not so sure you should do that now," Gessner answered.

"Why not?"

"You're thinking like a cop. I'm thinking like a prosecutor. Cops gather evidence until they feel they have enough to make an arrest. I want enough to ensure a conviction."

Gessner emphasized that Cynthia had the means to afford the best attorneys in the state, so the prosecution had to be irrefutable. "We'll need a lot more than we would prosecuting an average person," Gessner noted. "Let's listen to more calls, and see what we get." By the time the investigation ended, Felber eavesdropped on more than 200 taped exchanges.

Some themes became tiresome. Zaffino regularly mentioned that the Georges had "no choice" but to accommodate his needs. However, John also implied that Larry Whitney and the Georges' lawyers were working together. For example, Zaffino maintained that Cynthia's attorney, Michael Bowler, was willing to pass along information and funds from his wealthy clients.

John also spent a great deal of time talking about a letter that Cynthia was supposed to send him. Then, one day, the conversations about the letter stopped. Was this because it had finally arrived? If the letter could be located, Felber and Whiddon concluded, it might seal the case. But authorities had to act quickly.

Felber called the warden and asked to have Zaffino's cell searched. Because inmates are guaranteed minimal rights of privacy, an invasion of this type can trigger outrage in a prison. But the warden understood the imperative nature of the request. In order to protect the investigation, he ordered all cells in Zaffino's pod raided. As a result, Zaffino had no reason to suspect that he was being singled out.

On May 31, deputies swept in and combed through Zaffino's cell. They found letters from family and friends, as well as the Bible presumably sent from Cindy. Its transcription read, "To John, From Your Friend." But the much-coveted letter remained elusive.

FROM THE MOMENT that law enforcement began this phase of their probe, they'd tried their best to be discreet. Because of the clout wielded by the Georges and their affiliated attorneys, one reckless comment could expose the investigation. Still, Zaffino was able to learn that detectives had questioned his fellow inmates about his comments regarding the case—and Cynthia George. And on June 16, 2003—the two-year anniversary of the murder—John's sister, Judy, received a reproachful e-mail from Larry Whitney:

> I just heard a very disturbing thing. The courthouse rumor is that they have tapes of John's telephone calls, which are very incriminating in nature and may effect his appeal. I don't know what I have to do. I have preached to him over and over. His mouth is what put him where he is right now . . . Please pass this on for the umpteenth time. I just can't live in the joint with him.

Perhaps to alleviate this threat, Zaffino conceived a new tactic after his transfer to Trumbull Correctional Institution a short time later. He began using another inmate number when he made his calls. What he didn't realize was that deputies figured out this ruse quickly, and passed the information on to Akron detectives.

So detectives listened, as Zaffino worried that Whitney had "thrown him under the bus," while the Georges suffered no repercussions for the homicide, and Judy claimed that Cindy's lawyer, Michael Bowler, advocated communication via letter "or pay phone to pay phone" because "he believes that our lines are being tapped, too." Judy also noted that she kept two file boxes of material related to her brother's plight at the store that she ran in New Jersey.

"You know me," she stated. "I don't throw anything away."

YET, AS FAR as police brass were concerned, the Zack case was over. Jeff's killer had been convicted, and the pressure was on Felber and Whiddon to shift their full attention to other cases. No one opposed an investigation into Cindy George's involvement in the murder. But few believed that the manpower spent interviewing inmates and listening to tapes would yield a conviction.

Then, in December 2003, Whiddon was forced to take time off for back surgery. Technically, he was being treated for an on-the-job injury, but not because he'd hurt himself in a car chase, or grappling on the ground with a perp. Rather, the City of Akron had mandated that he take a physical agility test. Because the lieutenant was a weightlifter, official charts listed him as being overweight. Among the tasks he was asked to perform to justify his employment was scaling a six-foot wall.

He accomplished the challenge quickly. But on the way down, he jammed his back. After several months of discomfort, he received a two-month medical sabbatical.

Although the bedridden lieutenant managed to listen to many of the intercepted phone calls, Felber was largely on his own. Fortunately, the staff at Trumbull—particularly Sharon Chilson and Antonio Cardona—were knowledgeable about the phone retrieval system, sending the detective CDs of the taped exchanges, rather than forcing him to drive two hours back and forth to the prison.

Meanwhile, a voluminous amount of evidence had been collected, and Felber realized that if the case was ever going to be presented to a grand jury in a comprehensible format, he'd need technical assistance. The outdated equipment supplied by the police department was virtually useless. So on his own, he spent $2,000 on a laptop, and turned it into a digitized evidence vault. The actual physical evidence remained stored in the property room at the police station.

The monitored calls between Zaffino and his sister suggested an elaborate scheme to pass the Georges' money from their attorneys, Robert Meeker and Michael Bowler, to Whitney. Allegedly, Whitney would then transfer the money to Judy, who'd use it to assist her brother.

The detectives and prosecutors wondered, could it possibly be true that the Georges were using their attorneys to pay for Zaffino's defense to keep the killer quiet about the *real* details of the case? It was hard to believe that Whitney, Bowler and Meeker were involved in this.

They were not only powerful, but highly regarded. Felber knew that no one would believe that the trio had been brokers in hush money—unless it was proven beyond a reasonable doubt. Recordings of Zaffino and his sister speculating, griping and fantasizing weren't enough. The money would have to be passed all the way to Zaffino for the assumption to have merit.

By the end of January, Judy indicated that money had arrived. Not willing to discuss the issue at police headquarters—a source of too many leaks in the past—Felber rushed over to Whiddon's home. The lieutenant was amazed, as well as angered. But he was also cautious. Maybe, he suggested, Felber misunderstood what had transpired. The detective agreed. As soon as Whiddon returned to work in February, he and Felber met with prosecutors.

Carroll promised to start listening to the calls himself before anyone jumped to conclusions.

IN THE MEANTIME, Zaffino received the crushing news that the Ninth District Court of Appeals had upheld his conviction. Wrote Judge Beth Whitmore:

> Additional evidence of a developing plan between Appellant and Cindy George came in the form of telephone records from relevant time periods. Those records establish that the two were in extensive contact both before and after the purchase of the motorcycle, before and after the murder, and while the Appellant was disposing of the motorcycle in Pennsylvania.

In other words, it seemed, the judge all but took it for granted that Cynthia had played a key role in the plot. But Zaffino vowed to appeal to a higher court—while Felber and Whiddon pledged to continue their pursuit of Cindy.

Several weeks later, Zaffino and his sister began discussing a $500 check that had apparently come from the Georges—via Meeker and Bowler, and then Whitney. The money seemed to quell Zaffino's urge to talk to the media.

Around this time, a third prosecutor joined the team. Phil Bogdanoff was a legal expert for the Summit County Prosecutor's Office. While Mike Carroll's specialty was presenting evidence to a group of civilians whose knowledge of legal issues generally came from television, Bogdanoff focused on judges. Carroll relied on personality and people skills to win a case. Bogdanoff concerned himself with legal precedents.

Carroll knew that if Cynthia were ever brought to trial, her team of attorneys would manipulate every legal loophole available. And if she was convicted, they would appeal. But if it could be proven that she'd helped Zaffino plan the homicide, she was guilty of conspiracy and complicity.

In April, after Carroll and Whiddon had heard most of the phone calls, Felber decided that it was time to deliver a multi-media presentation to the heads of both the police department and prosecutor's office. For months, gossip-mongers at the Akron P.D. had accused the detective of neglecting his chores with the Property Unit, and "milking" the Zack investigation. In some circles, his nickname had become the Reiter Guy—after the local Reiter Dairy. If he didn't convince this crowd that there was a strong case against Cynthia, he'd be ordered to halt the investigation and move on.

He'd invested too much of his life to accept that.

As an audience of ten—including Major Michael Madden, Captain Elizabeth Daugherty and Summit County Prosecutor Sherri Bevan Walsh—listened, Felber exhibited 250 slides in a PowerPoint display that incorporated photos, documents and edited versions of the phone calls. When questions arose, the detective handled them deftly. Then, a silence filled the room. The presentation was over. This was the moment that both Felber and Whiddon were awaiting: the affirmation that it was time to sign an arrest warrant for Cynthia George.

Instead, the bosses stood and began walking toward the door. Everyone complimented the professionalism of the presentation. There were mutterings that Cindy was obviously guilty. But no one made the call to arrest her.

Then, the spectators melted away.

Turning to Whiddon, Felber held up his arms. "Well? What do we do now?"

"How the hell should I know?" the lieutenant answered. "I guess we keep doing what we're doing."

TWELVE

BY THIS POINT, the national media had discovered the Cynthia George story, and video crews from Court TV and A&E found their way to Akron to interview key players. On camera, Mike Carroll appeared at ease, and for good reason. As a lawyer, he was well versed in slander law, and careful not to divulge anything that hadn't been mentioned in court. For detectives, the task was more daunting. Although members of the press may accuse the police of withholding information during interviews, the reality is that detectives—already working for pitiful salaries—are reluctant to utter the wrong comment, and lose their homes in a lawsuit.

The show eventually produced by A&E was titled *Who Whacked Zack?*, and included interviews with Felber and Whiddon. At one point during the taping, the pair was asked to walk down a hallway past a number of detectives. It was more like running the gauntlet in some military initiation. The difference was that no one beat the men with rods or spurs. Instead, they were hammered with ridicule.

"Nice haircut. Are you shooting a promo for That Seventies Show*?"*

"Felber, your fly is open."
"Don't worry. There isn't anything for anyone to see."

IN PRISON, ZAFFINO was growing increasingly impatient. He asked his sister Judy to contact Cynthia's attorney, Michael Bowler, and demand $50,000 in legal fees—to be divided in installments of $30,000 up front, and $20,000 later—and grumbled about exposing the Georges to the national media.

Almost every week, Felber and Whiddon met with prosecutors. They knew that Judy Diggelman had assured her brother that she'd held on to all materials related to the case. If that were true, it was possible that she had letters between Cynthia and John, as well as correspondence involving the transfer of money from the Georges to Zaffino. That was enough to order a search warrant in Ohio. The problem was that Judy lived in New Jersey. It took Bogdanoff several weeks to work with the Middlesex County Prosecutor's Office in the Garden State, and obtain warrants for Judy's home and business. The next step was a road trip to New Jersey to execute the warrants.

Plane fare was out of the question. Instead, the day before the raid, a caravan of cars departed from Akron for the eight-hour journey.

Felber and Whiddon were together again—only this time the lieutenant's radio was broken. "Damn," Felber taunted, "I was really starting to like country music."

After some confusion over New Jersey's "jug handle" system—cars exit on the right and round a curve to reach the opposite side of the highway—the two ended up sharing a room at a roadside motel. But the lieutenant's snoring was so loud that Felber began repacking his bags.

Whiddon snapped out of his slumber. "Where are you going?" he asked.

"I'm getting my own room."

"Why? The city won't reimburse you for it."

Feigning emotional distress, Felber responded, "Because you no longer fulfill my needs, and I think it's time we went our separate ways."

"What?" Whiddon was completely befuddled.

Felber explained that the snoring was keeping him awake. Whiddon apologized, and promised to wait until Felber fell asleep. But the detective wanted his rest, and arranged to meet the lieutenant in the parking lot in the morning.

For weeks, Whiddon found himself apologizing for his snoring.

"It's no big deal," Felber answered. "It's not something you can control anyway." But he always made a point of emphasizing the fact that he'd paid 80 dollars out of his own pocket for a separate room.

Whiddon would offer to pay half the cost. Felber rejected the overture. It was worth the price to make the lieutenant feel guilty—and keep him in the dark about the fact that Felber snored, as well.

ON THE MORNING of July 15, 2004, while Judy Diggelman and her husband, Chris, were busy at their company, CJ's Home Decor & Fireplaces, LLC—a business that relied largely on the Internet to sell stone mantels, vent-free stoves, chimney pipes and other fireplace items—in the town of Hillsborough, detectives and prosecutors from New Jersey and Ohio presented their search warrants to a local judge, who granted them permission to raid the office, as well as the Diggelmans' house in New Brunswick.

No one was home at the Diggelman residence. Police later maintained that the house already looked like it had been raided; dishes were piled in the sink, and clothes were strewn about. Legally, the officers could search anywhere they wished for any piece of paper associated with the case. The detectives only discovered a handful of documents, as well as a box containing files related to Zaffino's defense.

In the office, Chris Diggelman—a short, thin man who spoke with a foreign accent—was respectful to the investigators. He claimed to know little about the machinations between his wife, her brother and the Georges, other than what Judy had told him. Judy, on the other hand, recognized Felber and Whiddon from court, and blamed them for locking up her brother.

As police scoured the office, they found a box of files actually marked with John and Cynthia's names, and asked Judy if she had other material related to the case.

She shook her head from side to side.

Detectives continued searching, and unearthed another carton of files.

"Which computer do you use to send e-mails?" Felber questioned.

Judy pointed at one of three computers in the main office. "So all your correspondence with Larry Whitney's on here?" said Felber.

Judy nodded. But as the detective probed, he discovered a number of e-mails to the attorney on other computers, as well. "What about these?" he asked.

"I forgot about them," Judy responded.

"Why do you and John expect the Georges to give you money?"

"I don't know, but I haven't gotten any from them."

"What about the five hundred dollars Larry Whitney sent you?"

Judy acted as though she didn't understand the question.

"The five-hundred-dollar personal check you just got?"

Judy claimed that the lawyer had sent the money because he was "a nice guy." She added that she'd never received any payments from Cynthia's attorney, Mike Bowler.

On the one hand, Felber felt sorry for Judy, since he believed that she was backed into a corner—her brother was doing time for murder, and he'd placed her in charge of finding an angle to set him free. But after about an hour in the office, the detective lost his patience over what he perceived as the woman's hostility and lack of truthfulness. At one point, Felber raised his voice, inducing Judy to rush over to Whiddon, grasp his tie with both hands and implore, "I'm not lying. I'm not lying."

What Judy didn't realize was that she was choking the lieutenant. As Felber watched Whiddon attempt to detach himself from the woman, the detective almost burst out laughing.

Judy then turned to the local police who'd accompanied the Akron group to the office. "Make them stop," she begged.

"All you need to do is start telling the truth," an officer answered.

Halfway through the search, the Diggelmans' office worker approached Felber, and asked if she could leave. When he granted her permission, she turned to Chris and quit.

"I want you to know that I think that you're just a pawn in this conspiracy," Felber told Judy. "And if you work with us, we can keep you out of trouble."

"How do you want me to work with you?"

"You could wear a wire when you talk to Whitney and Bowler."

Judy said that she was too scared to do something like that. "But I want to speak to my attorney," she added.

"I wish you would," Felber replied, sincerely believing that it would expedite the search to have a lawyer present, acting as a liaison between Judy and the police. The team had also discussed whether Judy could be charged with conspiracy. Although Carroll and Bogdanoff eventually shied away from pursuing this avenue, an attorney could have enlightened Judy to her predicament—and encouraged her to cooperate.

"What's your lawyer's name?" Felber said.

"I don't have one," she admitted.

Felber hoisted up the local yellow pages and placed it in front of the woman. "Just make sure it's someone who doesn't have any connection to this case—or to Akron."

Judy declined the offer, while her husband watched the police closely. "I know you have to take the computers," Chris said, "but this could really hurt our business."

He pointed out one computer that was particularly important to the operation.

"I'm going to do what I can to get this back to you quickly," Felber promised.

While still at the scene, he contacted the nearby Somerset County Prosecutor's Office, and spoke to their computer forensics expert, Andy Lippert, about the matter. After the business' eight computers were confiscated, Felber and Lippert examined the hard drives until 2 AM, copying three. Felber was amazed by the hardware at Lippert's disposal. At Akron police headquarters, the computer forensics division consisted of one highly qualified self-taught expert laboring in a 14-by-12-foot compartment. The Somerset County prosecutors had an entire floor devoted to computer forensics.

The next day, the computers were returned. Five of the hard drives were missing; police brought these back to Akron for analysis. However, the desktop that Chris Diggelman claimed was crucial to his business was completely intact.

Still, the Diggelmans eventually sued the city and Felber, Whiddon and Detective Russ McFarland, insisting that the search was groundless. Judy claimed that investigators had trashed her home, ruined her business and called her names. The city's law department affirmed that the detectives had done nothing wrong—but agreed to settle the lawsuit for $12,000 anyway. The rationale: it would cost more than $12,000 for the city to defend itself. Felber and Whiddon were appalled, but not surprised.

IT TOOK WEEKS to sift through the documents, e-mails and other correspondence found during the search. In a letter to his sister Laura, Zaffino mentioned the Bible that Cynthia had sent him, and wrote about entering a program that would allow him to keep a dog in his cell. The next part of the letter became a vital piece of evidence that prosecutors would use against Cindy. It included instructions for Laura to phone Larry Whitney. Word for word, Zaffino outlined exactly what he expected his sister to communicate to the lawyer:

> Larry, my friend and I had an agreement that if anything happened to me, they would do whatever it takes to set me free. Now, I did exactly what I said I would do. And now, I need my friend to do the same.

This was precisely what detectives wanted to find: written corroboration of Cynthia's involvement in the Zack slaying.

A short time later, John wrote a letter to Judy. After complaining that Laura wasn't doing enough to save him, Zaffino lamented:

> It's like now I'm in prison nobody has time for me anymore. My life isn't over yet. I still have a chance of coming home.
>
> . . . Judy, I need you to <u>take control</u> of <u>everything</u> (<u>please</u>). The longer we wait the less the media will want the story, and I think we may be able to use them to help me . . . If Larry [*Whitney*] wont [*sic*] act quickly then you can call you know who and explain what we need to do.
>
> . . . And they need to know the longer I sit here with nothing being done the madder I get, and before long, the shit is going to hit the fan!

I can still make a call and get a deal. It may be for 15 or 18 years, but it's better than 23 to life.

Within a week, John sent Judy another letter. However, he also included a message for Cynthia George. On April 14, 2003, Judy attached her own typewritten note to her brother's letter to Cindy:

I have refrained from writing to you hoping things would turn out differently for my brother. However, since John is still not home, I find that I need your help. It took a couple of days after the guilty verdict for my brother to realize that he was indeed stranded. . . . It is amazing the things that I have learned about the twisted relationship between the two of you. You had him so convinced that you were a Christian and a good, kind, loving person. He was so infatuated with you that I didn't have the heart to tell him that true Christians don't cheat on their husbands and families and live lives based on lies . . . I find it hard to believe that you would let this happen to John when you have the power and the financial means to help him. . . . I don't care what you have to do, but you must get additional lawyers . . . You and your family have the means to take care of this. I, on the other hand, have the media asking for interviews and stories. The more John talks to me the more I have to tell. . . . I will do what I need to do at this point.

John's accompanying letter to Cynthia left little doubt in the detectives' minds that she was directly involved in plotting Jeff Zack's homicide:

What are you going to do now? You said that you would not leave me here. I could have knocked 20 years off my sentence if I would implicate you.

I stuck by you, now I have lost my life. I will be 60

years old when I'll be up for parol [*sic*], and I may not get out then. [Zaffino's son] Alexander will be 36 at that time.

Your lawyers did not help me. Now I <u>need</u> some new lawyers to fight for my life . . . if you are worried about your business—<u>sell it</u>—and your house, if that's what it takes to get me out.

At <u>any cost</u> you need to help me now.

. . . Show me I have not went [*sic*] through this hell in vain. I would rather be dead than to live like this.

You need to tell your husband what I need and that he needs to help me <u>now</u>.

. . . You need to help me, I need some big lawyers and it will cost big money. Please do whatever it takes to free me.

Zaffino instructed Cynthia to send all future correspondence through Judy. As an apparent conciliatory gesture, he scribbled a crude cross at the bottom of the letter, next to the words, "May the Lord be with you and guide you."

CINDY'S RESPONSE HAD a decidedly religious theme as well, beginning with the inscription "Corinthians 13:1–13" ("And now abideth faith, hope, charity, these three;" the passage ends, "but the greatest of these *is* charity."):

There will never come a day that I shall perceive you as anything other than you are. That is, the strongest man I have ever known. No instance or person will ever change that image . . . You have to understand that if you really dig deep, Jesus will take your hand.

. . . I know how sorrowful you are and my heart aches every day . . . My day starts by going to church <u>every</u> morning and a mass is offered for you, your strength and safety.

. . . Yes, the storm is quite great and devastating, but plant your feet and dig. The spirit of God is within you

now, and always with me. His power is great, we will walk
into the storm with one who is more powerful than all.
    . . . We must, though, listen to counsel. God is also
working through them, too. Pray for their wisdom. We
cannot make one mistake.

To the detectives, there was nothing subtle about this
message. Cynthia appeared to be telling Zaffino to keep
quiet, and trust the attorneys to come up with a solution. If
they couldn't find one, it seemed that Cindy was implying,
God would eventually resolve the problem.

"Lastly," Cynthia continued,

I feel so badly that I cannot comfort Judy . . . She is in my
prayers daily . . . I look forward to the day I can meet her.

Here, Cindy appeared to be trying to pacify John as
well as his sister—the same sister who'd apparently contemplated exposing the couple's surreptitious exchanges
to the media.

On another piece of stationery—this one decorated
with angels—detectives discovered a second letter that
Cynthia had written to John. It included the following
postscript—an indication, police believed, of the role
Zaffino had played in neutralizing the quandary known as
Jeff Zack:

You are the eyes when I cannot see
You are the voice that's sent through me
You are the strength in the weakness . . . you are . . .

Again, the tone was pious. Cynthia wrote about receiving "a sign," and praying to St. Jude and St. Theresa for
John's prayers to be answered. "I miss all your stubborn
bullheaded, pigheaded ways," she said. "But most of all I
miss you." She drew a sad face next to these words.

And when you say you weep at never seeing me again, think again. You will always see me again, come what may.

You're stuck with the most gentle, levelheaded, patient, funloving, wonderful, not to mention <u>humble</u> person in the whole wide world.

And I on the other hand are [*sic*] stuck with the most obstinent [*sic*], cantankerous, stubborn, strongest person I've ever met.

She drew a smiley face nearby.

And you're all that and much more. So don't ever waste your tears on that subject.

. . . Remember, when confronted, always think about how Jesus would handle a comeback. His points were made very clear, and might I ad [*sic*], very clever. So study his words.

. . . You're very right that nothing has really changed, only that you don't have to bear to look at this terrible grotesque face of mine.

She drew an ugly face to add emphasis to the joke.

Johnie, Johnie, Johnie, Johnie, I so worry about you . . . We all love you and need you to come home safely.

. . . As you can see, I'm getting sloppy now. It's 12:30 a.m. Usually, I blow your candle out at 11:30 and take my cross to bed and say my prayers.

Sometimes I leave the candle lit and watch the shadows dance on the ceiling and wonder your thoughts.

. . . Remember what I used to say "It's like trying to put the ocean in a glass." It's quite draining. And I've only touched the surface. Please, take care of yourself. I will leave you in God's hands trusting in Him always.

I'll say Goodnight and thank you again.

Too da loo . . . I miss you terribly.
Sparky.

ALTHOUGH THE GEORGES failed to provide Zaffino with Johnnie Cochran or F. Lee Bailey, it appeared that Mike Bowler was now involved with his appeal. Bowler might not have had national name recognition, but he had represented Cindy George. In Zaffino's mind, detectives surmised, any lawyer good enough for Cynthia was good enough for him.

The detective felt this was a clear conflict of interest for Bowler—and possibly a breach of law. But Carroll and Gessner did not subscribe to this logic. Neither prosecutor believed that Whitney or Bowler would knowingly take part in a cover-up. And hiring an attorney, Carroll said, was a lot different from passing money. Plus, no one was sure whether Bowler was actually involved in the appeal.

Either way, the complexion of the investigation now shifted—from an intricate case involving the two lovers working in tandem to kill Jeff Zack, to a complicated plot that included a trio of prominent lawyers furtively passing money.

Even the prosecutors were awed. Carroll and Bogdanoff prosecuted what were essentially blue-collar crimes: rapes, homicides, robberies, assaults. White-collar felonies featuring elaborate money trails seemed out of their realm.

Detectives suggested that Carroll talk to the lawyers about the suspected money transfers, without revealing that police were also investigating. Carroll was not willing to deceive his colleagues. So on August 5, Whitney was invited to Akron police headquarters to be questioned by Whiddon and Felber.

By this time, the lawyer understood the detectives' motives; Judy had told him that she'd been asked to record her conversations with the attorneys. He also knew that the detectives were interested in discussing the $500 check that he'd sent to her. Nonetheless, he still agreed to an interview.

Because of attorney-client privilege, Whitney said that he was unable to answer many of the questions. He did say that Bowler was not representing Zaffino, but explained that it was possible for two co-defendants to have their attorneys work in tandem.

And, yes, he confirmed, he had sent Judy Diggelman the $500. It seemed that after Zaffino's conviction, Zack's widow had filed a claim with the state attorney general's office for victims' assistance, hoping to garnish whatever John received in the future. Whitney claimed that he'd mailed Judy the check so she could dole out commissary money to her brother in small increments.

When Felber insinuated that the source of the money may have come from elsewhere, Whitney insisted otherwise, a position consistent with Judy's assertion that the lawyer had mailed the money because he was a "nice guy." Taking a more direct approach, the detective then asked Whitney if he'd been channeling money from Bowler. The attorney appeared insulted, maintaining that he'd enjoyed a long, reputable career in the legal profession, and would never resort to acting as a conduit for money. Nor, he added, would a man like Mike Bowler.

Still, when the lawyer left, both Whiddon and Felber had an uneasy feeling. Both detectives simply couldn't help but assume that the man known as perhaps the most honest attorney in Akron was being less than truthful. When they expressed these sentiments to Mike Carroll, he remained unwilling to change his opinion about Whitney. The only way to learn the facts, the team determined, was to call in outside assistance to help them follow the money.

During the Zaffino investigation, FBI Agent Roger Charnesky had provided considerable support, along with the United States Postal Service and Ohio Department of Public Safety. This time, the team needed advice on which documents to subpoena, and the best way to review those records.

They decided to call the IRS.

As before, Felber believed that secrecy and confidentiality were imperative, and kept details about the continuing investigation from everyone but Whiddon. Needless to say, this behavior raised the suspicions of his other supervisors. They constantly asked him what he was doing and where he was going. His brief answers amplified their ire.

In the fall of 2004, a frequent felon—and sometime source for the Akron Police Department—phoned Felber from jail to warn about an upcoming truck hijacking. Felber explained that he did not have the authority to reduce the informant's sentence. Nonetheless, the detective was willing to notify the FBI about the scheme—as well as the man's cooperation.

Allegedly, the informant had learned that an inmate who'd once worked at a warehouse was developing a plan to rob several trucks from the company, and at least one Russian mob member was participating. The warehouse was outside of Akron, though—and outside of Felber's jurisdiction. The detective had had little contact with Captain Daugherty since she'd interrupted his interrogation of Zaffino. Now, however, Felber hoped to heal the relationship by reaching out to the captain. Together, they could avert a half-million-dollar heist.

Daugherty seemed interested, and told Felber to call the FBI. He did. Everyone agreed that more was needed than a jailhouse stoolie's allegations. So Felber continued communicating with the informant. Because the department had yet to requisition a cell phone to the detective, Felber used his own.

One night, the man called while Felber was off-duty, and demanded to see him immediately at the Summit County Jail. When the detective arrived, the informant showed him a hand-drawn map of the warehouse, its surrounding fence, guard house and nearby streets. The places where trucks were loaded were also marked. The informant named the inmate involved in the plot, along with a conspirator who worked at the plant. The trucks' color coding, the warehouse security schedule and other intangibles were also mentioned.

Several hours after he left the jail, the informant phoned again. Could Felber pose as a buyer for the stolen merchandise? The detective had no idea how to play this role, but assumed that he could either learn quickly, or enlist the FBI's assistance. But as these thoughts were running through the detective's mind, the informant handed the phone to a fellow inmate. Immediately, the man began discussing how the crime was going to be committed.

Felber hung up, believing that the robbery would not occur for several weeks—allowing investigators ample time to foil the scheme. Still, as soon as he arrived at work the next day, Felber briefed the captain on the exchanges, even showing her the map. Daugherty asked Lieutenant Ken Ball to join the consultation, then ordered Felber to leave the room.

Twenty minutes later, Lieutenant Whiddon and Sergeant Terry Hudnall marched toward the captain's office, casting curious glances at Felber along the way. Another twenty minutes passed before the pair exited with Lieutenant Ball, and alerted Felber that the captain wished to see him again.

Clear orders were now issued to the detective. He was not to talk to the informant any longer, nor work on the case. His involvement would end that morning. He was instructed to call the local police department, convey the information to them and let them take over.

Felber followed the instructions—learning later that the information he'd received from the informant was accurate. After calling, he ambled into the Crimes Against Persons Unit. Whiddon and Hudnall laughed, as they told Felber that the captain thought he should be placed under arrest for facilitating a crime.

"How did I facilitate a crime?" Felber asked.

Apparently, the captain believed that Felber had broken the law by agreeing to purchase the stolen inventory. Whiddon, Hudnall and Ball had taken great pains to explain to their boss that Felber's actions could be characterized as simple police work. After all, narcotics detectives set up buys and acted as criminals on a daily basis. Applying the captain's standard, the entire narcotics division would have to be detained before Felber was arrested.

THIRTEEN

ABOUT A MONTH after the murder, while suspicions largely centered around Ed George, Jeff Zack's mother Elayne was walking across a quiet golf course near her home, filtering small details about the case through her mind.

"I had a revelation," she said. "All of the sudden, it just came to me that it wasn't Ed George. If Ed George had murdered my son, no one would have ever known or found out. Ed George was too slick.

"I guess it was mother's intuition, but I talked to some friends, and they agreed with me. Yes, it was definitely Cindy."

Since the Zaffino conviction, Elayne made it a point to phone Lieutenant Whiddon about once a month, asking when police planned to arrest Cynthia George. Whiddon never gave her a direct answer, nor revealed what police were uncovering. He simply told Elayne that detectives continued to explore the possibility that Zaffino had a co-conspirator.

Elayne would hang up, a combination of anger and frustration welling inside her. But at police headquarters, events were in motion that would soon make her very happy.

• • •

FOR MONTHS, MIKE Carroll was hesitant to approve a warrant for Cynthia's arrest, even as Felber and Whiddon tried lobbying him to their side. Under other circumstances, jailhouse phone calls would have been considered hearsay, and inadmissible in court. But in conspiracy cases, conversations between co-conspirators could be introduced—if a judge ruled in favor of the prosecution. It seemed to be a risk worth taking. After reviewing the calls, as well as evidence confiscated from Judy's property, both Carroll and Bogdanoff agreed that they had a very strong case.

The team needed time to organize itself for a trial. But with Thanksgiving and Christmas looming, there was a shortage of working days on the calendar. The team opted not to arrest Cindy until January.

In the interim, they'd continue following the money trail.

With the help of the IRS, investigators discovered that, on January 15, 2003—a month before Zaffino's trial had begun—Ed George had written a $5,000 check to attorneys Robert Meeker and Michael Bowler. On January 31, Meeker and Bowler sent another $5,000 check to Zaffino's lawyer, Larry Whitney. The pattern was repeated later in the year when, on July 30, the Georges paid Meeker and Bowler $10,000, the same amount the pair sent Whitney on August 26.

Whitney and Bowler were given the opportunity to defend themselves in front of the grand jury investigating Cynthia on January 7, 2005. The panel learned little, as both invoked attorney-client privilege. After the hearing, the decision was made to charge Cindy with conspiracy to commit aggravated murder, and complicity to commit aggravated murder.

Felber and Whiddon couldn't grasp the difference between the two charges. The variants were so subtle, they seemed almost meaningless. But prosecutors wanted to cover their bases. The conspiracy charge related to Cindy's purported involvement in luring Zack to the park on May 8, 2001. To prove complicity, prosecutors would have to show that she either "solicited or procured" Zaffino to murder Jeff Zack a month later.

ON JANUARY 10, the arrest warrant was officially issued. Whiddon contacted the Northern Ohio Violent Fugitive Task Force for assistance. Because Cynthia lived outside the city, it was difficult for the Akron Police Department to set up surveillance of their target. For the task force, this type of operation was routine.

Still, there were problems. It was difficult stationing a detective outside the Georges' home, since they lived on a two-lane country road devoid of trees. As a result, a task force member had to sit on the house by illegally parking next to a ditch in the open. It was in no way inconspicuous.

As this was transpiring, Whiddon and Felber covertly prepared the arrest warrant. It was next to impossible. Whenever anyone in local law enforcement spotted the duo, it was understood that they were working on Cynthia's impending arrest. And once the paperwork was completed, the pair had to have the warrant activated in the clerk's office—a unit staffed by civilians with no particular penchant for secrecy.

Nonetheless, the wheels were in motion. At 3 PM, task force members saw Cindy walking into the Tangier, and phoned Felber.

"Should we arrest her now?" one of the members asked.

Felber and Whiddon discussed this, and decided that the timing was wrong. If Cynthia was arrested in front of her husband, he might warn her not to speak to the police. Of course, she'd probably been counseled to remain silent. But detectives hoped that the trauma of being arrested would loosen her resolve.

When Whiddon and Felber left work at 4 PM, they believed that the task force had called it a day. But members actually continued watching Cynthia and, in the early evening, saw her pull away from the Georges' home with two of her teenage daughters. Police followed her to the Bath & Body Works store in the West Market shopping plaza in Bath Township. Whiddon was called, and authorized the arrest.

If police didn't move now, the lieutenant feared, she might leave town.

The task force approached Cynthia and informed her that she was under arrest. "I think her reaction is what you'd expect," her lawyer, Michael Bowler, would later tell reporters. "She's deeply disappointed. But at the same time, it's not something she didn't feel like could happen someday.

"She knew that the investigation has been ongoing. It's been no secret that's the situation. So she was prepared . . . It could have happened any time, and it did."

She offered no resistance, as she was placed in handcuffs, good naturedly warning that she could probably free herself because she was "hyper-jointed." The task force phoned Ed to pick up the children. But he was busy in the restaurant, and couldn't drive out to the shopping center.

A nanny retrieved the children instead.

WHEN CYNTHIA ARRIVED at the station, around 8 PM, Whiddon and Felber were waiting for her. Anticipating the arrest, a nervous Felber hadn't slept in close to thirty-six hours. But now, his adrenaline was pumping. This would probably be his only chance to talk to Cindy George.

Both men entered her cell, where a now-frail-looking Cynthia sat on a metallic chair attached to a small steel table. She was facing life in prison, and the notion of that seemed to harden her pleasant features. Felber took a seat on the other side of the table, while Whiddon carried in a chair, and situated himself in a spot where both could see him.

Felber introduced himself: "I think we've all seen the

stories about you in the media, and they weren't very flattering. I imagine that must have been very hard for you, and we know you're not the person we've read about in the papers. But since we never had a chance to talk to you before, we could never tell the media that. Now, that can change. This is your opportunity to tell us your side of the story, let everybody know the truth. It's your last chance."

He read her the Miranda warning. "Having these rights in mind, do you wish to talk to us now?"

"I want to, but my attorneys told me not to."

"Do you want to talk to us?" Felber repeated.

"Not without my attorneys being present."

That was it. She'd been well coached. The interview was over.

WITH THE MEDIA still unaware of Cynthia's arrest, she was transported to the Summit County Jail with little fanfare. Now, as promised, Whiddon picked up the phone and dialed the numbers for Jeff Zack's mother and widow.

Both were tearful, relieved and grateful to police. "I'm thrilled," Jeff's mother Elayne said when a reporter finally reached her. "I'm elated. She had so much goddamn nerve to do it and to think she'd get away with it."

Each woman had more questions than Whiddon could answer. But he assured them that he'd provide more details in the days to come.

By the next morning, the press had been informed about the arrest and swarmed the courthouse for Cindy's arraignment. Interestingly, the star of the day was actually still at the Summit County Jail, clad in an orange jump suit, staring into the camera via a video hookup, as prosecutors argued for a $10 million cash bond. Bowler claimed that the figure was excessive. Cynthia had been a suspect almost from the day that Zack was murdered, the lawyer said. Yet she'd never been a flight risk.

Nonetheless, Common Pleas Judge Mary Spicer sided

with the prosecutors. Cynthia would remain in jail, as her legal team attempted to lower the bond. After telling the press that he believed that the amount was "unnecessarily high," Bowler responded to a question about the homicide.

"I'm not going to tell you exactly what she said about it, but she denies her guilt, just as she has from the start. She has always said she had no part in this, and will continue to say that."

Two days later, Cynthia's team managed to have her bond reduced to $2 million, just as Larry Whitney had done for John Zaffino. The difference was that Zaffino's relatives were unable to bail him out of jail. It cost Ed George $200,000 to take his wife home. Although she said nothing during the hearing, there was a glimmer of hopefulness in Cindy's eyes as she smiled at her husband and daughter in the courtroom. Until her trial, she'd be restricted to Summit, Stark and Medina Counties, and required to report to county pre-trial release officials every week.

NO ONE ON the team was shocked when Ed bailed out his spouse. But since the entire crime seemed to center around her infidelity, the question was "Why?" Some surmised that he'd played a role in the hit. Others theorized that he couldn't chance a bitter Cynthia turning on him and his family, revealing secrets about their business dealings that they didn't want authorities to know. But this was all pure speculation.

What bothered detectives the most was the way that a person of Zaffino's socio-economic status was treated by the courts, as opposed to someone with the means at Cindy's disposal. How could a judge possibly impose the exact same bond? Some legal experts argued that the bond was fair because both parties received the same amount. But what about the ability to pay? Strangely, Felber and Whiddon found themselves relating to Zaffino, the former truck driver forced to endure indignities an affluent socialite could avoid.

Because of the wealth disparity, neither detective was confident that the system would work for them. No matter how organized the evidence, they believed that Cindy's well-funded attorneys would discover a fissure in the process. Both Mike Carroll and Phil Bogdanoff contended that the detectives' attitude was overly pessimistic. Nonetheless, they vowed to seal any gap that they found.

The two contemplated having Meeker and Bowler removed from the case. It was an uncomfortable situation. These were the prosecutors' peers. Bowler was a former Summit County Prosecutor. Mike Carroll and Robert Meeker had both graduated from the same high school. Carroll had even visited the Meeker home to play basketball with the defense attorney's sister. Yet, the prosecutors believed that if the pair remained on the case, Cynthia could later appeal her conviction, maintaining that the two were more concerned with protecting themselves from cash-funneling charges than defending her interests.

On January 31, prosecutors filed a motion to remove Meeker and Bowler, characterizing them as witnesses to the conspiracy between Cynthia and Zaffino. As evidence, three separate checks—for $10,000, $5,000 and $500—were mentioned. Bowler had allegedly passed the money to Larry Whitney, prosecutors said, to help with Zaffino's appeal, and buy his silence.

If that was a strategy, it had been working.

But Bowler countered that his client had assisted Zaffino because she hoped to be exonerated by his acquittal. If Zaffino went free, the lawyer elaborated, prosecutors would have no foundation to charge George.

Bowler characterized their "joint defense agreement" as a "common legal strategy" utilized when two or more people were suspected of the same crime. "To me [the hush money claim] is ludicrous," Bowler told the *Akron Beacon Journal*'s Phil Trexler. "Their whole theory is nonsense."

Whitney maintained "our clients' defenses were joined . . . they were friendly defendants." Under the pact, the suspects promised to share expenses, as well as information. Whitney would provide data concerning evidence— material available to Zaffino, but not Cynthia. In turn, Meeker and Bowler offered constructive criticism of Whitney's performance at his client's trial.

Still, prosecutors wondered why there'd never been a written agreement between the two parties. When Carroll queried several defense attorneys he knew, it was difficult finding anyone who'd worked a case under this type of arrangement. And Judy Diggelman herself told the press that she'd never heard of the joint defense pact, pointing out that she and her father had doled out $15,000 for her brother's defense.

"Someone got their money's worth," she scoffed. "But it wasn't me or John."

MEANWHILE, ZACK'S WIDOW Bonnie attacked her late husband's purported assailants from another flank. On March 12, 2005, she and her son Brian filed a lawsuit against Ed and Cynthia George and John Zaffino, alleging that the three had conspired to kill Jeff. The suit also alleged that, four months after John's conviction, the Georges had attempted to shield themselves from this type of action by moving $2 million in property into a privately held trust. Detectives wished Bonnie luck, assured that, even if Cynthia triumphed in criminal court, Zack's family had a shot at justice.

As of this writing, the lawsuit was still pending.

WITH SEVEN MONTHS to prepare for the trial, the team tried telegraphing their adversaries' defenses. One of the scenarios they envisioned was the "blackmail" argument.

What if Cynthia's attorneys claimed that Zaffino was try-ing to shake down the Georges by lying about his lover's role in the homicide? That would have explained some of the language used in the letters and phone calls. But wouldn't these prominent defense attorneys have gone to the authorities with this information? After all, an investi-gation might well have vindicated Cindy.

Cynthia had recently hired two Cleveland lawyers to complement her defense team, Gerald Gold and John Pyle. Both had national reputations and powerful credentials. A fifth attorney, Patricia Millhoff, an associate professor at The University of Akron, would be added later on.

"This trial's her whole life, her whole family," Robert Meeker said. "It's huge for her, her husband and her chil-dren."

Because of this, Bowler claimed, Cindy was willing to testify in her defense.

TECHNICALLY, PREPARATION FOR the Cynthia George case should have been easier than the Zaffino trial. After all, 75 percent of the evidence was going to be identical. But the team soon realized that the data was scattered between the courthouse, the prosecutor's office and the police station. Much of the evidence had been haphazardly boxed, and not labeled.

During the first trial, the phone records had been blown up and glued to plasterboard. Although the strategy had worked, Felber was concerned that the documents looked bland, and wanted to ensure that jurors kept their minds on the evidence. As a result, the prosecutor's office agreed to hire an art director—recommended by Felber's friend from the ad agency where he'd once worked—to create mounted, enlarged phone records for the courtroom.

Tension levels had been high before Zaffino's trial, but the stakes seemed greater now—and the competition more formidable. An extravagant amount of time was spent re-examining the fine legal details that could form the foundation for an appeal. Every witness from the Zaffino trial had to be called in and re-interviewed.

Since many contend that, the evidence notwithstanding, the wrong jury can doom a case, Carroll wavered back and forth over hiring an expert on jury selection. Ultimately, he concluded that few of these specialists shared his experiences of picking thousands of jurors over a span of some twenty years, and resolved to trust his own instincts.

Common Pleas Judge Patricia Cosgrove requested that 100 potential jurors be screened, then ultimately whittled down to a panel of twelve and four alternates by the trial date. Dressed in a cream-colored blouse, burgundy sweater and gray skirt, Cynthia attended jury selection, appearing relaxed, as candidates were questioned about their television viewing habits—did they favor news magazine shows with a tabloid flavor?—and whether they or someone close to them had practiced infidelity, or been a victim of domestic violence. The 51-year-old defendant held a book, *Prayers and Promises for Women*, and failed to register a noticeable reaction when Cosgrove ruled on a pre-trial motion to suppress that Zaffino's phone calls with his sisters could be introduced into evidence.

The defense also asked the judge to bar testimony from Zaffino's fellow inmates—described by Cynthia's attorney Gerald Gold as "unreliable," "not trustworthy" and "self-serving." Although Cosgrove ruled in favor of the prosecution, it was a moot point. One inmate had left the penitentiary, but soon resumed his life of drinking and stealing. Felber had done his best to keep in touch with the man. But by the time of the trial, the ex-con had found his way to West Virginia, where he was hiding from police.

The other jailmates had also left prison for civilian life. When one was re-arrested for a weapons charge, and faced 7 more years behind bars, prosecutors were willing to cut a deal. The charges would be dropped if the man repeated Zaffino's story about collaborating with Cindy to kill Zack in the park.

A month before the trial, the former prisoner reiterated the tale for Felber and Whiddon. They were satisfied—until he told them that he would never testify against another former inmate. That was what snitches did—and he was no rat.

"What about our agreement?" Felber asked.

"What agreement? I never made no agreement with you."

The detectives were certain that they had the upper hand. If the man wasn't going to live up to his end of the deal, they'd re-arrest him on the weapons charge. Carroll told the pair that this wasn't possible. The charge had already been dismissed, and the process couldn't be reversed.

Another blow seemed to come when the defense handed the prosecution its list of witnesses. More than 100 names were printed—without phone numbers or addresses. After the initial shock—and a good deal of cursing—the prosecution team began reviewing the list. They weren't familiar with many of the names, and couldn't figure out their relationship to the case. Other names belonged to wealthy and powerful local citizens. Carroll spotted a person on the list whom he knew personally.

The detectives concluded that the whole thing was a trick; it appeared that the defense wanted to waste the prosecution's resources by forcing the team to hunt down and interview people with little relevance to the case. This infuriated Felber and Whiddon, since they were already above their heads in work. To verify the suspicions, Carroll phoned the one familiar name on the list, and asked the man when he planned to testify at Cynthia's trial.

As it turned out, he barely knew the Georges, and had never been contacted by any of the defense lawyers. "And if I had been, I would have refused," the man continued. "I have to tell you—I'm not very happy that someone put my name on a witness list."

Carroll had the confirmation that he needed, and wanted to toss the list aside and move on. But Felber and Whiddon were angry about being played, and persuaded the prosecutors to show the list to Judge Cosgrove, and order the defense to provide addresses and phone numbers. Although the work would be delegated to clerks in the various law firms, it would still take time.

When the abridged list was handed over to prosecutors, there were only five people on the register. The team was familiar with every name except one: Dr. Alan Kurzweil, a therapist who'd counseled Cynthia in 2001. Seven pages of notes were also included.

The visits had begun in February, when Cindy told Kurzweil about the way she'd always felt rejected by Ed's family. In time, she added, her bond with her husband felt more like one between a father and daughter than a husband and wife. Because of this and other factors, she'd developed a relationship with a friend, who'd shown her kindness and support. After a while, though, this person also disappointed her, stealing and becoming verbally and physically abusive.

In his notes, Kurzweil wrote that Cynthia had to do something immediately about the relationship. The friend appeared to have two personalities: one charming, the other vicious and controlling. Cindy was the object of his obsession. Whenever she tried to distance herself, he became even more frightening.

A week later, Cynthia said that she'd felt so helpless after the last session that she realized that she could not end the relationship right away. This would have to become a long-term goal. Kurzweil suggested places where Cindy might find support, like a victims' assistance or church group.

Three days later, she was back in the therapist's office, discussing what she categorized as her underprivileged upbringing. It took a great deal of effort, she stated, to work her way into a position where she could meet people of higher social standing.

Wrote Kurzweil, "Now patient's greatest fear is that her husband learns of her infidelity, he divorces her, she loses her credit, she'd be financially destitute."

Two days later, Cynthia complained that her friend was constantly calling her. His behavior was becoming more bizarre, and she worried about him taking out a contract on her if she severed ties. Kurzweil recommended that she call the police.

The last of the seven sessions took place on March 3. Cynthia appeared to be in better spirits. She had come up with a number of solutions for breaking the link to this menacing companion: obtaining a restraining order, hiring a bodyguard, procuring photos of the man in a compromising situation.

The therapist replied that he supported the first two ideas.

Felber read the observations carefully. The prosecutors were planning to argue that Zack's murder had come about after his romance with Cynthia had soured. Now, the defense was going to make the point for them. Kurzweil's notes, as much as anything else, demonstrated the motive behind the killing.

PRIOR TO JURY selection, there were many lively discussions about the kinds of people who would determine Cynthia's fate. Some members of the team hypothesized that Cindy's extramarital liaisons might disaffect jurors, particularly older, conservative women. Yet, at the same time, many would find it hard to imagine this type of woman— affluent, pretty, religious—becoming enmeshed in something as odious as murder. As before, prosecutors hoped to select analytical jurors capable of piecing together divergent bits of evidence, and convicting Cynthia on the basis of the big picture.

But it was not to be. On November 10—as forty-four potential jurors waited in court to be questioned—Cynthia's lawyers decided to have the case tried directly in front of the judge.

"We just didn't feel we could get a fair and impartial jury in this county," Meeker said. "Despite people seeming to be promising that they would make every effort, we just felt they were tainted so severely by this extensive publicity— so many news articles and so many news reports—that it was just asking more than a jury could fairly do."

Prosecutors were stunned by the move. The team had previously discussed this possibility, while trying to telegraph the defense attorneys' tactics. But it didn't seem like Cynthia's team would want to take their chances in front of the judge. Cosgrove, a prosecutor for eleven years, had worked in the same office as Mike Carroll, and was known to have a law-and-order sensibility. Logic dictated that Cindy was better off gambling her fate in front of a dozen civilians.

Carroll had been ready to make his case in front of a collection of jurors alien to the gradations of legal rationale. Now, he could skip all the extraneous explanations, and not worry about simplifying the evidence for a novice's ears. In Judge Cosgrove, the team saw an arbiter who would understand the pieces of the puzzle.

FOURTEEN

BEHIND THE SCENES, there was a dialogue between the defense and the prosecution, centered around a plea arrangement. The prosecution was willing to agree to a maximum of 13 years in prison, and have the judge decide the precise sentence. Cynthia's team rejected the proposal.

Prosecutors were also open to lightening Zaffino's sentence in exchange for his testimony. By now, he'd been transferred to a facility in Toledo—following a rumor (never substantiated) that the Georges planned to have him killed by an inmate at a prior prison. Zaffino appeared unconcerned. He'd hired an attorney from New Jersey, who requested having his client's sentence lessened to 5 years in exchange for cooperation. Prosecutors regarded this as a preposterous demand, and refused to entertain it. But they asked detectives to move Zaffino to the Summit County Jail—close to the courthouse—during the trial, in case he changed his mind. He did not.

He was sure that he'd eventually be released on appeal.

ON NOVEMBER 18, 2005, as a group of reporters listened to a simulcast from an adjacent overflow courtroom, Carroll made his opening remarks. In many ways, his comments were almost identical to the ones he'd delivered at John Zaffino's trial: "Cindy George had a problem in her life. That problem was Jeff Zack, and she solved that problem through John Zaffino."

The prosecutor detailed Cynthia and Jeff's dysfunctional romance, the story of their secret love child, the alleged hit in the park, bank records that indicated that Cindy had paid for Zaffino's motorcycle, and the phone calls between the killer and his paramour immediately before and after the homicide.

If it weren't for Cynthia George, the prosecutor reasoned, Zaffino might not have had a conflict with Jeff Zack at all. As Whiddon later elaborated to a reporter, "Whether [Zack] had threatened her for custody of the child, or to take the child, or was threatening [the Georges] for money, who knows? It all revolved around that."

In his opening remarks, Cynthia's lawyer Michael Bowler characterized the calls as evidence of an affair, not a murder plot. And since transcripts of the conversations did not exist, he emphasized, there was "little else to tie Cindy George to any of this."

By the time of Jeff's murder, Bowler stressed, his affair with Cynthia had already ended. Therefore, Cindy had "no reason on earth" to sponsor the shooting. "At this point, she didn't have a problem with Zack anymore. The relationship was over because Cindy George took steps in her life to end the relationship. She was gaining strength . . . The plan was working, and she could feel good about it."

Zack had also moved on, Bowler continued, after finding his "soul mate" on a flight to Arizona to see his family.

THAT EVENING, WHIDDON and Felber met with the next day's witnesses: Elayne Zack, Bonnie Zack Cook and former nanny Mary Ann Brewer. Since the Zaffino trial, Mary Ann and Bonnie had become close, but nothing could fill the gap caused by the nanny's estrangement from the George family. At one time, Mary Ann had been like a mother to the George kids, and she still loved them. But the Georges now viewed her as a pariah. When she took the witness stand, Mary Ann was bracing for the hateful stares of the children, as well as Ed—a man she admired, and viewed as a friend. And she dreaded the possibility of an awkward encounter with the Georges in the hallway. Felber felt guilty about the fact that the murder and the subsequent legal proceedings had cost Mary Ann her second family. Yet he was depending on her to testify.

To the detective, the nanny was just another in the long line of victims.

But in the courtroom, she easily maintained her composure. She told the judge about the time she'd overheard an argument between Cynthia and Jeff, and questioned Cindy about the nature of the relationship: "I asked her why she put up with him, why she took the abuse that she was taking from him . . . the arguing and the screaming, and she told me that he used to cuss her out a lot . . . She said, 'I have to put up with him. I have to see him. I have to talk to him.'"

If she didn't, Cynthia apparently told Brewer, Jeff was going to move the couple's child to Israel.

As for Ed, Mary Ann claimed that she was uncertain when the Tangier owner knew about his wife's infidelity, or the paternity of the youngest George child. But the restaurateur was apparently confused by Zack's unremitting calls to the house. "He didn't understand why there were so many hang-ups," Mary Ann said.

As Bonnie spoke about her own response to learning about the affair, and her husband's parentage of the youngest George daughter ("I just felt like I was hit"), a primly bespectacled Cynthia seemed to grimace slightly. Her discomfort continued when Jeff's mother replaced her former daughter-in-law on the stand, exuding a blend of bitterness and sorrow.

Elayne revealed how, early in the investigation, she'd arranged with police to call Cynthia, and tape-record the conversation, hoping to glean an insight or two from the woman's nebulous comments.

The courtroom now listened to Elayne trying, in her throaty, demonstrative manner, to prod Cynthia into letting down her guard. "Cindy!" Elayne exclaimed on the tape. "Cindy! What happened to Jeffrey? He was killed. Cindy, weren't you his best friend, and he loved you?"

"You know what?" Cynthia responded. "I didn't know whether to call . . . I don't know if he was drugged or . . ."

"You know Jeffrey would never take a drug."

Elayne asked why Cynthia had opted not to attend Zack's funeral.

"I kind of thought it might not be good . . . I was just afraid of Bonnie, you know, what she would think. I just stayed here . . . I never even learned the address."

". . . But you have no idea why this could have happened?"

"I don't know how this could happen."

". . . It's your worst nightmare."

". . . I know what it's like, and it's horrible."

"So you know how I feel, and I would love to know what happened, and how he was hurt by you. I really would. I would love to know that story. If you want to come over, I'd love to see you, and I'm sure Bonnie would accept it . . . It would give me some closure, because I know how hurt he was."

"How what he was?"

"Hurt. Hurt by you . . . He wasn't going to be friends with you anymore. And I know how persistent Jeffrey was, and I know that he had to have been trying to call you . . . He wouldn't take no for an answer."

". . . It seemed like he was, something, something was going on. I don't know what . . . He was acting . . . constantly, like, worried about something."

"And he never told you what? He probably confided in you more than anybody."

"The last thing he said to me was they were investigating him at work."

". . . The other thing that always boggled my mind was how he was able to talk to you the way he talked to you, and see you the way he saw you, without having your husband be suspicious. I mean, if I was involved with another guy, my husband would absolutely become suspicious."

"Right."

"I could never understand all that. I mean, I know he [Ed] works a lot. But didn't he wonder?"

"Um, yeah. I guess it was a problem here and a problem there. But he really, he really didn't care."

"He didn't care?"

The conversation switched back to Jeff's demise. "I know he was working for some family," Cynthia offered. "I don't know if he borrowed some money from them."

"Oh, really?"

"I don't know."

". . . I never understood how close you could be with Jeffrey, whether it was sexual or not. And not be in suspicion with your husband. It really amazed us. It amazed us! I mean, if my husband saw me go on bike trips and be with another guy, he would've wondered and said something . . . And I'm not accusing anybody. I know [Ed] had nothing to do with it. Believe me, it was probably a guy Jeffrey cut off. The guy that murdered Jeffrey, Jeffrey probably cut him off, and he had a fight with him . . . I know Ed had nothing to do with it. But I never could understand, and I just need to know."

Cindy didn't deliver a definitive response. Then, in what detectives interpreted as an effort to create a timeline for herself, she mentioned that she'd been at a wedding on the Saturday that Zack was killed, and didn't learn about the murder until the next day, when her husband told her the news.

But as Cynthia continued to speak, Elayne detected a

slip-up—when the suspect claimed that she'd been so distraught over the murder that she'd dropped out of a beauty pageant.

"She said that she was very nervous," Elayne later expounded. "And Saturday morning, she cancelled her beauty pageant. She had signed everything to appear in a Mrs. Ohio beauty pageant. And she was so nervous that she dropped out. But Cindy had told me that she didn't know about Jeff's death until Sunday."

CHRISTINE TODARO TOOK the stand on November 17. But this was a very different Christine from the anxious woman who'd lost weight during the John Zaffino trial, and carried around guilt over testifying against a husband who'd been both unfaithful and violent. She'd since left her boyfriend, Tim Cantanese, over what she claimed were his tendencies to abuse substances and mistreat women, and relocated to Florida. There, released from the canons of her Ohio social network, she'd flourished at a job setting up phone systems. Reinvigorated, she returned to Akron, confident that helping the authorities had been the right choice. Now, in court, her words flowed evenly, with Christine looking straight ahead, relieved that, at *this* trial, she wouldn't have to face down Zaffino.

THROUGHOUT THE TRIAL, prosecutors were unsure about whether to summon John Zaffino's sister, Judy, to Akron to testify about the jailhouse phone calls. Thus far, she'd refused to testify, and the only way that this could be remedied was by physically handing Judy a subpoena in New Jersey. In light of this situation, Judge Cosgrove adjourned court for one day to permit Felber and Gessner to meet with Judy, her husband, Chris, and her attorney at a neutral site.

Judy greeted Felber with an obscenity.

"Nice to see you, too," he smiled.

Judy's lawyer quieted his client, then led her into an office to speak to Gessner. Felber and Chris sat in the waiting area together.

As before, Chris was affable, even when describing how the investigation had inconvenienced him. He didn't seem particularly upset with law enforcement, though. Unlike his wife, Chris felt no particular responsibility for his brother-in-law, nor was he blinded by wrath born in family loyalty. As a result, he blamed John Zaffino for the disruptions.

When the meeting ended, Gessner motioned to Felber to accompany him to the car. There, the prosecutor described the conference. No, Gessner told Felber, he had no desire to place Judy Diggelman on the stand. A good lawyer never wants to risk not knowing what will come out of a witness's mouth.

THE NEXT TRIAL day would be buffered by the weekend. But members of the team were so burnt out that gathering on Saturday was out of the question. Over the last few weeks, families had been neglected. During those rare occasions when participants *were* home, they were so consumed by the stresses of the case that they were hardly pleasant company.

Once again, Whiddon and Felber realized that there was no way for them to prepare as much as they wanted. Time had run out. Everyone knew the facts, and would have to rely on experience to carry on through the rest of the trial. It was a cathartic deduction.

For the first time in the trial, Cynthia displayed real emotion, tearing up and dabbing her face with a handkerchief, when her spiritual missives to Zaffino were read aloud:

"You are the eyes when I cannot see
You are the voice that's sent through me
You are the strength in the weakness . . . you are . . ."

Whiddon had read every letter—and listened to each of the forty-six jailhouse tapes—so many times that he was amazed by his own knowledge on the witness stand. Nonetheless, on cross-examination, he had to concede that he'd never heard Zaffino say that he and Cindy had planned the crime. In fact, Whiddon admitted, at one point, John actually proclaimed, "I'm not going to lie on somebody to help myself."

Had the defense allowed him the opportunity to elaborate, the lieutenant could have added that Zaffino made this remark after hearing the requisite warning that authorities were recording the conversation.

When it was Felber's turn to testify, he struggled with the arrangement of the boards displaying the telephone records. But since he didn't have to enchant a jury, he recognized that in front of the judge content mattered more than style.

After completing his testimony, Felber was bequeathed the honor of sitting at the prosecution table for the remainder of the trial. Lieutenant Whiddon graciously relinquished the spot, watching the rest of the proceedings from the gallery.

Just before the defense started its case, Cynthia's lawyers asked the judge to dismiss the charges. Zaffino, they allowed, had likely murdered Jeff Zack. But they insisted that he'd acted alone. Despite the mound of circumstantial evidence, the attorneys said, proof of Cindy's involvement was non-existent.

"There is no basis to infer that she talks about any kind of killing—none," proclaimed her lawyer John Pyle. "The evidence wasn't there [at the time of Zaffino's arrest], and it isn't there now."

Not surprisingly, Judge Cosgrove declined the motion.

DR. ALAN KURZWEIL was the first witness for the defense. Cynthia had been referred to him by her psychiatrist in

2001, he testified. At their early sessions, he added, she'd appeared to be disheartened and stressed. Her husband, she'd said, was 62 years old and "severely depressed," while Zack appeared to have developed a split personality that could be terrifying. Although Kurzweil claimed that Cynthia had never mentioned Zaffino—nor a desire to have her harasser harmed—prosecutors believed that the therapist represented the defendant's motives as clearly as any other witness.

"IT'S THE BUSINESS I chose."

Ed George was on the stand—hair thinning, in silver-framed glasses and a blue, pin-striped suit—describing in a grandfatherly tone how the long hours he'd logged at the Tangier had driven a wedge in his marriage. Still, he professed to have known neither about Cynthia's affairs nor the true paternity of his youngest child—until police had begun investigating the murder.

Meeker asked why Ed chose to remain with his wife.

"Well, the first reason is, I took a marriage vow," George answered, "for better or for worse. I firmly believe in that. I'm a devout Christian.

"I think a mother is important in raising children. I don't think you can raise a family without a mother. I look at my wife and the things we have gone through . . . I see this person I met . . . and I always hoped that person would return. And she has."

Some six months before the murder, Ed remembered, he was genuflecting at mass on Christmas Eve, when his wife's cell phone rang. An agitated man was on the other end, spewing foul language. "I heard a loud voice, but I couldn't decipher what was being said," George testified. Cynthia "became very upset in church. She said it was Jeff Zack and she asked him to please just leave her alone. She just wanted to be with Jesus tonight."

It was a month later when Ed called his friend, Akron

Police Major Paul Callahan, about the persistent hang-ups, but the restaurateur chose not to file a report with his local police department: "I felt like I didn't want to put all our dirty laundry out, and have the media and other people find out."

But when Zack was killed, the family became a staple of local gossip. Ed testified to reading about the murder in the Sunday newspaper, then showing the article to his wife: "She was stunned. She said nothing. She was just speechless . . . We both stood there. We couldn't believe it."

He insisted that his wife didn't blanch when he'd later questioned her involvement. "She said she had nothing to do with it."

Unfortunately for the prosecution, Cynthia chose not to take the stand. "Her silence," Whiddon would later tell a reporter, "not being able to talk to her, not being able to sit down and have her answer some of our questions, that definitely was the most frustrating. I wanted to know exactly what was going on. If she didn't have anything to hide, then she could've come clean. She never has."

Here, on the last day of the trial, the defense followed Ed's testimony with a series of recordings featuring John denying Cynthia's involvement in the crime. With this point established, closing arguments began.

GENERALLY, THIS IS one of the most exciting points of a trial, when defense attorneys perform for the public, affirming that they are worth their lofty fees, and colorful prosecutors audition for higher office. Insinuations not allowed earlier in the proceedings are now all but encouraged. The dry nature of courtroom rules are pushed aside, as the lawyers attempt to stir the emotions of the jurors.

But this case would be an exception. Judge Cosgrove had seen her share of theatrics, and wasn't impressed by flash. She simply wanted the facts, the less melodrama the better.

Gessner drew the judge's attention to the phrase "we

can't make one mistake" in Cindy's letter to Zaffino. "Cynthia George confesses right there, Judge," the prosecutor said. "If 'we' did nothing wrong, why would 'we' have to worry about making a mistake?"

As with the Zaffino trial, the defense maintained that law enforcement had tossed together random bits of information, hoping that something would stick to the defendant. And, it was noted, Zaffino, not Cynthia, was the one who'd initiated the phone calls on the day that Zack was slain.

The prosecution countered that the phone records all but confirmed Cindy's guilt. Even if you couldn't hear her speaking to Zaffino, then Zack, then Zaffino again in the park—or with the killer on June 16, 2001—anyone with a degree of common sense would know that Zack was being set up, prosecutors asserted.

But was this intuition enough to find a prominent mother of seven guilty?

WITH THE CLOSING arguments completed, the detectives went back to work, attempting to concentrate on their other cases. Still, the next few days dragged. Twice, they gathered with the prosecutors to receive updates, and speculate about the impending decision. Everyone agreed that they'd presented a strong case. Of course, there were a few things that each person could have done differently. But the team had fought a giant with vigor and ingenuity.

The Thanksgiving weekend came without a verdict. As Judge Cosgrove spent the holiday reviewing evidence in the courthouse, the George family departed from the conventions of their annual Thanksgiving brunch to utter a silent prayer. In their own homes, the various prosecution team members tried keeping busy. Whenever there was a lag in activity, though, each man found himself contemplating critical moments of the trial—and Judge Cosgrove's mindset.

Finally, on Monday, November 28, 2005, the call came in. Everyone was to assemble back in the courtroom. Reporters piled into their seats, while others positioned themselves in the adjacent courtroom to listen to the simulcast of the ruling. Cynthia arrived with her attorneys Patricia Millhoff, Bob Meeker and Mike Bowler. At a table just three feet away, Felber squeezed in next to Carroll and Gessner.

The back of the room looked like the pews of a church, with Bonnie Zack Cook and her relatives sitting with Mary Ann Brewer. In another section, Ed George gathered with his family's supporters. Three of his children moved up to the front and hugged their mother. A younger daughter clutched a crucifix and moved her lips in prayer. Cynthia's sister looked on, preoccupied.

Friends gestured assuredly at Cindy. She responded with smiles and blown kisses, jutting her head toward the ceiling to send a "chin up" message. This was Cynthia the hostess, the woman who could work a room as well as anyone in Akron.

"How are you?" she asked her husband, softly, but loud enough for observers to hear.

"I'm okay," Ed answered.

Everyone was supposed to be in the courtroom at 11 AM. But Judge Cosgrove remained in her chambers. Ten minutes passed, then twenty. Felber tried not to glance at Cynthia, but he noticed that Millhoff was holding the defendant's hand.

Then, the judge entered, and the place went dead quiet.

"THE COURT FEELS it is important to state some of the salient reasons for its opinion," Judge Cosgrove began. On May 8, 2001, she continued, it appeared that Cynthia and Zaffino were working together to draw Jeff Zack into the park near the Everett Covered Bridge: "Although phone records—calls between the defendant, Zaffino and Zack—certainly point to a conspiracy to lure Zack into the park, without more, this court cannot prove that the state met its burden of proof on this count."

Cynthia clenched her eyes shut.

". . . For the foregoing reason, the court finds the defendant not guilty."

Cindy's supporters cheered, clapped and cried. The defendant placed a hand over her mouth, then shrieked a joyful "Yes!" with the same spirit she'd exuded as a Pep Club member at North Canton High School. But the judge quickly extinguished the party.

"Not guilty of the *conspiracy* charge," she scolded.

Attention turned back to the bench as the judge resumed reading her opinion. "Additional evidence at this trial," Cosgrove stated, "not presented at John Zaffino's trial, included letters that were seized during a search of Judy Diggelman's residence. There were several letters written by the defendant to Zaffino after he was convicted in the death of Jeff Zack. In one letter, written on stationery lined with cherubs, the defendant tells Zaffino of her continued love and her promise to see him again . . . In another letter . . . George also praised Zaffino for his incredible strength . . . The defendant went on to caution Zaffino . . . 'We cannot make one mistake.'

"In conclusion, there is no smoking gun in this case. What there is, is an abundance of direct and circumstantial evidence proving beyond a reasonable doubt that the defendant procured and/or solicited John Zaffino to commit aggravated murder in the death of Jeff Zack."

Cynthia was crying now, her hands intertwined with Millhoff's on the defense table, her head resting on the lawyer's knuckles. But the judge wasn't finished.

"Without the financial assistance to Zaffino, who had barely enough funds to support himself, he could not have purchased the weapon . . . He could not have afforded to purchase the motorcycle used . . . in the slaying. He could not have paid for the trip after the homicide, when he attempted to dispose of the distinctive and much-sought-after motorcycle.

"Without the defendant's encouragement and influence in procuring and convincing Zaffino to commit this murder, it could not have been accomplished on June sixteenth, 2001."

Cynthia's wails were loud now, as were the sobs of her daughters. Ed George threw his arms around them.

"Based on the totality of the evidence produced at this trial," the judge said, "the court finds beyond a reasonable doubt that the defendant, Cynthia Rohr George, is guilty of complicity to commit aggravated murder."

Cynthia's daughters shook with grief, as their mother was asked to approach the bench. Cosgrove ignored the defendant's tears and asked, "Is there anything that you want to say to the court prior to the imposition of sentence?"

Cindy was so distraught that she could barely enunciate her words: "First of all, I just want to tell you I didn't do it. I know it points that way, but I didn't do it. I was just seeking help. I know this has been a tough decision for you, and I know you are fair, and I know how it looks . . ."

Felber listened and shook his head. Sure, Cynthia was seeking help, he thought. That's what he'd known all along. Jeff Zack was the problem. John Zaffino was the help. If Cindy was ever going to utter something close to a confession, this was it.

"Under Ohio law," the judge continued, "there's only one sentence the court can impose in this matter. Pursuant to the revised code, the court hearby imposes a life sentence."

"Oh my God!" someone shouted from the gallery.

"I just remember looking at my children," Cynthia would later tell *Dateline*, "and the horror on their faces, and how this could happen to our family."

A 3-year mandatory sentence was added to the penalty

because a gun had been used in the commission of the crime. Cynthia would not be eligible for parole for at least twenty years. Although she had the right to appeal the conviction, her chances looked slim. It was the price the defense paid for trying the case in front of a judge.

"You always second-guess yourself when you have the wrong conclusion," Meeker conceded to the media.

As Cynthia was led away in handcuffs, Ed George shouted, "We support you!" Through their tears, his daughters yelled, "We love you!" Several turned toward Mary Ann and glared at her.

"It's your fault!" one of the children scowled. "It's all your fault!"

The former nanny felt like breaking into tears. "It hurts me deeply that I can't be a part of their life anymore," she says. "They can't e-mail me. They can't call me. But I don't see where I'm to blame. I didn't have anybody murdered. I just told the truth.

"Cynthia deserved what she got. She deserved it for what she did to her family—to the George family, and to her own children. And her poor mother. She was a very selfish woman."

Elayne Zack watched Ed lead his children past a horde of reporters onto an elevator, and felt a sense of compassion: "I think about all these children losing their mother for life. And I'm very sad for them. But I also feel sorry for my grandson, Brian, who lost his father.

"Justice was served."

Just before Ed George left the building, a tight grasp around one of his crying children, he spotted Vince Felber. For the two years that the detective had worked at the Tangier, the owner had never exchanged a word with him. Now, all this time later, the former bartender was suddenly worthy of acknowledgment.

"Felber," Ed George stated. "I hope you are proud."

"I am," said the man who wouldn't let go of the case. "Thank you."

As the local news stations led their programs that night with the report of the fallen socialite, Cynthia was in the Summit County Jail, looking at a plate of meatballs, vegetables, rice and corn cake. On the side of the building reserved for male inmates, Zaffino ate the same meal, and prepared for the trip back to the penitentiary in Toledo, still unwilling to betray his former lover.

And that was it. In Ohio, even the wealthy couldn't get away with murder. Or at least it seemed that way—for nearly two years.

FIFTEEN

THE NEWSPAPERS RAN Cynthia's booking photo, taken in the county jail less than an hour after her conviction, clad in prison garb, smiling faintly into the lens. Everyone had a good time with that one.

At the Ohio Reformatory for Women in Marysville in Union County, about 130 miles from Akron, she settled into a routine. Her family visited between eight and ten times a month, and spoke with her every day.

"Cindy has a lot of faith," Ed George would later tell the *Akron Beacon Journal*. "She is an eternal optimist about good things happening if you stay on course."

He conceded, "Does Cindy have some things in her life that she has to revisit herself? Yes. But this is not about that. This was a criminal matter. It was not a moral matter."

Behind prison walls, Cynthia tried aiding her cause by granting a rare interview to the NBC television show *Dateline*. With the cameras rolling, she admitted providing the money for Zaffino's motorcycle, but insisted that she'd never suspected that it would be used in conjunction with a crime. She explained the timing of the phone calls from Zaffino on June 16, 2001, as an unusual coincidence. And, she contended, it was her lawyers who'd encouraged her to write those letters to John after he began serving his sentence.

"Do you take responsibility for anything that happened?" asked correspondent Victoria Corderi.

"I take responsibility for adultery," Cindy said. "I take responsibility for allowing fear to keep me in a place of not getting help."

In August 2006, Cynthia's new lawyers—Bradley Davis Barbin, Max Kravitz and Jacob Cairns—filed a thirty-page appeal with Ohio's Ninth District Court of Appeals. The defense team criticized Judge Patricia Cosgrove for not granting the prosecutors' motion to dismiss Robert Meeker and Michael Bowler. Because the pair had passed on money to Zaffino's lawyer, the appeal stated, "they were in fact witnesses; they could no longer be George's advocates."

The two "had to be concerned about their reputations and licenses," the appeal alleged, "and that concern had to impact every decision they would thereafter make" defending Cynthia.

"She certainly got a pretty tough deal," Barbin told a reporter. "I mean, here's a mother of seven who is told by her attorneys to keep her mouth shut and everything will work out. And certainly, it didn't. And she's been sitting in jail . . . and she didn't need to sit in jail."

The document also noted that Zaffino's taped conversations should have been barred because he "intended to extort money from [Cynthia] by threatening to provide false information implicating her in Zack's murder."

It was the argument that prosecutors had prepared for prior to the trial. But Cindy's original defense attorneys had never utilized this tactic.

Legal experts said Cynthia's chances of acquittal were slim—1 in 1,000, according to one estimate. But her appellate attorney Barbin projected confidence: "We're aware that criminal appeals are very difficult to win, but the percentage increases when you have an all-circumstantial case like we have with this one."

The week of March 19, 2007, was a rough one for the Akron Police Department. Over the weekend, two officers had pulled over a vehicle leaving a known drug house at 3 AM. Inside the car were two male teens, several rocks of crack cocaine and a loaded .45-caliber handgun.

When police approached the auto, the 19-year-old driver grabbed the gun and pointed it at one of the officers. The officer's partner pulled out his own weapon and shot the suspect three times before he could fire a round. The officers took cover behind a cruiser and called for backup. That, police said, was when the driver, Demetrus Vinson, fatally shot himself in the head.

Whiddon came in over the weekend to investigate. The story was initially corroborated by the 15-year-old passenger, who claimed that Vinson was "acting crazy" before the incident, vowing to kill himself if police tried to arrest him. So, technically, this appeared to be a "good shooting"—the sometimes-callous police term for an incident that justifies gunfire. Then, the boy changed his story, and hired an attorney.

The only reason Vinson was killed, the teen said, was that he was black.

Soon, protestors would gather in front of police headquarters, and at city council meetings, wielding signs with slogans like, "It Don't Add Up." Police grumbled that none of the demonstrators seemed to wonder what two teens were doing in the middle of the night, in a car stocked with drugs and a handgun. But the rhetoric did much to batter police morale, and keep Whiddon busy for weeks to come.

Meanwhile, Felber was working with prosecutors on an upcoming homicide trial. On March 21, he called Mike Carroll to discuss the case, and asked if he'd heard anything about Cynthia's appeal. The day before, a *Dateline* producer, putting the final touches on the story about the lovers' quadrangle murder, had questioned Felber about this—raising the detective's curiosity.

"Nothing yet," Carroll answered. Then, there was a pause. Phil Bogdanoff had just sent his fellow prosecutor an e-mail with the ruling.

Carroll tried opening the document, but couldn't. "It says I performed an illegal operation," he griped.

"Uh, oh," Felber replied. "Don't say another word until I read you your rights."

"Hold on. Phil is calling me on the other line."

Carroll put the detective on hold. When the prosecutor came back on the phone, there was an ominous tone in his voice: "You might want to come over here."

Immediately, Felber went looking for Whiddon. But he and Sergeant Hudnall were busy preparing a search warrant related to the Vinson shooting, and Felber didn't want to interrupt. He went to the prosecutor's office alone.

When he arrived, Carroll's door was locked. That was a first. "He obviously knew I was coming," Felber cracked to Carroll's assistant.

She chuckled.

Felber knocked, and Bogdanoff let him in. No one told the detective to unlock the door when he closed it behind him. Both prosecutors appeared to be in a state of shock.

"Let me guess," Felber began. "She won her appeal."

"She was acquitted."

"So we have to retry her? Right?"

The prosecutors shook their heads. In a 2–1 decision, the appeals court had reversed the conviction. Because of the constitutional guarantee against double jeopardy, this meant that Cynthia could never be tried on the same charges again. The appeal was heard by the same panel that had sustained Zaffino's conviction and had talked about Cynthia's role. Yet now, appellate Judges William Baird and Beth Whitmore maintained that even though the collection of circumstantial evidence proved Zaffino's guilt, it was not enough to convict Cindy on the complicity charge.

"Such a conclusion would be based on mere speculation," Baird wrote, "not on facts in evidence."

Although the pair had clearly spoken around the time of the murder, Baird elaborated, "There was no evidence presented about what the two had discussed or what either of them said . . . It would be purely speculative to come to any conclusions."

Yet the judges felt free to speculate themselves:

> Zaffino had a motive to want his competition out of that scene. Moreover, Zaffino might have wanted to be his lover's hero and take it upon himself to end her problem with Zack. . . . The fact that Zaffino had his own reasons to kill Zack negates any argument that George "must have solicited him to kill Zack."

Appellate Judge Lynn Slaby cast the lone dissenting vote, writing:

> Viewing the totality of all the evidence . . . a reasonable fact finder could then weigh the evidence beyond a reasonable doubt that Defendant procured Zaffino to murder Zack.

With a distraught Carroll listening, Bogdanoff tried explaining the ruling further. According to the appellate court, the prosecution had not presented a case that would convince any rational human being that Cynthia had known about the murder in advance.

"So, in other words," Felber sneered, "the police department, the prosecutor's office, the grand jury, the jurors in Zaffino's trial, Judge Cosgrove, even the one dissenting judge on the appeals court—none of those people are rational?"

"Basically," Bogdanoff replied.

"So we have two judges ruling that another two are irrational, and that gets a murderer out of jail?"

Bogdanoff took a breath.

"I still don't understand," the detective continued. "I've never heard of a case being overturned on appeal and the prosecution not being allowed to retry the case. We went over this possibility hundreds of times, and you always said that we'd be able to retry her."

Bogdanoff explained further: The Appeals' Court had reached the extremely rare conclusion that the prosecution had not presented *any* evidence of George's guilt. According to this premise, authorities never even had the right to arrest her in the first place.

The prosecutor seemed to draw into his own thoughts. "She is out forever," he uttered.

IN ANOTHER PART of the city, Bradley Barbin was significantly more verbose. "I don't think the crime ever occurred," he told WAKR radio. "I think the reality is . . . people make mistakes with who they choose to be associated with. But when you call somebody a murderer, you better have some evidence . . . Anybody that ever met Cindy George would know that she doesn't have it in her. She just doesn't have it in her . . . The version of Cindy George that was reported in the Akron and the Cleveland media was probably the worst vilification seen since [Richard] Jewel," the private security guard falsely accused of planting a pipe bomb in a heavily populated park during Atlanta's 1996 Olympic festivities.

"Everybody just wants to believe that a wealthy woman who has everything going for her in life must be evil. And . . . that's not who she is. And it took a long time for people to figure it out."

After 16 months behind bars, Cynthia left prison, dressed in a blue sweat shirt and white sneakers, 7accompanied by her husband and daughters. Surrounded by the assembled media, the 52-year-old exonerated felon wept, expressing gratitude to friends and strangers who'd written to her.

"I'm just so thankful for God," she enthused. "I just need to go home. I just want to go home."

Said Barbin, "They can't get her. The bottom line is, she is going home, and she's never going to be charged with this or any related offense again."

Cindy returned to a house packed with flowers and over-joyed relatives. "We're all ecstatic," her husband told WAKR. "But I was always in her corner. I always felt that Cindy was innocent of any crime. The kids and I have been with her through all this ordeal . . . When you hear the real story, as the appellate court has, then justice does prevail, and our prayers have been answered."

In Arizona, Elayne Zack's revulsion over the latest turn of events set off a tremor felt all the way in Ohio. "You know damn well that woman was involved in the murder, and now she's getting out?" she barked to the *Beacon Journal*. "This is outrageous. So the poor guy with no money sits in jail forever, and the rich beauty queen gets off. Only in Akron. You have a crooked city, and you can quote me on that."

Along the drab hallways of the Akron Police Department, a number of detectives approached Felber.

"Don't feel sorry for me," Felber would respond. "Feel sorry for the system."

He pointed out that everyone who wore a badge played a role in perpetuating that system. "It's up to us to fix it," he'd explain.

The responses were always the same. The organism known as the legal system was corrupt and unhealthy. But what could you do about it? "Vince," Felber would be told, "it isn't worth the trouble. You can't change the way things work."

Felber came back with the same argument he'd always espoused—only with a little less conviction:

"If nobody tries, it'll never change."